Controlling
Illegal Drugs

Controlling Illegal Drugs

A Comparative Study

SANDRO SEGRE

Translated by Nora Stern

Aldine de Gruyter
New York

About the Author

Sandro Segre Professor, Department of Political and Social Sciences, University of Genoa, Italy

Originally published as Le politiche sociali in tema di stupefacenti: Un confronto fra Svezia, Stati Uniti e Italia, copyright © 2000 Carocci Editore, S.p.A., Rome, Italy.

ALDINE DE GRUYTER
A division of Walter de Gruyter, Inc.
200 Saw Mill River Road
Hawthorne, New York 10532

This publication is printed on acid free paper ∞

Library of Congress Cataloging-in-Publication Data

Segre, Sandro.
    [Politiche sociale in tema di stupefacenti. English]
    Controlling illegal drugs : a comparative study / author, Sandro Segre ; translator, Nora Stern.
        p. cm. — (New lines in criminology)
    Includes bibliographical references and index.
    1. Narcotics, Control of—Italy.   2. Narcotics, Control of—Sweden.
3. Narcotics, Control of—United States.   4. Drug abuse—Italy—Prevention.
5. Drug abuse—Sweden—Prevention.   6. Drug abuse—United States—
Prevention.   7. Drug abuse—Italy.   8. Drug abuse—Sweden.   9. Drug
abuse—United States.   I. Title.   II. Series.
    HV5840.I8S4313   2003
    363.45—dc21

                                                                        2003012790

Manufactured in the United States of America
10 9 8 7 6 5 4 3 2 1

Contents

Introduction

This study presents and compares the drug policies in use in the United States, Sweden, and Italy to limit the use and abuse of narcotics (such as marijuana, hashish, cocaine, heroin, and amphetamines) and to suppress the traffic in these drugs. A primary objective of this study is theoretical: to evaluate and explain, by means of a comparative method applied to the study of individual cases,[1] the respective level of success of these policies, measured according to conventional criteria. The aim of this comparison between Swedish drug policies (a positive case) and U.S. and Italian policies (negative cases) is to evaluate the effect of these policies, taken in their entirety and considered on the whole as a sufficient condition, on drug use. Therefore, this study proposes to come to a general conclusion. The existence of a causal relationship is deduced from the association between Swedish policies and the limited diffusion of narcotics in Sweden on the one hand; and from the association between U.S. and Italian policies and the wide diffusion of these substances in the United States and in Italy, on the other hand (Kohn 1987:721; Ragin 1987:47; Ricolfi 1993:302–3).

Social policies or welfare policies, considered as a whole (financial benefits in the sphere of assistance and social security programs, services and policies in the job market, and social security programs in general), constitute a condition that is merely sufficient. This study does not propose to ascertain whether this condition is also necessary, that is, it does not aim to give a complete explanation of the high or low use of narcotics. This level of consumption could be the consequence of other causes, which are not considered here as independent variables but on the contrary sometimes as intervening variables. The literature in this field has dwelt particularly on sociopsychological causes. Examples are the influence of parents and peers, attitudes toward the use of drugs or abstention from them, the positive or negative images that persons have of themselves, and the possibility or, on the contrary, the difficulty of establishing significant forms of interpersonal communication (Baraldi 1994a; Ravenna 1994).

There are some logical problems inherent to the comparative method: the deterministic, rather than probabilistic, nature of causal inference and

1

the small number of cases examined (three in all), so that measurement errors have a great impact on the conclusions. Furthermore, there is the difficulty of analyzing a multiplicity of causes, or variables, which are plausibly present, and the possibility that these causes exert reciprocal influences (Berk 1988:156; Lieberson 1991; Scheuch 1990:31–32). However, these logical problems are not beyond solution. The ideal type that constitutes the independent variable—the social policies of the individual countries—is in fact composed of a plurality of other concepts, each of which describes a particular aspect or "dimension" of the ideal type (Lazarsfeld and Rosenberg 1955:15–16). Many of these are expressible in terms of continuous variables that make use of interval and ratio scales, therefore permitting rigorous comparisons. Examples are the incarceration rates, the inequality of the income distribution, and the proportion of national income spent on enforcing the laws on narcotics, rehabilitating drug addicts, and providing specific social services in the field of assistance or social security (Teune 1990:54).

These independent variables are strongly correlated (as we will see) and can thus be subsumed under the more general concept of social policies (Ragin 1994:84). They may also be correlated with intervening variables (such as the percentage of single-parent families or families with an income below the official poverty line) or with dependent variables, which measure the level of drug use within a population. Thus, they lend themselves to a multivariate analysis for which the logical problems previously mentioned do not exist. The multivariate analyses of the partial correlations between specific variables are obtained from the literature in the field, for example,

- between the probability of receiving social assistance and of being nonetheless obliged to seek employment because of insufficient income (Harris 1993);
- between the probability of a deprived ethnic group's poverty conditions worsening (e.g., blacks in the United States) and of the group increasing its economic isolation (Jargowsky 1996; Tigges, Browne, and Green 1998), so making it more difficult for a member of that group to find a job;
- between the probability of being out of work and of taking drugs (Osgood, Wilson, O'Malley, Bachman, and Johnston, 1996).

The use of multivariate analyses serves exclusively to compare the drug policies of Sweden, the United States, and Italy and to evaluate their effect on the diffusion of drugs. In an attempt to keep the methodological problem of equivalence under control—that is, the comparability of measurements dealing with different social units (Smelser 1982:251; cf. also Kohn 1987:720–21; Teune 1990:50, 53–55)—the analysis concentrates on specific dimensions of the social policies of these three countries. These dimensions are the component elements of unitary models of social policy, which constitute the object of the study (Kohn 1987:714). In the course of this analysis we will make use, as much as possible, of aggregated data collected with uniform criteria and published by government or international sources (such as statistics relative to health and educational conditions, to the job market, and to national income). The analysis also uses representative samples of homogeneous populations (in terms of age, ethnic group membership, and other aspects relevant to the research) and the same variables (repressive interventions on drug use and trafficking, the rehabilitation of drug addicts, and preventive measures).

The choice of object cases for comparison (the social policies of the United States, Sweden, and Italy) and the period (from the midsixties to the present) is justified by a particular theoretical interest for sociology and the social sciences in general (Kohn 1987:726–27; Ragin 1994:111–12).

Concerning the choice of cases, the social policies that characterize the United States, Sweden, and Italy share major aspects, which plausibly have the same causal significance for each country (Smelser 1982:283, 287). In particular, a common aspect that could have the same causal relevance for the potential diffusion of drugs is that these social policies have been put into practice in countries that share a high level of economic development, and thus a high capacity for public spending in the field of social services (Wilensky, Luebbert, Reed, and Jamieson 1989:100). To measure how much this applies to the individual countries, it is possible to make use of frequently used indicators of socioeconomic development and of social spending. International organizations such as the OECD, the World Bank, and the United Nations make use of such indicators (Jaffee 1998:99–115; Marklund and Nordlund 1999:21–29).

Equivalent indicators of the same concepts may thus be formulated, thereby limiting the risk that the differences noted between the effects of different social policies are the consequence not of these policies, but of methodological problems (Kohn 1987:720). As authoritative sources point out, these social policies differ in terms of their guiding principles. They also differ in terms of their effect on the respective populations, regarding living conditions, the diffusion of poverty and social exclusion, the distribution of income, and especially the level of drug use (Esping-Andersen 1999; Hagan 1994:Ch. 3; Kautto, Heikkila, Hvinden, Marklund, and Plough 1999a:10–12). "Macroanalytical studies [in this case the comparative study of concrete systems of welfare] cannot completely substitute for general theory-building" (Skocpol and Somers 1980:196). Still, it is possible to reach general conclusions by considering each system of welfare as a model, that is, as an abstract conceptual and theoretical construction.

Conforming to the theoretical objective of this study, the comparison of distinct models of welfare policies then permits general conclusions on

4 Introduction

their social effects. The U.S. model is of a residual character, in the sense that the welfare system provides goods and services only to those who cannot purchase them on the market. The northern European model—focusing on the example of Swedish welfare policies—shows instead a relative balance in the redistribution of income and has a universalistic character, since it gives all citizens and residents access to social welfare services. Finally, the Italian model does not possess a unitary inspiring principle to which the policies enacted or put into effect may conform in a consistent manner.[2] The theoretical (rather than historical) objective of the study determined our choice of the period from the midsixties to the present. This choice is also an attempt to limit the temporal variation of the independent variable (social welfare policies).[3] Furthermore, a significant part of the existing knowledge of the effects of U.S., Swedish, and Italian social policies is almost entirely available only for that period.[4]

The comparison we make aims at a knowledge that is not only theoretical but also practical, i.e., usable for changing practical circumstances (Stehr 1991:10), and so it also has relevance for the political authorities. Obtaining knowledge that has, at least potentially, a practical interest (in this sense) constitutes a second aim of the study. The unit of analysis is the social policies planned and put into effect by the U.S., Swedish, and Italian authorities, with the purpose of repressing and preventing drug use, and rehabilitating drug users. Accordingly, the comparative research has a macrosociological character. Each variation within the three countries (in particular, local differences in the functioning of the respective welfare systems and the existence of social and ethnic inequalities within each country) will be shown to be accounted for by overall social policies, which constitute the unit of analysis (Teune 1990:50–51). The units of observation (Rossi 1988:135–45) are either particular individuals who use and abuse drugs, or public institutions, such as the political, administrative, and police authorities. These authorities are situated at distinct jurisdictional levels and their activity and decisions are addressed, at least to some extent, to these individuals.

Chapter 1 is a systematic comparative description (Smelser 1982:215–16) of the policies carried out in the United States and Sweden. It compares the modes of intervention, the social services offered, the intended public of destination, and the administrative organizations charged with realizing and financing these policies. While both countries show a strong commitment to repressing the traffic in and consumption of drugs, the study will try to demonstrate that the United States and Sweden differ in their commitment to other common objectives of their public policies. These policies concern both drug use and the objectives of primary prevention, such as policies on the redistribution of income and intervention on behalf of disadvantaged ethnic groups in the housing and job market. It also makes some introductory observations concerning the effectiveness and the efficiency of public policies in the United States and Sweden. Chapter 2 is a comparative evaluation of the success of these policies, bearing in mind the different distribution of the respective populations between urban and country areas, and also the different demographics of the young people involved. To evaluate the success of the policies, indicators of both internal effectiveness ["intended as the capacity to achieve the objectives or expected results established ex ante by the public agency" (Palumbo 1995:323)] and external effectiveness ["intended as the capacity of the product/service offered to meet the needs of the public" (ibid.:331)] are employed. The benefits of the respective policies are defined in a strict sense as the capacity to achieve the objectives pursued, in terms of social services and the recipients of these services. These objectives must, however, show some agreement between the two countries, and their achievement cannot be arguably attributed to other causes (ibid.:323–31; cf. also Ginsberg 1994:162–74).

Since the effect of social policies, as far as preventing and repressing the use of and traffic in drugs is concerned, is generally speaking modest (Reiss 1994:15–16), benefits not far from those expected are considered as indicators of success. Chapter 3 evaluates the respective direct costs. The respective efficiency of U.S. and Swedish social policies is measured in this work by the correlation between costs and benefits. Chapter 4 looks at some of the presumed reasons for the relative success or lack of success of these public policies and evaluates the consistency of the objectives pursued with the results expected, according to the knowledge available in the social science field. Chapter 5 considers the perverse effects of the U.S. and Swedish policies, which are objectively verifiable or simply claimed. Chapter 6 contrasts Italian drug policies on the one hand, with U.S. and Swedish on the other. This involves a comparative analysis of the respective policies that have been established, the benefits of the policies of rehabilitation and primary and secondary prevention, and the efficiency of these policies in different spheres (assistance, employment, education, and health care). Particular reference is made to the Italian authorities' objective to limit the use and abuse of drugs. Also for Italy, coherence between the objectives pursued and the results expected is evaluated. An indication of the perverse effects of Italian drug policies is shown by a parallel evaluation with indicators for the United States and Sweden. Chapter 7 and the conclusion offer a summary of the comprehensive argumentation, showing how it was used to achieve the theoretical objective of the work.

The sources of data are government publications, published in English, Swedish, and Italian, and recent studies that deal with themes relevant to this study. They are, in particular, the socioeconomic causes of the diffusion of drugs, and deviance in general, and the efficacy or efficiency of the policies employed to limit and prevent the traffic in and use of these substances.

NOTES

1. This is Mill's indirect method of difference (Ragin 1987:39–42).

2. See in this connection Esping-Andersen (1990:222–29), Ginsburg (1992:18–28), Kautto et al. (1999a:12–15), Negri and Saraceno (1996:12–19), and Plough 1999.

3. As has been remarked (see, for example, Skocpol and Somers 1980:193–96) the method of controlled comparison between cases, which has been followed here, presupposes that the single cases—namely, the single welfare systems—be internally homogeneous. Including a less recent historical period may involve excessive internal heterogeneity.

4. This is precisely the period exclusively or chiefly considered by comparative investigations on the social policies of different countries. See Esping-Andersen (1990), Ginsburg (1992), and Teune (1990:43–44). Studies concerning Sweden and Scandinavia in general (such as Kautto, Heikkila, Hvinden, Marklund, and Plough 1999b), the United States (for example, Danziger and Gottschalk 1995; Jaentti and Danziger 1994; Jencks 1992), or Italy (for instance, Negri and Saraceno 1996; Rei 1997:83–129) also refer to this time period.

1 Social Policies on Drugs in the United States and Sweden

PRELIMINARY OBSERVATIONS

In this first chapter we compare the social policies aimed at preventing and combating the use of and traffic in drugs and show how these policies have been implemented and employed differently in the United States and Sweden. The specific public policies followed in Sweden are intended to repress the traffic in drugs, to treat drug addicts, and to carry out primary and secondary prevention of the use of these substances. The term *drug addiction* is used here to signify that condition in which drugs are used daily or almost daily, so that the user becomes physiologically dependent on them. This definition conforms both to the definition of heavy drug abuse provided by the Swedish National Institute of Public Health, and also to the traditional definition of dependence. The traditional definition considers only physiological dependence and not psychological dependence, and continues to be preferred by some influential U.S. academics (Akers 1991:790, and in general 773–93; Swedish National Institute of Public Health 1995:14; Walters 1996:947). A distinction is drawn between use, misuse, and abuse, taking into account the difference between cases where consumption constitutes respectively a minimum, significant, or great risk to oneself or others (Nicholson 1994:235).[1]

Primary prevention is directed toward the whole population or toward broad sectors of it, such as the school-going population. In a frequent application of the term, primary prevention aims to ensure that those who up to now have not used drugs do not begin to use them. In a more general sense, the term is used to refer to programs that intend to persuade all those—users or not—who do not use these substances to a harmful degree from increasing their consumption. *Secondary prevention* is addressed to that part of the population who may be considered potential users or "at risk." Also in this case it is usual to distinguish between two definitions of the term. First, secondary prevention designates efforts to prevent those who use drugs for experimental or recreational purposes from, as a result, increasing their consumption to harmful levels, or from becoming dependent. Second, the term is suitable to describe those programs that propose to prevent those who already use drugs to a harmful degree from becoming dependent on them (Uhl 1998:151–53).

U.S. and Swedish policies have for the most part pursued the ambitious objective of preventing all drug use through measures of primary and secondary prevention. In this last case the policies attempt to persuade or coerce subjects at risk from using drugs. Programs to reduce the damage have pursued the less ambitious objective of limiting the harmful consequences of practices of ongoing consumption (ibid.:154). These programs—such as the free distribution of sterile syringes—have had very limited implementation in the United States and only on the initiative of private organizations. In Sweden these policies have been implemented by the government, but only on an experimental level, on a local and limited scale, and with great caution. The political authorities and public opinion of both countries, in fact, fear that such types of policies with a different orientation have the undesirable effect of promoting the use and abuse of narcotics. Thus, one can affirm that Swedish policies, like U.S. policies, are prohibitive (Nadelmann 1998:294–95; Nicholson 1994:244; Swedish National Institute of Public Health 1995:24). This is not necessarily the case elsewhere. Notwithstanding the universal prohibition of the sale of hard drugs, a partial liberalization of soft drugs has taken place in Holland, on which there is available a more or less apologetic literature (Nadelmann 1998:298; Scienza Nuova 1998). Moreover, in some countries, for example, Switzerland, the authorities and public opinion are generally more open-minded toward large-scale programs that reduce the damage in progress (Zimmermann et al. 1991:168–71).

The repressive nature of both U.S. and Swedish drug policies makes it possible to avoid taking a position on the much-discussed question of the effectiveness of, and so the opportunity for, the partial or total liberalization of the use of drugs (Inciardi and McElrath 1998b:285–87). The supporters of the liberalization point of view claim to be able to obtain, in this way, results generally considered desirable: a reduction in use and of the connected crime, and the cancellation or reduction, depending on the cases, of the inherent costs of drug repression (Nadelmann 1998). Accordingly, we will focus on the differences between U.S. and Swedish policies. Our thesis is that, except for some local initiatives, public policies implemented in the United States do not correspond to those in Sweden. They do not correspond, in particular, in terms of meeting their established objectives, the degree of their achievement, the modes used to achieve these policies, and the proportion of recipients effectively reached. A comparison between the two countries will then be made in the modes of intervention followed; the activities of repression, rehabilitation, and prevention; the specific recipients of these activities; and the respective administration (centralized or decentralized) conducting the activities.

INITIAL OBSERVATIONS ON EVALUATING THE EFFECTIVENESS AND EFFICIENCY OF THE DRUG POLICIES PURSUED IN THE TWO COUNTRIES

The indicators used in this evaluation are:

1. The capacity to achieve the benefits. Benefits are achieved if the following objectives are reached: the prevention of the use and abuse of drugs by repressing the trafficking, the rehabilitation of those abusing drugs, and the primary and secondary prevention of use (singling out in this last case the actual and potential number of users).

2. The relationship between costs and benefits.

3. The congruence (or consistency) between objectives pursued and results expected.

4. The capacity to avoid or limit perverse effects, that is, the congruence between results achieved and results expected.

The first indicator is of internal effectiveness, ex post taken from the social policies. The second indicator is of efficiency. The third is of external effectiveness, ex ante taken from the specialized literature in the field. The fourth is of external effectiveness, taken ex post (Palumbo 1995:326–27; cf. also Stame 1998:126–32).

The benefits of the social policies on drugs are defined as the achievement of the objectives, previously noted, that have been set by the respective U.S. and Swedish authorities. However, not having followed in a systematic and continuous manner objectives other than the repression of drug trafficking and drug use in the United States, only in Sweden can the benefits of public policies on social rehabilitation and primary and secondary prevention be evaluated. These policies involve the commitment to reach a significant part, if not all, of the actual and potential drug addicts with adequate social services to achieve these objectives. In fact, only in Sweden have public policies included repression, rehabilitation, and prevention at the same time.

Even if the specific costs cannot be ascertained, we can estimate the approximate costs of social policies that aim—as the Swedish policies do—to achieve general welfare objectives, including policies on drugs. We conduct the comparative evaluation of efficiency by considering the relationship between the costs of the social policies (as a percentage of the gross national income) and how effective they are in achieving the intended benefits. There is also the question, in both countries, of "intangible" benefits, that is, benefits that cannot be measured directly through market prices, such as the capacity to provide adequate assistance to that part of the population most disadvantaged, to maintain a high level of health care and education for the whole population, and effectively to rehabilitate most if not all drug addicts. Since the relationship between costs and benefits cannot be evaluated in monetary terms with sufficient precision, we consider instead the relationship between costs and effectiveness (*cost-effectiveness analysis*) (Dunn 1994:298, 329; Uhl 1998:195–96).

The congruence between objectives and results, that is, a causal relationship between specific objectives pursued and results expected, can be deduced from the specialist literature in the field: for example, between the objective of preventing the use and abuse of drugs and the expected result of imprisoning as many actual and potential drug dealers as possible (as in the United States); or instead, between the objective of limiting ethnic and social segregation, and the anticipated result of reducing the level of unemployment of the economically marginalized levels of society and reducing the inequality in the distribution of income and opportunities (as in Sweden). Finally, the capacity to avoid perverse effects, that is "the undesired and undesirable effects" (Boudon 1981:15; cf. also Ginsberg 1994:159–60; Stame 1998:155–59), is evaluated here from the presumed points of view of the respective populations. Undesired and undesirable effects, in the strict sense, are considered to be those effects of public policies that hinder the policies' explicit objectives and expected results (Palumbo 1995:323, 326–27, 329–30, 336). Uhl defines more in general the impact evaluation as an estimate of effects that have not been explicitly expected (1998:176).

DRUG POLICIES IN SWEDEN

Drug policies in Sweden have been consistently repressive, in keeping with a culture that "has shown its disapproval of drunken and disorderly behavior" (Gould 2001:9). These policies, which aim to repress the traffic in drugs, to socially rehabilitate drug abusers, and to contain the diffusion of drug use, have been elucidated in official publications.[2] From these one can learn the following:

(a) In Sweden, the law (passed in 1968 and amended many times since) prohibits the procurement, the encouragement of the diffusion, the processing, the transportation, the storing, and the possession of drugs or the equipment for their use, and the use itself. In terms of drugs then, the Swedish authorities have consistently kept to a rigorously prohibitory course. The procurement of drugs is punished with particular severity. Moreover, the punishment varies according to the quantity of drugs involved, the type (heroin and cocaine are considered the substances posing the most serious social threat), and the individual involved (it is held that young subjects should receive more protection from the law). The existence of a standard criminal code throughout the country makes the application of centralized directives on drug repression, rehabilitation, and prevention possible, even if they are coordinated with the local authorities.

(b) The various police forces (central, regional, local, and border) retain a traditional bureaucratic-professional orientation, with diligent and energetic repression of supply and traffic on a very large scale, in an attempt to leave no area without police control. However, this traditional model of police activity does not mean that the police force does not actively seek the support of pubic opinion.

(c) The judiciaries, the police, and the authorities charged with the repression of drug smuggling operate in strict and continuous collaboration. Correspondingly, there exists complete collaboration between the local police and the central and regional police authorities, and also between the police authority, the prison department, and the social services. A common goal, which explains their close collaboration, is the rehabilitation of all drug addicts including those serving prison sentences. A punitive aim has been affirmed for the last ten years, in line with the repressive character of Swedish drug legislation. However, the aim to rehabilitate remains and helps to explain the brief duration—from one to a few months—of the sentence for the majority of those imprisoned for drug offenses. It also explains the high proportion—40 percent—of the population of open prisons who are drug offenders. The rehabilitative operations make up part of a series of social services of welfare, to which the government and Swedish population trust not only the task of preventing drug addiction and criminal deviance in general, but also of meeting the wider demands of assistance, obligatory social insurance, and social security.

(d) The self-same social services and other authorities, in particular, those of the police and prisons, by virtue of a law passed in 1982 have leave to oblige drug addicts (including alcoholics) considered dangerous to themselves and others to undergo compulsory treatment. This treatment is considered the last possibility of rehabilitation and is provided for a maximum of six months. Afterward the patient is offered the possibility of receiving voluntary treatment. This service involves a minority (10 percent) of the drug addicts subject to rehabilitative treatment on the part of public or private institutions. In the majority of cases, these individuals are completely dependent on public assistance, homeless, and without occupation. For the rest, the law expects rehabilitation to be carried out with voluntary collaboration between the recipient and the services themselves.

(e) In the case of voluntary or noncoercive treatment, rehabilitation is, for the most part, carried out by means of a recuperative period in a residential center, the majority of which are private but are provided with public funding. This treatment is also often made available to alcoholics. These centers are under the organizational responsibility of the social services of local councils, which are subsidized by the councils and by the state. There are also families willing to offer hospitality to individuals who abuse drugs. In both cases the authorities control the methods of treatment. While the families are chosen, prepared, and assisted by specialized personnel, the residential centers endeavor to provide their guests with a therapeutic regimen (or "career" in the sense of Goffman). This therapy includes a first phase to change the attitudes and behavior of the patient, a second phase in which the patient's emotional life is attended to, and a final phase to achieve an improved adaptation to social life.

(f) Policies that produce the undesired effect of legitimizing drug use for potential users are not encouraged. Programs to reduce the damage, such as the distribution and sale of sterile syringes, have been adopted at a local level and are of an experimental nature. Centers that administer methadone—the heroin substitute—have been in operation since 1984, after a long trial period, and accept strictly only voluntary patients, who are twenty years old or over and who have been dependent on opiates for at least four years.[3]

(g) The Swedish authorities strive to identify all the drug addicts in their operational area and encourage them to undergo treatment. Initially, in the seventies, the social services made not very successful attempts to single out and socially recuperate all those who abused drugs, or those deemed potential abusers. Thereafter, a policy of cooperation between the social services, the police, the prison authorities, and the judiciaries was put into effect with precisely this objective. The social services try to approach all young people believed to be actual or potential users and also those drug abusers not undergoing rehabilitative treatment. Moreover, a systematic and detailed activity of secondary prevention, undertaken since the beginning of the eighties, has involved information campaigns. These campaigns are directed at all parents with adolescent children, as well as teachers and other adults in contact with young people, and to young people between seven and nineteen years old.

Although the drug prevention campaigns are centralized, the informational activity is conducted locally. It is left to the collaborative efforts of the school authorities, the police, the social services, and private nonprofit organizations—for example, foundations and associations, in particular voluntary recreational and sporting associations—to which more than half of Swedish youth belong. Collaboration between private organizations and public services has been consolidated as accepted practice in Sweden and in other Scandinavian countries.[4] The insistence on rehabilitative therapy and the repressive nature of its instrumentation, precisely with the aim of achieving this rehabilitation, is shared by almost all the personnel who have contact with drug addicts, including prison guards (Feeley and Simon 1992:457, note 17). The success of these policies of cooperation between public institutions to rehabilitate drug addicts is referred to later in this volume.

(h) Notwithstanding the commitment of the Swedish authorities to re-duce the traffic in and use of drugs and to rehabilitate those who abuse them, the principal objective is to prevent the diffusion of drugs and so to achieve, according to the expression used in governmental publications, "a drug-free society." The official criterion of evaluation of the Swedish drug policies is the level to which this ambitious objective has been achieved. To achieve this aim, on the one hand, is instrumental, i.e., the effort to closely coordinate repression, rehabilitation, and prevention; and on the other hand, is a commitment to keep to a minimum the level of ethnic and social segregation, the amount of relative deprivation, and the number of people unemployed, above all, youth. This task is carried out in the sphere of pri-mary prevention. Preventive activity in schools, in particular, has been conducted for many years in a systematic manner in every school in the country. It has involved a continuous effort to update the information given, to adopt the most effective methods, and also to coordinate with the police and social services.

Secondary prevention is directed toward those who already abuse drugs; tertiary prevention toward those who are judged to be potential abusers of alcohol or drugs and toward the social group to which they belong. Sec-ondary and tertiary prevention has involved a continuous commitment on the part of the social services to exert social control on, and give informa-tion to, local youth in schools and other meeting places like discotheques and subway stations. This activity is carried out in collaboration with the public authorities, especially schools and the police, parents, and members of voluntary organizations. The social services, represented by groups of young social workers, have the task of identifying and approaching young people already known to be drug addicts or potential drug addicts. To these young people and their families, the social services offer advice, psycho-logical counseling, help in the search for a job, and other services.[5]

Thus the Swedish authorities entrust the prevention of drug addiction, as a social problem, to their welfare institutions (National Board of Health and Welfare 1996:98). The activity of these institutions has traditionally been and continues to be based on the support of the population. Consen-sus is much greater for those public policies of general advantage, such as health care and pensions for the elderly. By way of contrast, nonuniversal-istic programs, which benefit only specific categories, such as unemploy-ment benefits and child allowances, are less popular, and programs for economically disadvantaged citizens and residents (for example, housing allowances and social assistance) are less popular still. However, not only do even these latter programs have the support of the direct beneficiaries, but more than 50 percent of the population think that they should not suf-fer cuts in their financing (Andersen et al. 1999:247–249, 254).

The social services and other public institutions are given the task of providing income support and social security, which should consequently lead, in the eyes of the Swedish political and administrative elites, to the primary prevention of drug addiction. This primary prevention activity requires, according to Swedish authorities:

1. Limiting relative deprivation by means of a variety of policy instruments: a relatively equal distribution of income, achieved by means of a high and very progressive taxation system; poverty-reducing programs; high-quality health service available to all; various types of support—in close cooperation with voluntary organizations subsidized by the state—for people in difficulty, in particular, young people and families with children.[6]

2. Keeping the number of people unemployed to a minimum. The intention of the Swedish political elites has been for many years to achieve full employment. The social democrats currently in power have maintained a commitment—as have the conservatives during their periods in office—to "active" policies in the job market. Active policies are measures passed to facilitate the geographical mobility and the professional retraining of the workforce, and also to create jobs subsidized by the treasury ("sheltered jobs") and to help finance businesses in difficulty in order to safeguard jobs. In Sweden, active employment policies have been in use since the end of the fifties. However, at that time they had already been legitimized by the rigid and institutionalized separation, since the thirties, between job placement and "passive" policies, that is to say, the provision of income support for the unemployed. Arranging job placement is trusted to the unions, but is coordinated by an organization set up by the central government. The local public authorities administer passive policies. When income support is made available, it is because of entitlement to social security (for workers who have paid the mandatory contributions to unemployment insurance), rather than entitlement to public assistance for the poor. Therefore, an effort has been made on the part of the authorities to include everyone who is eligible for work in the job market.[7] Furthermore, in the first five years of the nineties measures to combat youth unemployment, which had been relatively neglected up to that point, were introduced or extended.[8]

3. Pursuing a housing policy of building low-rent homes to prevent ethnic and class segregation. Its objective has been to place at the disposal of all residents, and in particular the most disadvantaged socioeconomic and ethnic groups, an affordable and comfortable home.[9]

SOCIAL POLICIES IN THE UNITED STATES

Despite the enormously widespread diffusion of drugs in the United States, public policies, in substance, have been extremely limited in their objectives, active intervention, and social services offered to the public. In particular:

1. Laws of an extremely repressive nature regulate drug policies, as in Sweden. There are both federal laws, which set the minimum penalty (the Comprehensive Drug Abuse and Control Act of 1970, followed by the Anti-Drug Abuse Control Act of 1988, which made the penalties heavier) (Inciardi and McElrath 1998a:xiv; Reuter 1998:318), and also state laws. Not only is the supplying of drugs penalized, but also simply the possession of drugs for personal use and their use (in most of the United States, even in private). Federal organizations like the Federal Bureau of Investigation (FBI) and the Drug Enforcement Administration (DEA) (Jacoby and Gramckow 1994:152) and municipal organizations like the police conduct the repression. The different municipal police forces have been gradually moving toward a "community" style concept of their duties. These duties have been accordingly intended as the results of the combined efforts of the police, citizens, and local community organizations, rather than the effect of a bureaucratic-professional organization—the police itself (Mastrofski, Worden, and Snipes 1995; Uchida and Forst 1994). This new concept has been applied with particular vigor to the repression of drug-related crimes (Davis and Lurigio 1996:99–109). It has not changed, however, the emphasis placed by the authorities on the repression and so the imprisonment of individuals suspected of having committed this type of crime (regardless of their attested behavior). Measures to rehabilitate and reduce the damage have not been accordingly favored (Feeley and Simon 1992:455–57, 461–62; Nadelmann 1998:290–91, 295), although their limited use has been able to demonstrate their effectiveness (Anglin and Hser 1990:424–28; Donziger 1996:201–4).[10]

The conviction that energetic intervention on the part of the police and the judiciary can significantly reduce the supply and demand of drugs is indicated by the frequent rhetorical recourse to the "war on drugs" by presidents, presidential candidates, and other politicians, even in the absence of preventive and rehabilitative measures. Also, laws that threaten heavier penalties for crimes related to the supply and use of drugs, and which in their application take away judicial discretion, support this conviction. It seems to permeate the self- and public image of the role of the agents of social control as soldiers who must demonstrate energy and decision, engaged as they are in a "war" against a dangerous internal and—regarding drug trafficking—also external enemy. This repressive orientation also characterizes most, if not all, of the activity to check the traffic in and the use of drugs, carried out by citizens in areas in which these phenomena are considered to be particularly intense.[11]

2. The repression of drugs remains the primary objective of U.S. drug policy (the consequences of which are discussed in our evaluation of these policies). Nevertheless, the U.S. authorities have made an effort, for many years now, to finance and organize the rehabilitation of some of the large population of drug addicts. This effort has involved, at the expense of the

municipal budget, the creation of centers for the provision of methadone treatment; at the expense of the state and federal budget, the payment of vast amounts to residential centers, or to centers of psychological support for drug addicts in difficulty. Also private organizations, often religious, carry out drug rehabilitation, thereby in fact assuming public functions.[12] A number of factors would appear to have hindered the development, if it ever began, of a coherent national drug rehabilitation policy, coordinated by the various administrative authorities: the condition of municipal, county, or state budgets; their judicial autonomy; the generally poor attitude and lack of commitment to drug rehabilitation programs on the part of public administrators (for example, their hostility toward the methadone centers and their reluctance to finance them, notwithstanding the proven effect of methadone in the social rehabilitation of drug addicts; Platt, Widmann, Lidz, and Marlowe 1998:180–81). In addition, the various public administration apparatuses face great difficulty in coordinating the multitude of private service companies that have been given contracts to provide public services (DeHoog 1993:122). The presumably poor effectiveness of such a drug policy can best be evaluated in comparison with the corresponding Swedish drug policy.

3. The potential recipients of these programs are therefore not the total number of drug addicts, and much less all the subjects at risk, but only those who are motivated to detoxicate, at least for the period of rehabilitation. The recourse to coercive intervention is avoided, maybe because it is considered unconstitutional. Many municipalities prefer to close the private places where drugs are sold and so to sustain the relative costs in the legal disputes with their owners (Davis and Lurigio 1996:105–9, 114–16). Very little systematic research into the potential benefits of rehabilitative treatment has been carried out at the national level, perhaps because it is too costly. The research that has been done has been methodologically badly conducted (Anglin and Hser 1990:429–32; Deschenes and Greenwood 1994:267–70). Nor have drug addicts been provided with sufficient opportunity to detoxicate and to reinstate themselves in society (Inciardi, McBride, and Surratt 1998:46; Knight et al. 1996). Limited budgets have not been the only reason (Hunt and Rosenbaum 1998:195–99). Finally, we should mention the trust that politicians and, it would seem, the majority of public opinion continue to demonstrate in the repression of the traffic and use of drugs as the main public weapon in the fight to contain their diffusion.

4. The emphasis placed on repression has also meant a limited commitment, on the part of the responsible authorities, to the prevention of the use and abuse of drugs, so much so that there is a lack of coordination between the different authorities, those both at the same and at different administrative levels. The preventive programs that have been adopted have remained limited in their breadth and financing. The most recent presidents

of the United States, from Reagan to Clinton, and numerous state governors have declared a "war on drugs," stating in this way, with the possible exception of Clinton, to be at least implicitly in favor of repression rather than prevention (Donziger 1996:115; Hagan 1996:156–157; Kornblum and Julian 1995:152, 154). A consequence of this policy implementation has been a lack of damage limitation programs (Springer 1998:43), which in contrast have been tried in certain European countries. Another consequence has been that in the United States preventive activity has frequently been projected and implemented alongside repressive activity.

Apart from local organizations, such as some schools whose teaching personnel and educational programs have moved in this direction (Eggert, Seyl, and Nicholas 1990), only certain city authorities have developed preventive activities, sometimes also availing themselves of state funding. These preventive activities have always been planned and accompanied by repressive intervention. Some important cities have put into effect, or at least have undertaken to put into effect, preventive programs—for example, the recent Weed and Seed program, referred to below. These programs combine the traditional bureaucratic-professional orientation of the police force with its new "community" orientation and with other measures, like the closure of private places noted as centers of drug dealing. Such interventions have been concentrated on socially disaggregated urban areas where both the supply and the use of drugs are widespread, and also among groups of youths (Fagan 1996:46–51). In line with the community orientation, municipal authorities have often acted together, and in agreement, with neighborhood community associations, whose formation they have promoted.

5. Preventive programs against drug addiction have generally been conducted in schools or in local communities and therefore have had—in the majority of cases—a circumscribed impact and effect (Kornblum and Julian 1995:192–93; Rosa, Spizzichino and Tempesta 1986:53; Weingart 1993:96–101).[13] Some programs are nevertheless noteworthy for their effort to coordinate local initiatives as well as, sometimes, for the attempt to systematically evaluate their effects (a task that is methodologically very difficult (Botvin 1990:499–500; Hawkins, Arthur, and Catalano 1995:361–64; Uhl 1998). In this sense the Weed and Seed program is noteworthy. A preventive program on a vast scale, realized in nineteen cities of different sizes, this program succeeded in coordinating the intervention of the authorities situated at different administrative levels, above all the police.

It is still too early to know the results of another preventive program against alcohol and drug abuse, called Fighting Back and aimed especially at the younger section of the population. Financed by private foundations, it was carried out by members of these institutions and ordinary citizens. In any case this is one of the most wide-ranging preventive programs ever carried out in the United States (in terms of financing and the number of urban and rural communities involved) (Klizner 1993; Davis and Lurigio 1996:74–75). Another vast program of prevention called Community Partnership Program was based on federal financing, by means of which as many as 252 communities, heterogeneous in terms of territorial dislocation, population size, ethnic composition, and other characteristics, have tried to coordinate their preventive activity. They did this by developing joint programs and holding periodic meetings between their institutional and voluntary representatives (Cook and Roehl 1993).

Although the meetings have revealed the difficulty of coordinating diverse programs and personnel, overall they are considered to have been very useful (ibid.:238, 241), so much so that—while waiting for a definitive evaluation of the preventive programs—it is hoped that a systematic coordination can make some contribution to solving the drug problem in the United States. Nevertheless, there have often been many obstacles in the way, for instance a lack of funds, as well as unforeseen effects and an absence of planning. At times this lack of funds—as with the Weed and Seed program—has affected the most innovative part, the "sowing," that is, the encouragement of nondeviant behavior and relations, which constitutes primary prevention. All these difficulties have been augmented by the difficulties ensuing from the relatively high deprivation that afflicts the recipients of the programs of secondary prevention of drug addiction and criminal deviance in general. Thus—in the absence of programs of primary prevention—the preventive activity takes place in an extremely difficult social context. Such a context is determined, from among many factors, by extreme disparity in the distribution of income to the detriment of families, mostly single parent, who are very poor and not adequately assisted; by unemployment, particularly among young people, and concentrated among young people from disadvantaged ethnic groups; and by public housing policies that are lacking in every aspect. According to qualified experts, such unfavorable living conditions preclude any possibility of success for preventive policies against drug addiction and criminality in general, which they do not manage to change to a significant degree (Davis and Lurigio 1996:130; Massey 1990:353–54).

The United States lacks "a consensus on the question of a coherent national drug policy" (Ginsburg 1992:99). It is also important to note the aversion of most white Americans to welfare policies—inspired more by their conservatism than by prejudice (Dillion 1999; Quadagno 1999:5)—above all if the policies would be of advantage to ethnic minorities, especially blacks.[14] Keeping this in mind, we turn to the domain and the methods of intervention and the recipients of these policies, which propose to reduce a condition of relative and absolute deprivation. We also compare them with the corresponding Swedish policies. After examining their effective capacity to reduce the deprivation (absolute and relative) of their intended population, we analyze their corresponding benefits.

The unequal distribution of income in the United States, particularly among families, has not been the target of redistributive intervention on the part of the authorities for more than thirty years, not since the time of President Johnson's War on Poverty. On the contrary, it has been the object of comparative research into the corresponding distribution of per capita income in the United States, in less recent times, and in other comparable countries, like Germany, Great Britain, and Sweden. These studies have highlighted the following:

1. The distribution of family income, measured according to conventional criteria, is especially unequal in the United States and especially equalitarian in Sweden (Ginsburg 1992:199–200; Keister and Moller 2000:63–69). Consequently, considerably more favorable conditions exist in Sweden for the economically disadvantaged levels of society. The lowest salaries in Sweden are 60 percent higher than the lowest salaries in America (Gynnerstedt 1997:200).

2. In the course of the eighties this inequality increased in the United States as elsewhere. However, in the United States, as opposed to in Sweden, there has been a significant polarization of family income to the detriment of those with lower incomes (Fritzell 1993; Danziger and Gottschalk 1995:39–66, 111–20; Nielsen and Alderson 1997:13–14).

3. In the United States much more than in Sweden, poverty is concentrated in certain urban areas and has struck specific ethnic groups (above all blacks) (Abrahamson 1988:34–35; Jencks 1992:136–37; Small and Newman 2001; Wacquant and Wilson 1993:26–27).

4. Finally, in the United States much more than in Sweden poverty has struck female heads of families with children, particularly black women with children residing in poor urban areas.[15]

In the United States public policies to support the unemployed and fight unemployment originated in the social legislation of the thirties, under the presidency of Roosevelt. Since then they have been consistently eroded as a budgeting principle, so that now only those who have previously paid the compulsory insurance contributions have the right to receive unemployment benefits. For some time this has been a percentage of previously earned income, which varies from state to state. In contrast to Sweden, U.S. unemployment policies have put the emphasis not on active but on passive employment policies. They provide unemployment benefit for a maximum of six months to those workers who have paid the compulsory social security contributions for a minimum number of years (usually ten). The remaining programs of income support, aimed at those citizens who live in conditions of poverty but are not up to date with the payment of their social security contributions, are not specifically addressed to the unemployed. Programs such as Aid to Families with Dependent Children (AFDC), Supplemental Security Income (SSI), and Medicaid provide the necessary health cover for specific categories of economically or physically disadvantaged people.

Active policies went through a revival in the sixties and seventies, above all with the Comprehensive Employment Training Act (CETA) of 1973. The legislators intended this act to create jobs in the federal, state, and municipal sectors, with funding provided by the federal government. The end of the CETA program, in 1985, came about for many reasons: the organized opposition of private economic powers to this federal program, dating back to the end of the seventies under the Democratic presidency of Carter; its incapacity to fully deliver the foreseen benefits despite the high costs; and finally, the hostility of the Reagan presidency. Federal support for these policies was drastically reduced at the beginning of the eighties. Their implementation was regulated by a program much more limited in its objectives, the Job Training and Partnership Act, the financing of which was reduced to less than a third of that of the CETA programs. The Omnibus Budget Reconciliation Act of 1981, also under the Reagan presidency, required those making a request to receive federal assistance for children in their care (excluding mothers with small children) to do voluntary work. Furthermore, the federal contribution to state programs of income support for the unemployed has been made dependent on the participation of a minimum quota of beneficiaries in compulsory work.[16]

Public housing policies have a noteworthy effect on limiting or, on the contrary, promoting deviant behavior and relations (Coleman 1987). In the United States, such policies have put at the disposal of the poorest citizens accommodation at a reduced rent (no more than 30 percent of the income of the occupant). This has been done in the double form of the construction of housing blocks under public subsidies and the provision of subsidies to private building contractors (Horton et al. 1994:272; Jencks 1992:9–10, 20). However, in the United States these policies are characterized by a lack of quantitative commitment and by a lack of quality in the planning, construction, and maintenance. Certain attempts of reclamation or reconstruction of neglected areas were made in a less recent period (from the midthirties to the end of the seventies. Apart from them, not one project has been completed that has not been limited to simply moving the urban ghettos from one area to another, as detailed in the following paragraph. The demolition of uninhabitable public housing, without the obligation to construct new homes for the tenants lacking adequate income, has received legislative sanction through two recent federal laws. This is referred to in Chapter 5, on the perverse effects of U.S. social policy.

In the fifties, sixties, and seventies, a period of maximum public commitment to the construction of public housing projects, less than 2 percent of the new homes constituted affordable accommodation constructed with funds made available by the authorities. Since then, this commitment has been drastically reduced. In comparison with 127,000 low-rent new homes built in 1970, in 1991 only 7,500 were constructed. Urban reclamation embarked upon in the United States has suffered from a lack of coordination between municipal authorities, between them and the state and federal authorities, and also between the different federal agencies, even when they have managed to revitalize the economy of a city and so give greater possibility to the financing of programs to prevent deviance. The problem of coordination persists in the Department of Housing and Urban Development, which has precisely the task of coordinating the various municipal, state, and federal building programs, even though it was established in 1965 under the presidency of Lyndon Johnson.[17]

NOTES

1. The distinction is not, however, universally accepted among the specialist scholars. They often prefer to make generic reference to the nonlegal use of drugs (Reilly, Leukefeld, Gao, and Allen 1994:124), or more frequently do not distinguish between their "non-proper use" and "abuse" (Uhl 1998:140–41).

2. For a short introduction to the Swedish and other Scandinavian welfare states, cf. Coluzzi and Palmieri (2001:151–61), Ginsburg (1992:30–66), Gynnerstedt (1997), Kautto, Fritzell, Hvinden, Kvist, and Uusitalo (2001a), Olsson Hort (1993, 1995), and Palme (1999). Nordic welfare states, including Sweden, have been recently subject to a thorough investigation. See Kautto et al. (1999b) and Kautto, Fritzell, Hvinden, Kvist, and Uusitalo (2001b).

3. Cf. Feeley and Simon (1992:457, note 17), National Board of Health and Welfare (1994:41–42, 1996:98–99), Swedish National Institute of Public Health (1995:24–30), and Von Hofer, Sarnecki, and Tham (1997:64–66).

4. Cf. Klausen and Selle (1997:167–68, 171–73), National Board of Health and Welfare (1994:42–43), Swedish Institute (1995), and Swedish National Institute of Public Health (1995:15–18, 21, 25, 27–28).

5. Cf. Nersnaes (1998), Swedish Institute (1995), and Swedish National Institute of Public Health (1995:8, 10–11, 16–18, 25, 32–33).

6. Cf. Ginsburg (1992:128), Klausen and Selle (1997:167–70), Halleroed (1996:146), Ministry of Health and Social Affairs (1997:1), and National Board of Health and Welfare (1994:42–43, 52–55, 58–59, 1996:66–80, 122–29).

7. Concerning the conceptual distinction between active and passive policies, see Dropping, Hvinden, and Vik (1999:134–37), Furaker, Johansson, and Lind (1990:150–51), Hvinden, Heikkila, and Kankare (2001), and Reyneri (1996:379–86). Concerning the historical origins of Swedish active policies, and the effect of legitimating them by distinguishing them from social assistance, cf. King and Rothstein (1993:147–55, 161–63, 169–73).

8. Cf. Dropping et al. (1999:146–57), Esping-Andersen (1990:182–83), Gynnerstedt (1997:194–95, 200–1), Ginsburg (1992:32, 39–42, 202–3), Halleroed (1996:146), Pontusson (1997:60), Stein and Doerfer (1992:56–57), and National Board of Health and Welfare (1994:49).

9. Cf. Arnell-Gustafsson (1982:40, note 2), Gynnerstedt (1997:199), and Lindahl (1979:100).

10. Governor George E. Pataki of New York State has moved away from traditional repressive interventions, by decreeing to keep in state jails only violent crim-

inals. Other convicted criminals are set free, provided they attend training courses to better qualify in the labor market, and also rehabilitation programs, if they are drug addicts (Hernandez 1998).

11. Cf. Donziger (1996:15, 115), Feeley and Simon (1992:457), Hagan (1994:154–57), Hawkins et al. (1995:355–57), Horton et al. (1994:115–16), Inciardi and McElrath (1998b:285–87), Jacoby and Gramckow (1994:151–53), McNamara (1997), and Weingart (1993:89–94).

12. Cf. Anglin and Hser (1990:417–29), Cohen (1997:31–32), Davis and Lurigio (1996:130–31), Deschenes and Greenwood (1994:268), and Horton et al. (1994:122).

13. Cf. Botvin (1990:472–99), Hawkins et al. (1995:357–61), and Springer (1998:39–43). For the Italian reader, cf. Rosa et al. (1986) (a thorough and well-informed, but not recent review of preventive programs, with particular reference to the United States).

14. Most white people do not favor redistributive policies, in contrast to blacks, who tend to be in favor irrespective of their social class (Innis and Sittig 1996).

15. Cf. Ginsburg (1992:103–4, 201), Horton et al. (1994:355), Jencks (1992:204–35), Kornblum and Julian (1995:236–39), McLanahan and Garfinkel (1993:113–18), Neckerman, Aponte, and Wilson (1988:397–00), and Sanders (1990).

16. Cf. Danziger and Gottschalk (1995:20, 24–28, 173–74), Esping-Andersen (1990:181), Ginsberg (1994:110–19), Ginsburg (1992:107–11), Horton et al. (1994:360–61), Iglehart (1999c), Kornblum and Julian (1995:283), Mead (1993:180, 184), and Social Security Administration (1997:8–11, 23–25). On the ability of workfare programs to contain poverty and unemployment, we shall elaborate later.

17. Cf. Davis and Lurigio (1996:75–76, 102–4), Gruberg (1979), Handler (1979:494–95), Howlett (1998), Kornblum and Julian (1995:226, 460, 465–67), Wagner, Joder, and Mumphrey (1995:206–10).

2   The Benefits of Social Policies

PRELIMINARY CONSIDERATIONS

Our analysis now turns to the benefits of the social policies that have been implemented in Sweden and in the United States. First, we compare the ability of both welfare systems to develop effective (primary and secondary) rehabilitation and prevention actions, and then we look at the different prevalence of drugs in Sweden and in the United States. Reference will be later made to research concerning the social causes of drug use in order to discuss whether rehabilitation and prevention have limited the spreading of these substances into the population.

THE BENEFITS

The Different Ability to Implement Rehabilitation and Prevention Measures in Sweden and in the United States

In this section we continue to analyze Swedish and U.S. social policies, but now from the viewpoint of their ability to actually provide the expected benefits.

In Sweden, considerable results have been achieved thanks to a strong and continuous commitment of the government as well as of the central and local administrative authorities in rehabilitating those who abuse drugs (alcoholics included), and in systematically implementing secondary and primary prevention. A longitudinal study done toward the middle of the last decade focused on the change of behavior of over four hundred persons subject to voluntary rehabilitation treatment in twenty-two centers (unfortunately, a control group was not then available). The study found that approximately one-half of the patients had abstained from taking drugs, and over one-third of them had avoided any contact with substances that might alter their mental functions (not only drugs but also alcohol, mind-altering drugs, and solvents). Similar results have been also reported by a more recent survey. Encouraging success has been achieved through the rehabilitation of persons subject to preliminary compulsory treatment, and through secondary and tertiary prevention measures. The latter, in particular, reached an estimated 80 percent of those who abuse drugs. These measures have also allowed information on the effects of drug consumption to be spread among young people, their parents, and other adults who during their professional or voluntary activities have the opportunity to meet young people (Swedish National Institute of Public Health 1995:16–18, 28–29).

Primary prevention involves an effort to limit relative deprivation as much as possible, that is, differences in the distribution of income, the extent and intensity of poverty, unemployment—mostly long-term—and the concentration of disadvantaged social classes and ethnic groups into some urban areas. Though not completely, the aim of controlling relative deprivation has been achieved to a great extent. Bearing in mind this aim, and that the benefits of the Swedish welfare system are similar to those of the other Nordic welfare systems, a balanced evaluation of these benefits should consider the following elements:

1. The income distribution in Sweden is one of the most egalitarian ones in the advanced capitalist countries. Poverty rates are particularly low with respect to other developed countries, though in the course of the 1980s and 1990s the differences in income between more or less privileged social/professional classes have grown. Furthermore, the proportion of persons who live in relative or absolute poverty is particularly small, much lower (approximately one-third) than in the United States, and—despite an upward trend—has remained small in the early 1990s. Relative or absolute poverty conditions are either defined through a conventional standard establishing a poverty line, or by establishing through a sampling inquiry those who cannot enjoy a standard of living corresponding to their minimum personal requirements.

2. The risk of poverty in economically marginal persons (particularly mothers with dependent children, long-term unemployed people, and groups or individuals of foreign origin) has been in general effectively opposed by the social services. Nonetheless, the risk of social exclusion is—like in the United States—very high in young mothers as head of a family who have low qualifications for the labor market.

3. The level of quality of the Swedish social services, from which the whole population benefits, is generally considered high, and the results of their performances—as well as overall welfare performances—are excellent. Though some limitations have been recently introduced to reduce public expenditure, access to the benefits offered by the compulsory health, accident, and invalidity insurance is still very wide, their amount very high, and the quality of services one of the best in the world. In particular, Sweden (together with Japan) enjoys the lowest child mortality rate in the world and (after Japan) has the most long-lived population, with a life ex-

pectation exceeding by some years the average life rate in all other developed countries. Furthermore, social services are in a position to approach a very high percentage—estimated between 80 and 90 percent—of drug addicts who use intravenous injection, and to submit those who may have contracted an HIV viral infection to medical treatment.[1]

There are, however, some differences in the health conditions of the neediest social/economic classes compared to the richer ones. This is accounted for by the fact that the latter have the opportunity to avail themselves of the more expensive—but also more immediately accessible—private health service (Ginsburg 1992:63; Lehto, Moss, and Rostgaard 1999:114–15; Lundberg and Lahelma 2001). The modest reductions made in these benefits during the 1990s have been balanced by greater opportunities to find placement for children through six years old in public or private nursing centers operating within the National Health Service. The quality standard of children's nursing, which was already very good in the past, has likely increased in this decade because municipalities tend now to recruit specialized staff, which is currently the majority, despite a slight worsening of the ratio between the number of children and available staff.[2]

4. During the 1980s, the average unemployment rate was very low in comparison with the average rate in OECD countries. This rate grew during the first years of the following decade and surpassed the U.S. rate, staying however below 8.5 percent, but since the mid-1990s it has considerably decreased. Currently, it ranges between 5 and 6 percent, one of the lowest in the world, though it is higher than the U.S. rate.[3] About one-third of the subjects examined have been unemployed for a long period (this proportion also grew rapidly in the early 1990s and then decreased). As regards the age cohort that is most affected by unemployment—sixteen to twenty-four years—the average rate has never exceeded 20 percent and is currently 15 percent. Nevertheless, the relative disadvantage of young people (twenty to thirty years) in comparison with other age segments of the labor market, and consequently the available economic and social resources, became very pronounced after the 1992–95 slump, mostly for nonspecialized young people in the area of manual work. Young people were previously not disadvantaged, and the nonspecialized labor force was less disadvantaged than now.[4]

The effectiveness of the active labor policies that have been implemented for a long time in Sweden can be inferred in particular from the improvement—according to a 1991 government survey—in job qualification and security that one-half of those who attended professional training and retraining courses were able to achieve. Considering that Norway has the same welfare model as Sweden, some Norwegian surveys made in the 1990s show that retraining courses improved the chances of finding a job by 5 percent, and allowed an estimated 30–45 percent of participants to find a job immediately after having completed a course. Among those who had attended a course, the proportion of those who found a job almost equaled the rate of those who had lost one (Abrahamson 1993:127; Dropping et al. 1999:158).

5. The conditions of people of foreign origin are still much better in Sweden than in any other European country,[5] and they are incomparably more favorable than those of the more disadvantaged ethnic groups in the United States.[6] That "the second generation of immigrants breaks the law less frequently than the first generation" (Barbagli 1998:135–36) has been imputed to the success of the integration—especially welfare—policies that the Swedish authorities have addressed to the children of immigrants. Their greater law-abiding behavior may be explained by an efficient social control exerted by the welfare organizations on young people, as we have already noted. Nevertheless, the same author notes that the second generation of immigrants commits crimes "more frequently than natives" (ibid.; cf. also Martens 1997:225–26, 228–29, 236, 239–40, 243–44).

This phenomenon might be explained by the more severe social disadvantage suffered by immigrants. As a matter of fact, immigrants suffer—despite the efforts of governmental and municipal authorities—the most deprivation in terms of income (since immigrants more frequently resort to public assistance than Swedish native families), health conditions, quality and quantity of jobs in the labor market (considering that low-prestige and low-wage manual labor prevails among immigrants, especially in the case of unskilled services, and also considering the relatively heavy incidence of unemployment, including long-term unemployment), often unsatisfactory housing and residential areas, and finally, the sometimes discriminatory treatment immigrants receive from some representatives of the established authorities (although it does not appear that the judiciary system operates in a discriminatory way toward immigrants).[7]

To be effective, measures for the prevention of social and ethnic segregation should include the building of a suitable quantity of good-quality working-class housing that satisfies the needs of the disadvantaged social/economic segments and ethnic groups. In Sweden, this has been in general achieved: in fact, there are no real slums in Sweden, and a great deal of working-class housing with reduced rent and overall good quality standards has been built (Gynnerstedt 1997:199). However, it should take public housing policy in Sweden several years to provide the expected benefits to the whole population. As a matter of fact, it is "easier to redistribute money than it is to move buildings and people" (Arnell-Gustafsson 1982:35). Thus building new houses can only very slowly begin to effect a policy aimed at lowering residential segregation for classes and ethnic groups. In the year 1980, the overall quantity of housing units in Sweden—only a part of which includes public buildings—increased by less than 2 percent (ibid.:38). Moreover, the lack of low-rent working-class housing has resulted in long waiting lists (Lindahl 1979:100). Furthermore, some working-class quarters, which seem to contain a large number of immigrants and persons receiving social assistance, also are the locus of a great deal of vandalism and drug abuse (Von Hofer et al. 1997:64, 70). The attempts to discourage residential segregation by classes have not therefore been completely successful. It should be remarked, however, that in Sweden, like elsewhere, crimes against persons or property—rather than in particular segregated quarters—are mostly committed in well-trafficked areas, where strangers can easily meet and where it is difficult to implement effective social control (Wikstroem 1995:441–45, 456–60).

As a matter of fact, those who live in peripheral low-income residential areas are mainly persons belonging to nonprivileged classes and to ethnic groups of foreign origin (these categories partially coinciding). The characteristics of these areas do not always conform to the aims of the decision-making public authorities. Official publications and ethnographic surveys show that immigrants, due to their strong residential mobility, tend to gather in poorly kept working-class housing that is not attractive to the local population, who tries in turn—as soon as economically possible—to leave those unpleasant and unexciting areas, or at least the buildings where the new and poorer immigrants crowd together. Nonetheless, ethnic segregation is not total, since in the better working-class buildings local people and relatively well-integrated foreigners live together. There have also been some attempts to renew the decayed quarters without resorting to a perverse gentrification effect, which we shall discuss later with reference to the United States (Abrahamson 1988:35; Sjoegren 1992:10–11; Von Hofer et al. 1997:64, 68).

In the United States, public policies on drugs have stressed repression, which has had (disregarding the perverse effects, upon which we will later elaborate) some negative consequences:

- A relative shortage in public financing for and an absolute insufficiency in rehabilitating interventions.
- The absence of a coordinated, continuous, and unified (that is, combining repression with rehabilitation and prevention) intervention policy among local, governmental, and federal authorities.
- The inadequacy of primary prevention policies aimed at limiting poverty and at controlling relative and absolute deprivation.

1. The insufficiency in the allocation of public funds for the rehabilitation of drug addicts (Horton et al. 1994:469) has been worsened by cutting federal support programs (Nahon 1997:42).[8] This situation has been a great problem for the many American drug addicts who have been looking for rehabilitation but have not been in a position to bear the expenses of private organizations or to avail themselves of treatment locally or elsewhere (Donziger 1996:204; Knight et al. 1996; Kornblum and Julian 1995:151). Fur-

thermore, the widespread practice—almost everywhere in the United States—sanctioned sometimes by governmental regulations, of providing the same small doses of methadone to everybody is insufficient as an alternative to heroin. These amounts do not meet the needs of the single person. The supply is also often limited to a period of six months, which is usually inadequate without medical control and psychological or social support. This has been the case even though some government experts and the American Medical Association recommend medical control and support for substitutive treatments to be effective (Anglin and Hser 1990:417–21); Marsden, Gossop, Farrel, and Strang 1998:254).

Strong private participation in interventions aimed at rehabilitation, prevention, or both has only partially balanced the quantitative and qualitative deficiencies of the public service. A widespread tradition in the United States, as well as in Scandinavia and elsewhere, of collaboration between public and both profit and nonprofit private organizations in providing public services has not been sufficient to overcome this inadequacy. We should note the methadone programs are implemented by religious or nonconfessional, often nonprofit, organizations with federal and/or public financial support. These private programs provide interventions that not only benefit the young inhabitants of poor and socially disorganized neighborhoods, but also their families and the neighborhoods.[9]

Despite this private participation in rehabilitation programs for acknowledged drug addicts who can be approached by the authorities, the proportion of those who have received rehabilitation treatment is still small. Only one-tenth of imprisoned drug addicts receive comprehensive treatment from health authorities. The approximately 115,000 heroin addicts who in 1995 underwent methadone treatment were perhaps 15–20 percent of the total number. This is a very small percentage compared with an estimate of the corresponding rates in Italy, and especially in Sweden. This has happened in spite of the proven effectiveness and low cost of drug addiction and crime prevention programs in general, and particularly those aimed at the medical and social rehabilitation of drug addicts and criminals. Furthermore, the environment in which rehabilitation is supplied, particularly methadone supply centers, is often viewed with hostility and mistrust toward users, which can jeopardize their rehabilitation skills.[10]

2. The negative effects of insufficient public support for rehabilitation and secondary prevention programs might have been balanced by adequate primary prevention policies (financial support, continuity, and widespread extent), but unfortunately this has not happened. Since these programs were aimed at limiting relative and absolute deprivation, the dramatic reduction of federal funds increased the negative consequences of the lack of a systematic and continuous primary prevention policy. In

particular, the disparity in the distribution of income and the resulting percentage of people below the official poverty line grew from about 11–13 percent of the population in the 1970s to 13–15 percent in the following decade. This was a significant increase in comparison with the 1960s, and much more so in comparison with the 1950s. In comparison to other developed countries income distribution has remained very equal in Sweden, while both income and wealth distributions are very unequal in the United States, and have become even more so in the last decades.[11]

As most experts agree, the fact that the number of persons and families considered needy with reference to the official poverty line, as well as according to other not exclusively monetary criteria, should be also ascribed to a change in the aims of U.S. social—i.e., welfare—policies. Demographic and economic factors may also have been influential. At first, these policies significantly increased both financial and nonfinancial aid to persons and families considered poor, but they later reduced them. Nevertheless, as the comparative data supplied by a source that is generally deemed reliable—the Luxembourg Income Study—show, in 1980 (before these reductions took place), the proportion of needy persons receiving assistance was the highest in the United States and the lowest in Sweden, by a ratio exceeding 3:1. In particular, the proportion of poor women with dependent children receiving assistance was about six times higher in the United States than in Sweden.

Under Reagan's presidency in the 1980s, these differences grew, largely because of the reduction in income of single-parent, mainly black, U.S. families. This was so despite the reduction in the number of poor people eligible to receive welfare services, and the promulgation by Congress in the second half of the 1980s of federal laws granting support to needy families with dependent children. These laws marked a temporary return to welfare policies by a Congress then dominated by the Republican party. In the early 1990s, the proportion of poor children of preschool age (a very high rate of which—perhaps 40 percent—did not receive and still does not receive any welfare subsidy) increased enormously in the United States by comparison with 1979. As a consequence, the gap with other developed countries increased: the percentage of poor children in the United States became about eight times higher than in Sweden.[12]

The extent of poverty among the children of these two countries continues to be different, even if we limit our comparison—as regards the United States—to the white population (though poverty is even more widespread in groups like blacks and nonwhite Hispanics). This difference cannot be ascribed to a higher percentage of children living only with their mothers, who run a higher risk of poverty (since the rate of single female-headed households is the same in both countries). The higher percentage of poor children in the United States derives on the contrary—as it has been demonstrated by a recent survey—from the overlapping of three factors:

1. A wider labor force participation of Swedish parents.

2. A more egalitarian distribution of income (since in Sweden the marginal labor force is better remunerated).

3. A much more liberal Swedish welfare system, both in terms of performance and the proportion of minors (below the age of eighteen) who benefit from assistance among those who are entitled to it—almost all of them do in Sweden, while little more than one-fourth do in the United States. Furthermore, since the United States reduced social security subsidies in the early 1980s, these already considerable differences in the respective rates of poor children between the two countries have further grown (Jaentti and Danziger 1994; cf. also Lichter 1997:125–27; Rostgaard and Lehto 2001:152–62).

3. Like in Sweden, public economic support for assistance to poor people changed according to the will and capabilities of local administrations, despite the distribution of funds from the central administrations to municipalities (Sweden) or directly to the concerned persons (United States). However, unlike in Sweden and other OECD countries, in the United States the subsidy is so small that in many cases, it does not even cover minimal requirements and does not raise the family income over the threshold of poverty. The greater liberality and efficiency of the Swedish welfare system, compared to the United States, can be better appraised if the following consideration is made. The amount of direct Swedish aid is similar to the U.S. average, but by comparison it amounts to much more because of contributions to rents, pensions—such as survivor's pensions for children under the age of twelve—children's care and medical expenses, in addition to a variety of other benefits and social services provided to families.[13]

With regard to the latter, Medicaid, the U.S. medical assistance program for the poor, is deemed absolutely insufficient for its quality of services and the range of the needy population that actually receives services. This has especially been the case since the reductions made in the public expenditure on Medicaid in the early 1980s. Almost one-third of the poor cannot legally access to this program either for themselves or for their children. An undetermined number of them, which is considered to exceed half of the overall poor, have no health coverage. They cannot afford the medical expenses that are not included in Medicaid, or have not paid social security contributions due to their irregular work, or—in the case of clandestine immigrants—because they fear being discovered and expelled from the country. Furthermore, a high and continuously growing proportion of needy persons is not covered by any private health insurance: according to official estimates, about 16 percent of the U.S. population does not receive any public or private medical assistance.[14]

Thus, the low-quality medical standards of the poorest part of the population have increased the national average rate of child mortality (8.4 percent—the highest in the developed countries—against 5.8 percent in Sweden). It has also lowered, comparatively speaking, the average life expectancy (75.8 years—among the lowest in the developed countries—against 78.1 years in Sweden).[15] Finally, the welfare subsidy granted in Sweden almost doubles when the assistance is provided not to single adults but to couples, even unmarried, provided they consist of two persons continuously living together. In this way, Sweden does not encourage the trend of poor mothers to stay alone or to hide from social workers their partners who could contribute to the family budget (National Board of Health and Welfare 1994:46).

The coverage of basic family requirements for goods and services, which is granted in Sweden but not in the United States, probably contributes to a better quality of family life. It has been well known for a long time that there is a connection between poor economic and social conditions and family violence (McKinley 1964). As more recent surveys have shown, there is a causal relation between poverty, poor quality of family life, and the likelihood of deviant behavior by minors, particularly drug use. Indicators of deviant behavior are early motherhood outside marriage, educational disruptions, or other indicators of school failure (Bianchi 1999:326–28; Van Voorhis, Cullen, Mathers, and Chenoweth Garner 1998).

As a consequence, in the United States the absence or insufficiency of welfare services for needy families contributes to the use and prevalence of these substances, whereas the functioning of Swedish social services exerts a preventive influence. In the United States economic aid to needy families is not only insufficient, but the rate of poor persons in the overall population is also over three times higher than in Sweden, and the state of poverty on average lasts much longer. Under these conditions relapse is also frequent, especially among needy women. One half of U.S. families getting assistance have received subsidies for at least twenty months, and two-thirds of those with children have been aided for at least eight years, whereas only 6 percent of the Swedish families supported by the public services have been aided for twelve months or more.[16]

The intensity, prevalence, and duration of the state of poverty, and consequently the differences in income distribution, have grown considerably as a result of the cuts in welfare programs made in the early 1980s. The faith President Reagan and other conservative politicians had that assistance supplied by private organizations would be able to compensate for these cuts has proved groundless. As a matter of fact, charitable contributions, though favored by the tax regime, have been absolutely inadequate to meet the budget requirements of organizations and consequently to the fulfillment of welfare requirements. Furthermore, a number of these organizations—since they partially operate in the market framework as enterprises—provide some of their services only for payment, which therefore remain inaccessible to those who do not have sufficient income. Moreover, since the federal government has entrusted many social and health tasks to local organizations, it has placed an unbearable financial burden on them as well. So, a number of organizations operating in the tertiary/service industry that depended on public financing have been forced to give up their activities. On the other hand, several associations with strong political clout, which did not represent the interests of socially and economically marginal citizens, have continued to receive funds. Finally, the cuts made to social expenditure during the 1980s have reduced public financing to associations and jeopardized in this way their ability to supply public benefits.[17]

The inability to reach the entire needy population through welfare measures seems more marked in the United States than in Sweden. In the United States, perhaps a little less than one-half of those who are in a state of extreme poverty, children included,[18] as a matter of fact, do not receive any assistance, at least not the assistance they would be entitled to receive. In Sweden, thanks to public welfare, the proportion of persons who cannot afford an acceptable lifestyle, for example, a house equipped with modern conveniences, is very low—less than 2 percent. Finally, the scarce amount of unemployment subsidies, their short-term duration, and the impossibility of getting them for most of those who constitute marginal workers encourage in the United States an increase in the number of persons who can live only on assistance. (We consider those who do not have a regular job and are not up to date on their social security contributions as marginal workers.) Bearing in mind the existing differences between the two welfare systems, we can therefore understand why Swedish social services have been more efficient than U.S. ones in achieving the aim of reducing poverty and differences, but also why in the United States the expenditure for welfare as a percentage of national income has been higher than in Sweden.[19]

The earned income tax credit (EITC) law, which provides tax credits or rebates to those with low incomes, promulgated in 1975, was later widened several times to give more people access to the expected economic benefits. This law, which initiated a social policy to ameliorate relative and absolute deprivation, is quite relevant, but still insufficient. Currently, after a further widening proposed by President Clinton and approved by Congress in 1993, EITC may contribute to raising the income of full-time poor workers with dependent children over the poverty line. The income of those who do not work at all or have a part-time job may not, however, be raised. Only if these workers have dependent children are they entitled to receive—like the aforementioned workers—federal and governmental aid.

This subsidy was granted until 1996 within the federal program of economic aid to families with dependent children (AFDC). Since 1997, a Temporary Assistance to Needy Families program (TANF) has come into force and has been financed by state budgets instead of the federal budget. This program has been established within the Personal Responsibility and Work Opportunity Act, with the apparent purpose of reducing welfare expenditure, and bringing into the labor market those who have been receiving social assistance. If, on the contrary, those who receive subsidies do not have dependent children, they only have the right to receive welfare subsidies paid by municipalities. In either case—with or without dependent children—public support is not enough to bring these people out of their state of poverty (Danziger and Gottschalk 1995:158–59; Kenworthy 1999:1135–36; Quadagno 1999:3). The sense of the inadequacy of U.S. social policies becomes stronger if we consider interventions into unemployment and lack of affordable working-class housing. Like in Sweden, in the United States political authorities also have more liberally distributed welfare benefits to unemployed persons who have previously paid their compulsory insurance contributions, rather than to needy people without jobs (Ginsburg 1992:101; National Board of Health and Welfare 1994:49; Pontusson 1997:60; Von Hofer et al. 1997:63).

Nevertheless, there are considerable differences between these two countries with regard to the extent and liberality of their unemployment subsidies. In Sweden, unemployment subsidies are available to over four-fifths of the overall labor force. They are paid, furthermore, for a maximum period of twelve months, and they amount to 70 percent or more of the recipient's income, whereas for uninsured people the available aid has a much more limited duration and is a smaller amount. At the end of the period in which subsidies are distributed, the unemployed can obviously resort to public assistance, which is usually sufficient to cover their vital needs. These cases are, however, rare, though their incidence probably grew during the first half of the 1990s,[20] in concomitance with a lower labor market participation rate as an effect of the discouragement caused by the recession.

For a great part of the labor force, these subsidies are liberal and have a considerable duration. Practically, the alternation of jobs created by the government with periods of unemployment subsidies puts Sweden in the position of guaranteeing a nonwelfare income without end. The liberality and duration of unemployment subsidies can be explained by the relatively low (until the early 1990s) rate of unemployment—particularly long-term unemployment. This allowed Sweden to bear the financial costs of benefits, and the high unionization rate (about 85 percent of the overall labor force) has made possible the extended diffusion of subsidies among the unemployed, since trade unions themselves control the administration of benefits. Examples of recent cuts to welfare services include the reduction of subsidies from 90 percent to about 80 percent of a worker's pay prior to the state of unemployment; the obligation to wait five days before receiving aid; and the introduction of a ceiling that in 1995 totaled 565 crowns per day (approximately $60). These cuts have only slightly reduced the liberality of such aids.[21]

In the United States, on the contrary, unemployment subsidies are distributed only for a maximum period of six months (instead of a maximum period of 300 days until the age of fifty-five, and 450 days thereafter, in Sweden). Differently from Sweden, they also involve a considerable reduction in income for those who do not have private insurance. Both the amount and duration of these subsidies decreased in the early 1980s. These reductions were only partially balanced by some increases that took place in the early 1990s. Currently, the average aid corresponds, with strong variations from state to state, to an amount that in any case is below the official threshold of poverty for a family consisting of two parents and two dependent children. Furthermore, these subsidies are not very extensive if we compare them with the real extent of unemployment. Though 90 percent of the overall regularly employed labor force is entitled to receive a subsidy, as a matter of fact in the year 1985 about two-thirds of the unemployed (compared to one-fourth during the previous decade) did not receive any monetary aid at all.

This rate becomes much higher if we consider long-term unemployed persons, who on expiry of the coverage period lose this benefit. Moreover, their state of continuing unemployment (the incidence of which in comparison with the active population can less reliably be evaluated than in Sweden)[22] does not entitle them to receive public assistance. It is, however, possible, of course, to receive aid for other reasons like disability, old age, or for dependent children. This condition is therefore strongly related, in the United States, to enduring poverty. Long-term unemployed people very often belong—and in the 1990s more frequently than before—to two or more particular social categories:

1. Those who lost their jobs as a consequence of production reorganization,

2. Those who did not finish secondary school,

3. Those with little or no professional specialization that could be readily utilized in the labor market,

4. The young (about one-third of the U.S. unemployed are sixteen to twenty-four years old in comparison with one-fifth of the unemployed in Sweden),

5. The black underclass,

6. The homeless.[23]

The impact of active and passive unemployment policies has been very weak in the United States in comparison with Sweden, especially for what concerns policies specifically addressed to fight long-term unemployment in young people and adults belonging to the urban underclass. The effectiveness of active labor policies in favor of the preservation or growth of employment can be measured not only through the overall rate of unemployment, but also through the rate of long-term unemployment (over one year). After 1982, the CETA program no longer received any federal contributions. The program was terminated in 1985, though in 1978 it had provided job opportunities—mainly in the public area—to 12.5 percent of the unemployed. Later, in the 1990s, unemployment policies regulated by the Job Training Partnership Act (which has been poorly financed, provides no economic aid to participants, and is exclusively addressed to private enterprises) were affected by the attitude of the dominant conservative political forces. They did not trust the effectiveness of professional retraining programs for the unemployed labor force (despite a growing number of signals to the contrary), which provided jobs only to about 0.4 percent of both young and adult unemployed, against 7–10 percent of adults and 2–3 percent of young people in Sweden (Danziger and Gottschalk 1995:20, 25, 27, 153, 173–74; Ginsburg 1992:iii; OECD 1997:189–90). In Sweden almost 40 percent of the unemployed who in 1994 completed professional retraining courses were able to find a job within six months. The high level of education—higher than the average level in the OECD countries—of the Swedish labor force (Economist Intelligence Unit 1996–97:22–23) perhaps helped them.

In light of these facts, the benefits the U.S. compulsory work program produced for the unemployed in exchange for subsidies (so-called workfare programs) seem almost negligible: the programs have involved not only a very low number of the unemployed, who have not achieved much improvement in their job prospects, but have also provided jobs for unemployed persons who in any case had better employment prospects (not then the young people of the ghettos); in addition, these jobs do not require a high level of skill and do not lead to career advancement, and salaries have not been sufficient to enable the beneficiaries (often mothers with dependent children) to escape from their state of poverty. So, it is easy to understand why many needy women with dependent children have chosen illegal jobs while continuing to receive social assistance. As a matter of fact, over 90 percent of the public—federal and local—subsidies to needy families with dependent children are distributed to households with a mother as head of family. The opportunity to escape poverty through a job has been in fact only possible for those with particular characteristics, such as a decent level of education. They can hardly be found in the needy women heading families living in urban ghettos, if we consider the close correlation between poverty and lack of education in the United States.[24]

In spite of a higher per capita standard of living in the United States, family income in Sweden is generally higher for two reasons. First of all, though in both countries the head of a family is usually a man and his income is the most important one, male part-time jobs (which pay less than full-time ones) are more widespread in the United States. Furthermore, in the United States, unlike Sweden, the number of families enjoying two incomes is lower, which affects the standard of living and the level of family consumption of a great part of the population. In Sweden, the proportion of women in the labor force is higher than that in the United States. Unlike the United States, furthermore, unemployment generally affects women less than men. In comparison with the United States, in Sweden there has been a concentration of women in jobs that are more connected with the welfare state than with the market. This more effectively protects women, and in turn Swedish families, from the risk of unemployment. At an aggregate level, families with two incomes are more common in Sweden and women's contribution to the family income is higher, thus better safeguarding family revenues from market instability.[25]

In order to control unemployment, in the United States Republican administrations in the 1980s and early 1990s placed their trust, rather than in active labor policies, in the limited extension and low level of unemployment subsidies, and most of all in the flexibility of the labor market. The results are, however, questionable: though the rate of unemployment, even the long-term one, since the mid-1980s has been lower than the corresponding European rates (and, as regards Sweden, since the 1990s), exactly the opposite had previously occurred. Thus, flexibility and low subsidies do not necessarily reduce unemployment. Furthermore, new job opportunities provided in the United States in general pertain to jobs that do not require a high level of skill, do not lead to advancement, and are poorly remunerated. They are consequently inadequate for improving in a steady and significant way the economic situation of the marginal labor force (Mullard 1997:55–56. 68: OECD 1997:180; OECD, Statistics Directorate 1987:12, 76).

Finally, since 1980 federal housing programs for new working-class housing underwent, during the Reagan and Bush presidencies, some dramatic financial reductions: the 1987 budget was one-tenth of the corresponding 1981 budget. These reductions further worsened the already heavy lack of low-cost housing, and contributed to an acceleration of the decay of the existing ones. Currently, because of the shortage of public— namely, federal—funds, the availability of public housing and its maintenance are absolutely insufficient. Accordingly, those who belong to the poorer classes are homeless or can only find dilapidated housing. Sociological literature has underlined not only the wretched quality of living that many housing projects inflict on residents, but also the scanty proportion of people having an income below the official poverty line living in public housing. They amount to merely 10 percent, that is 3.5 million people out of about 35 million persons who are officially considered poor. Thus, the benefits of U.S. housing policy, which by the 1970s were already modest, have almost completely vanished, thereby worsening the public and private disadvantages of the ethnic and social segregation process.[26]

The Different Prevalence of Drugs in Sweden and in the United States

These two countries are characterized by a quite different diffusion of drugs, as can be gathered by comparing their respective prevalence during the 1980s and early 1990s. According to official estimates, there were about 10,000–14,000 drug addicts in Sweden in 1974 and 14,000–20,000 in 1992 (National Board of Health and Welfare 1994:40). Based on an appraisal made by another public organization, the Swedish Institute, , the overall number of opiate addicts at the beginning of the 1990s was 10,000–14,000. In this case, these figures would have been not increasing, but remaining constant throughout the 1980s. Assuming a total number of opiate addicts ranging between 10,000 and 20,000 persons in the early 1990s, in those years there would have been a prevalence of 0.11–0.23 percent out of a population of about 8.6 million inhabitants.

If we also consider alcohol addiction, which is estimated to affect about 300,000 persons in Sweden (a very low share of the overall population in comparison with other countries),[27] there would be a 3.6 percent prevalence of drug addicts. According to a governmental source (Swedish Institute 1995), during the 1980s and early 1990s the incidence of the use of intravenous injected drugs among young people showed a clear downward trend. These people were in general (and probably still are) users of different drugs, mainly amphetamines and other stimulants of the central nervous system. Only one-third of them included heroin addicts (that is, about 6,000 persons; from 2,000 to 3,000 according to other official estimates), the latter showing a downward trend. Based on these estimates, the number of heroin addicts would be 0.02–0.07 percent out of a population of about 8.6 million inhabitants.

The corresponding estimates, concerning heroin consumption only, in the United States during the same period (around 1990) indicate approximately 600,000 drug addicts out of a population of about 260 million people, giving the United States a rate 3–10 times higher than Sweden. The estimates on the number of regular heroin consumers—which are always very uncertain—showed considerable fluctuation during the 1980s and 1990s: some of them ranged around a number of 500,000–750,000 persons, while others placed this number in a range of 500,000–1,000,000 subjects. Finally, the estimates on the overall number of heroin users, occasional ones included, during the same period (around 1990) were in the range of about 2 million people, though some sampling problems suggest that these figures are underestimated.

In addition to heroin addicts we should also consider cocaine addicts. The National Institute on Drug Abuse estimated the number of those who take this drug at least once a year to be about 5 million in the early 1990s, on the decrease in comparison with the previous decade,[28] with about 250,000–600,000 weekly users of this drug, and consequently addicts. The number of regular users (once a month at least) of other opiates was estimated as amounting to several millions, according to the same source. Toward the early 1990s, according to the estimates of the National Institute on Drug Abuse, about 11–12 million people were dependent on psychotropic drugs, a 4.4 percent average prevalence, which is 20 to 40 times higher than in Sweden.

The consumption of heroin and cocaine, and consequently the number of addicts, after a heavy increase in the early 1970s, seems to have had minor variations later on. A decrease in the use of heroin and a concomitant aging of heroin addicts were offset by an increase—at least throughout the 1980s—in the use and abuse of cocaine (also in its concentrated form called "crack"). The level of diffusion of these drugs is, however, very high: about 60 percent of the worldwide consumption of illegal drugs occurs in the United States, where the overall population represents less than 5 percent of the world's population. The use and abuse of drugs, like violent crimes occurring there, are concentrated in the underclass living in the urban ghettos (Johnson, Williams, Dei, and Sanabria 1990), the members of which are generally not included in the sample of the National Institute on Drug Abuse (Mieczkowski 1996:373–74).[29] Also including alcoholics in this comparative analysis, the number of whom was estimated to be 15.1 million in 1990 by a federal source, and considering that this kind of addiction may also combine with opiate addiction, the following estimate may be made. In the early 1990s the total number of psychotropic substance addicts was perhaps 25 million people, a 9 percent prevalence, more than twice the prevalence in Sweden.[30]

There is a further indicator of a much greater diffusion of narcotics use in the United States than in Sweden. There were 42,000 U.S. drug addicts affected by AIDS until 1990, and over 60,000 until 1993, respectively equal to about 17 and 23 persons per 100,000 inhabitants. In Sweden, until 31 March 1997 (and for a few years thereafter), there were about 1,500 cases, one-quarter of which occurred among drug users, with a prevalence of 4 subjects per 100,000 people. In the United States, the overall incidence of AIDS cases until the end of 1996 was 220 cases per 100,000 inhabitants, in comparison with 17 cases per 100,000 inhabitants in Sweden. Therefore, the incidence rate was in Sweden about thirteen times less than in the United States. The occurrence of new cases in the two years 1995–96 was ten times smaller: Sweden (together with Japan) has one of the lowest rates of diffusion among industrialized countries, four to six times lower than the rate of the United States. In the United States this disease has assumed an epidemic character. The number of new cases of HIV viral infections in 1993 has been estimated at a little less than half a million (equal to about 200 cases per 100,000 persons). Over 30,000 new cases of AIDS were also registered that year (with a prevalence of over 11 cases per 100,000 persons). All these figures grew in succeeding years, though the data for 1996 show a reversal of the trend. Considering the enormous spreading of HIV infection, we can assume that the prevalence of manifest AIDS disease will further grow—and considerably—in the forthcoming years.[31]

In both countries, drug use is more widespread among young or relatively young people, especially those who live in big cities.[32] Still, Sweden is the country with the highest rate in the world of people over sixty years old (Golini 1991:252–53; Gynnerstedt 1997:202; Kautto 1999:59; National Board of Health and Welfare 1996:12). It also has, compared to the United States, a relatively smaller number of young people, though these differences are not very marked. About 19 percent of the Swedish population is under fifteen, compared to 22 percent in the United States (National Board of Health and Welfare 1994:52, 1996:175; Wilson 1985:150).

Bearing in mind that drug use is more frequent among the young, the difference between the respective demographic structures might explain, at least in part, a greater diffusion of these substances in the United States. However, in both countries drug users are proportionally more numerous in urban environments. According to some U.S. surveys, this holds mainly for marijuana, but also—though to a smaller extent—for heroin and cocaine.[33] The slightly higher percentage of young people living in the United States, compared to those living in Sweden, is more than offset, with respect to drug use, by a quite different level of urbanization. Already in the 1970s about 70 percent of the U.S. population lived in nonurban areas, and this percentage has since grown (Okun 1979:535; Stahura 1986:131). In contrast, in Sweden there has been a marked trend toward urbanization and therefore since the early 1970s the Swedish population has lived mainly in urban areas (Lindahl 1979:103).

If it is assumed that in both countries the young are geographically distributed in a way that does not radically differ from the rest of the population,[34] we can infer that most young Swedish people live in urban areas, whereas most young Americans do not. As a consequence, the much smaller diffusion of drugs in Sweden, compared to the United States, cannot be explained by differences in the demographic composition, since they are too small. Nor can they be explained by differences in the spatial distribution of the respective young population, as they would involve, on the contrary, a greater diffusion of drugs in Sweden. The reasons for a higher prevalence of drugs in the United States than in Sweden should then be sought elsewhere. As we have asserted, this different prevalence should be rather ascribed to different—and in fact contrasting—public policies. They regard not only the way in which drug traffic is repressed (for the authorities in both countries oppose any liberalization of consumption), but also the rehabilitation process of drug addicts, and the prevention of use and abuse of these substances.

From a methodological point of view, the different demographic structures are not however irrelevant. Because of this difference, in comparing the proportions of drug users in Sweden and in the United States, it is advisable to refer these percentages to the overall size of the youth population, rather than to the whole population irrespective of the distribution of the age cohorts.[35] Sample surveys have been conducted on the prevalence of the use, either regular or occasional, of drugs like marijuana or cocaine among the young in Sweden and the United States. The data confirm in general that "Sweden has a relatively minor drug problem compared to many other Western countries" (Von Hofer et al. 1997:65; see also Swedish National Institute of Public Health 1995:33). In particular, they confirm that use and abuse of drugs are a much more serious problem in the United States.[36]

Among U.S. teenagers (twelve to seventeen years old) attending secondary school the number who in the years 1988–91 had used marijuana at least once a year was estimated by the National Institute on Drug Abuse to be around 12–13 percent, compared to 24 percent in 1979. In the early 1990s, about 4 percent used it regularly and 9 percent used it at least once a week. Monitoring the Future, another source also based on self-reported information, provides data on samples of the entire population of high school students in the United States. This source reports (with reference to those who use marijuana at least once a year) a percentage almost double.[37] Nonwhite ethnic minorities do not seem to stand out in the inclination of U.S. teenagers to experiment with drugs. The subcultural characteristics of these minorities, as far as they are concerned, on the contrary showed a smaller inclination to take them during the last year of reference.[38] This is significant for a comparison between U.S. and Swedish users, who are ethnically more homogeneous.[39]

In Sweden, governmental surveys report that the rate of school-age teenagers who have used marijuana or hashish is about 4 percent, with a slight (from 4 to 6 percent) upward trend according to a 1995 inquiry. During the first part of the current decade the proportion of teenagers who use these drugs regularly (about 1 percent) did not change. The percentage of seventeen-year-olds who had experimented with marijuana or hashish during the period 1979–81 was higher (about 8–9 percent). Still, it was much lower than the proportion of fourteen- to seventeen-year-old Americans who in the same years had used marijuana (Swedish National Institute of Public Health 1995:13–14, 33, 1996:105–6, 204). By adopting a careful estimate of the number of young American users, the diffusion of soft drugs in the United States was, at the beginning of the current and during the previous decade, more than three times higher than in Sweden. Furthermore, diffusion was higher in the late 1970s.

During the 1980s, the same downward trend in both countries was observed with regard to teenage drug use and the aging of hard drug addicts. This trend has continuously kept the inclination of the Swedish teenagers to use drugs—evidenced by having taken these substances at least once—within a 1:3 ratio, in comparison with American teenagers.[40] On the other hand, there are reasons to believe that not only among teenagers, but also among the overall population, drugs are less widespread in Sweden than in the United States. In both countries, as mentioned, not only the sale but even the simple possession—and in Sweden even the mere use—of drugs are considered a crime. About 1 percent of the Swedish population has in recent years been suspected by the authorities of crimes in connection with drugs, whereas in the United States 4 percent of the population has been put under arrest (and thus not simply suspected) for this kind of crime. Furthermore, as reported, in 1991 almost 30 percent of young (eighteen to twenty-five years old) Americans and 10 percent of older adults used illegal substances, compared to 7–8 percent of the sixteen- to seventy-four-year-old Swedish population.[41]

Finally, if we consider imprisonment as an indicator of a previous condition of social marginality, drugs seem also less widespread among the Swedish than among the corresponding U.S. population. Among those who are in jail for serious crimes, the percentage of persons in the United States who had recently taken drugs was estimated to range from one-half to three-quarters. Roughly the same proportion emerged from investigations based on an objective indicator (urine samples), with strong variations from city to city. As a matter of fact, 20 percent of them had recently ingested cocaine (Kornblum and Julian 1995:149; Mieczkowski 1996:391–93, 402).

On the contrary, the Swedish data report that the total number of drug users among prisoners prior to their arrest was about 40–60 percent (Swedish Institute 1995; Swedish National Institute of Public Health 1996:255). The growing rate of drug addicts among Swedish criminals, and the heavy social and institutional marginality of chronic drug addicts in this country (Swedish National Institute of Public Health 1995:29), might be interpreted as a signal of concentration of drug addiction in some particular subjects. Even the efficient Swedish social services can hardly detect, reach, and socially rehabilitate them. Heroin addicts in the early 1980s were 28 percent of those who robbed passersby in the streets of Stockholm (Wikstroem 1995:459).

To be sure, we cannot speak of a failure in this case, but it points to the not completely successful results of secondary and tertiary social policies in Sweden.[42] To the partial success of these policies, an equally partial—

though considerable—success corresponds regarding primary prevention policies. Not only are drug addicts more numerous in relatively poor urban areas, but among Swedish drug addicts those of foreign origin are slightly overrepresented, in the sense that, according to a recent survey, they are 20 percent more numerous than they would be if their number were proportional to the share of the immigrant population living in Sweden. A slightly higher diffusion of drug addiction in this category of persons, in comparison with the native Swedish population, corresponds to a stronger (though relatively modest) relative deprivation among immigrants (Von Hofer et al. 1997:64, 68, 70, 78). Generally speaking, for what concerns the differences between these two countries in the use and abuse of drugs, our comparative analysis has examined the respective ability of their welfare institutions to implement a control of the rate of relative deprivation in the more disadvantaged social segments. We have already indicated the reasons why some alternative explanations, which emphasize different demographic composition and geographic distribution of the population, or the subcultural characteristics of the ethnic groups in which drugs are particularly diffused, are not persuasive.

Finally, we should also note that the so-called war on drugs, which the different strata of the U.S. public administration have waged, has produced few or no direct benefits. This has been so, even disregarding its perverse effects (which we shall examine later) and its possible indirect benefits (for example, improving the image of a neighborhood, or the feeling of public safety, by repressing the visibility of drug traffic).

We can make many arguments why this "warfare" has not achieved the expected results:

- Heroin use did not undergo any significant variation during the 1980s (Mieczkowski 1996:365–68), though "drug warfare" had begun in the first years of that decade.
- In the United States, experts of the National Development and Research Institutes have not imputed a decreasing prevalence in the use and abuse of hard drugs (heroin, cocaine, crack) in the youth of the urban ghettos during the 1990s) to police repression. This is apparently rather easily eluded, though its effectiveness has increased. Rather, this decrease has been accounted for as a reaction of today's generation of marginal teenagers to the damages produced by hard drugs to the body and mind of their parents or relatives of the preceding generation (Johnson, Golub, and Dunlap 1999). This reaction has produced the growing of a particular subculture, supported by internal rules, in the juvenile groups. This subculture encourages marijuana and alcohol consumption, while strongly condemning crack and heroin abuse.[43]
- The decreasing prevalence in the United States in the use and abuse of hard drugs during the preceding decade, and of other drugs since the

end of the 1970s, roughly corresponds to a fluctuation in drug consumption in Sweden. There is however a significant difference: only in Sweden, a country in which governmental policies have never privileged repression to the detriment of rehabilitation and prevention, has heroin consumption, too, decreased in the last twenty years. The progress achieved in fighting drug abuse cannot therefore be ascribed to this "drug warfare" (Mieczkowski 1996:362–72; Swedish National Institute of Public Health 1995:12–15).

NOTES

1. For a "balance sheet" of the benefits provided by the Swedish Welfare State in the 1990s, see Palme (2001). For the complete information, cf. Censis (1999:315, Table 23), Fritzell (1999:178–80), Ginsburg (1992:62, 206), Gustafsson et al. (1999:215), Gynnerstedt (1997:198), Halleroed and Heikkila (1999:206–13), Hagemann (1995:37–41), Kautto, Fritzell, Hvinden, Kvist, and Uusitalo (2001a:263–67), Kenworthy (1999), Kvist (1998), Lehto et al. (1999:104, 128), National Board of Health and Welfare (1996:12), United Nations (1997:23), and World Health Organization (1996:A3–A8).

2. Compare Kvist (1998:11, 13), Lehto et al. (1999:128), and National Board of Health and Welfare (1994:10–11; 1996:61).

3. This is an official evaluation. Other evaluations are lower. All point to the decreasing rate of unemployment in Sweden. Currently, the unemployment rate of the young, and in general, is lower than in most European countries, while long-term unemployment is lower than in the United States (Censis 1998:245–46, Tables 41 and 42, 1999:178–81, Table 1, Fig. 1; Economist Intelligence Unit 1997a:21, 1998c:20, 1998–1999:14; *La Stampa*, 14 May 1998, p. 15, 25 August 1998, p. 14, 11 May 1999, p. 17, 7 July 1999, p. 16; OECD 1999:120).

4. Cf. Fritzell (1999:169–73), Gynnerstedt (1997:200), Ginsburg (1992:39–40, 201, 203), Halleroed (1996:144–45, 154–58), Halleroed and Heikkila (1999:203), Hvinden et al. (2001:179, Table 8.1), National Board of Health and Welfare (1994:47, 1996:13, 137–38, 178), OECD (1997:180, Table 14), and OECD, Statistics Directorate (1997:72).

5. For an introduction to immigration policies in Sweden, cf. Marta (1991), Runblom (1992), Von Hofer et al. (1997:66–69), and Zucchini (1994:44–47). See also Bjorgo (1995).

6. There are in Sweden, as elsewhere, hostility to immigrants and refugees, and discrimination against them (Loow 1995:153; Zucchini 1994:57). Still, according to one survey Sweden is one of the least racist countries in Europe (cf. Sociodata 1998:4–5). Swedish policies of economic and social integration may have been effective in this sense, though causes and effects are hard to disentangle. U.S. research has focused on racist attitudes on residential segregation, racial discrimination, or equal-rights legislation, rather than on racist sentiments concerning the alleged superiority or inferiority of particular racial groups (Bakanic 1995; Bobo and Zubrinsky 1996; Steeh and Schuman 1992:348–56). Comparisons cannot therefore be made.

7. Cf. Esping-Andersen, Assimakopoulou, and van Kersbergen (1993:45), Ginsburg (1992:47, 63), Martens (1997:195–99, 246, 248), National Board of Health and Welfare (1994:47, 1996:13, 135), Schierup (1990:130–31, 151), Sjoegren (1992:10–11), Von Hofer et al. (1997:68, 76), and Zucchini (1994:51–52, 54).

8. Federal and local administrations during the Reagan presidency substantially reduced outlays to methadone distribution centers. This policy has not subsequently been reversed (Knight et al. 1996:925).

9. Cf. Cohen (1997:32), Davis and Lurigio (1996:130–31), DiMaggio and Anheier (1993:42), Donziger (1996:202, 246–47, 251), Gidron, Kramer and Salamon (1993:163, 172–73), Horton et al. (1994:122), Kornblum and Julian (1995:150–51), and Kuhnle and Selle (1993:199).

10. Cf. Donziger (1996:202–4, 231–53), Grosso (1999:37), Hser, Longshore and Anglin (1994:27–31), Hunt and Rosenbaum (1998:209–11), Kornblum and Julian (1995:192–93), Nahon (1997:42), and Walters (1996:948, 951).

11. Cf. Danziger and Gottschalk (1995:55–58), Fritzell (2001:24–28), Horton et al. (1994:355–56), Jencks (1992:72–79), Keister and Moller (2000:62–69), and Kornblum and Julian (1995:236–37).

12. Cf. Danziger and Gottschalk (1995:25–37, 89–92, 174), Donziger (1996:29), Ginsburg (1992:111, 200–1), Jencks (1992:76–79), Kornblum and Julian (1995:237–39), Lichter (1997), and Pierson (1996:28).

13. Cf. Danziger and Gottschalk (1995:34–35), Ginsburg (1992:108–9), Hatland (2001:126–27), Jaentti and Danziger (1994:50–52), Jencks (1992:226), Kjeldstad (2001:87–91), and National Board of Health and Welfare (1994:46).

14. Cf. Ginsburg (1992:129–32), Gortmaker and Wise (1997:160), Iglehart (1999c:405–6), Kornblum and Julian (1995:32–33, 37–39, 243), Kuttner (1999a), Physicians for a National Health Program (no date), Quadagno (1999:8), and Ruggie (1992:926–27).

15. The data refer to 1993 (cf. Kornblum, Julian 1995:29). Subsequently, child mortality has been reduced and life expectancy increased in both countries, but the United States has not caught up with Sweden (cf. World Health Organization 1996:A-5, A-13). Poverty is related to child mortality (Gortmaker and Wise 1997:163–64).

16. Cf. Harris (1996), Kasarda (1993:62), Kornblum, Julian (1995:241), National Board of Health and Welfare (1994:48, 1996:135–36), and Wacquant and Wilson (1993:36).

17. Cf. Colozzi and Bassi (1995:23–24, 1996:45–46), Gidron, Kramer, and Salamon (1993:168), and Kramer (1992:438, 440).

18. The services provided to U.S. preschool and schoolchildren are inadequate in all respects. Cf. Kornblum and Julian (1995:374).

19. Cf. Danziger and Gottschalk (1995:91), Ginsburg (1992:200–1), Halleroed (1996:149), Jencks (1992:80–85, 225–26), Kangas and Palme (1998:16–17), and Kornblum and Julian (1995:241).

20. The number of those who have received assistance increased from 516,000 in 1990 to 720,000 in 1995 (National Board of Health and Welfare 1996:132). Though the reasons for this increase are certainly connected with Sweden's economic difficulties in the early 1990s, they have not been fully accounted for (Arsanogullari 2000).

21. Cf. in this regard Clasen, Kvist, and Van Oorschott (2001), Ginsburg (1992:41–42), Gynnerstedt (1997:194), Marklund (1990:136), Pierson (1996:36), Pontusson (1997:58, 60, 63), and Ramaswamy (1995:13–14).

22. In the United States, socially and economically marginal people living in the ghettos are especially likely to be nonregistered, long-term unemployed. The number and rate of long-term unemployed in the United States are therefore more severely underestimated than in Europe, and Sweden in particular (Ginsburg (1992:109–10; Lichter 1988:776, 779). Bearing this in mind, in 1996 the proportion of long-term unemployed in Sweden was officially estimated to be one-sixth the corresponding proportion in the United States (OECD 1997:180, Table H).

23. Cf. Danziger and Gottschalk (1995:25, 35), Economist Intelligence Unit (1994a:21), Ginsberg (1994:116), Ginsburg (1992:108–10), Jencks (1992:87), Horton et al. (1994:352), Kornblum and Julian (1995:235, 241–42, 422–23), Lichter (1988), Neckerman et al. (1988), O'Connor (2000:549–52), OECD, Statistics Directorate (1997:12, 76), Rossi and Wright (1993:153), Simpson (1999), Singh (1991), Small and Newman (2001), and Wacquant and Wilson (1993:37).

24. Cf. Danziger and Gottschalk (1995:12–13), Ginsberg (1994:112, 116–117), Ginsburg (1992:111), Harris (1993), Jencks (1992:218–25), Kornblum and Julian (1995:241–43), Mead (1993:181, 184–85), and Wacquant and Wilson (1993:34–35).

25. Cf. Esping-Andersen et al. (1993:43), Esping-Andersen (1997:42–47), Jaentti and Danziger (1994:52–54, 57–59), OECD (1997:178), and OECD, Statistics Directorate (1997:12–13, 76–77).

26. Cf. Berry (1985), Fong (1996:209–14), Gotham (1998:16), Horton et al. (1994:272–73, 279), Jencks (1994:Chapter 6), Kornblum and Julian (1995:235, 204, 460–62), Rossi and Wright (1993:153, 157), Shihadeh and Flynn (1996), Skogan and Annan (1994:129–30), and Wilson (1985:136–38).

27. In 1993, in terms of individual alcohol consumption, Sweden ranked thirty-first out of thirty-eight countries covered by relevant statistical information. Cf. Swedish Institute (1995).

28. This decrease has been confirmed by another source, Monitoring the Future, which is also based on self-reporting, but focuses on high school and college students.

29. Along with the concentration of heroin use among the underprivileged ghetto population, a "heroin culture" has spread among young people of a particular milieu, who enjoy more favorable social and economic conditions. Their number is, however, limited (Chitwood, Comerford and Weatherby 1998:62–63; Grund 1998:220–22).

30. For quantitative information on the prevalence of the consumption of narcotics in Sweden, cf. Nordic Committee on Narcotic Drugs (1994:3), Swedish Institute (1995), and Swedish National Institute of Public Health (1995:14–15, 22, 1996:42). In the United States, cf. Davis and Lurigio (1996:1–5), Deschenes and Greenwood (1994:255–57), Grund (1998:219–20), Haen Marshall (1997:9, 30, note 3), Horton et al. (1994:114, 115, 117), Inciardi and Harrison (1998:xi—xii), Johnson, Thomas, and Golub (1998:116–21), Kinlock, Hanlon, and Nurco (1998:14–15), Kornblum and Julian (1995:133), Mieczkowski (1996), Silbereisen, Robins, and Rutter (1995:500–3), Stark (1975:91), Reuter (1998:321–23), and Wilson (1998:304, 309).

31. Cf. Horton et al. (1994:218), Inciardi et al. (1998:34–35), Johnson et al. (1998:124–25), Kinlock et al. (1998:18–19), Kornblum and Julian (1995:45–46), Reuter (1998:325), and United Nations, Department of Economic and Social Affairs, Statistics Division (1997:104, 107).

32. Cf. for the United States, Cole and Weissberg (1994:104–7), Davis and Luri-

gio (1996:4–5), and Steffensmeier, Allan, Harer, and Streifel (1989:815); for Sweden, Swedish National Institute of Public Health (1996:42, 123–26).

33. Cf. for the United States, Cole and Weissberg (1994:105); for Sweden, Folkhaelsoinstitutet [1996:223, Table B68 (the table indicates the geographical distribution of those drug consumers who have injected heroin in their veins, and have tested positive for HIV)].

34. The average age of U.S. citydwellers is lower than the average age of the U.S. population as a whole, due to the presence in the cities of ethnic minorities in which the younger population is overrepresented. Still, these differences in the two average ages, both across and within ethnic groups, are very small (Wilson 1985:149–50).

35. About one-fifth of the unemployed in Sweden, vs. about one-third in the United States, are young (OECD Statistics Directorate 1997:12–13, 76–77). This difference may account to some extent for the difference in prevalence of drug use in the two countries. The difference is, however, too great to be fully accounted for in these terms.

36. While both countries are strictly prohibitionist, it is incomparably more difficult in Sweden than in the United States to find heroin in illegal markets, as indicated by ethnographic investigations conducted in both countries (Persson 1981:151, 155–56; Weeks et al. 1996:565–66, 569).

37. Cf. Cole and Weissberg (1994:110), Deschenes and Greenwood (1994:255), Horton et al. (1994:115), Kornblum and Julian (1995:144–47), Mieczkowski (1996:360–73), Sussman, Stacy, Dent, Simon, and Johnson (1996:708–9), and Wallace and Bachmann (1991). The most complete and detailed data, with a discussion of the methodological problems of their validity and reliability, may be found in Mieczkowski (1996:373–80).

38. Cf. Mieczkowski (1996:362, 364, 372–73). Subcultural differences between blacks and Hispanics influence their choice of drugs and modes of use. Cf. Weeks et al. (1996:576–82).

39. In Sweden, people of foreign origin are slightly overrepresented among drug-related crimes, other circumstances being equal. This fact is, however, of little consequence, given the low number of these crimes (Von Hofer et al. (1997:71–73).

40. Cf. for the United States, Horton et al. (1994:114), Kornblum and Julian (1995:144–45), Mieczkowski (1996:363–65), and Silbereisen et al. (1995:501–2); for Sweden, National Board of Health and Welfare (1993:40, 1996:43), Nordic Committee on Narcotic Drugs (1994:2), Swedish Institute (1995), and Swedish National Institute of Public Health (1995:13–15, 32–33, 1996:105–7, 204).

41. Cf. Donziger (1996:14, 16–17), Kornblum and Julian (1995:145), Nordic Committee on Narcotic Drugs (1994:1), and Swedish National Institute of Public Health, (1995:19, 1996:242).

42. Felson has tried to argue that the Swedish welfare system, and in general social causes and preventive public policies, have played no role in limiting the crime rates. He has argued his thesis by showing rapidly increasing crime rates in Sweden and other developed countries from the 1950s to the 1980s (Felson 1998:19). The author is apparently unaware of the problems of validity and reliability of crime statistics, which make such comparisons difficult. The International Crime Survey, which has followed the same criteria in the procedure of gathering quan-

titative information on crime, has indicated that victimization rates in 1989 were in Sweden little more than half the corresponding rates for the United States (Smith 1995:416–17). Furthermore, murder rates in the 1980s were eleven times higher in the United States than in Norway, and nine times higher than in Sweden (Hagan 1994:23–24). The causes of the general increase in crime rates have been debated (Smith 1995:460–80), but strong differences among different nations remain.

43. These conclusions refer to in-depth ethnographic research conducted on the behavior of addicts and dealers in New York ghettos in the last twenty years (Johnson et al. 1999).

3   Costs of Social Policies

PRELIMINARY CONSIDERATIONS

The subject of this chapter is the specific costs of public policies on drugs, disregarding the estimates of the overall social costs produced by drug abuse.[1] It is very difficult, if not impossible, to distinguish between two distinct sources of costs: on the one hand, costs exclusively referred to public policies against drug traffic and use (concerning specific or secondary repression, rehabilitation, and prevention actions); on the other hand, costs depending, as a general rule, on public policies aimed at repressing and preventing crime, and at rehabilitating into society those who have committed them (in this case, whether they are the real or only the alleged authors). Similarly, the benefits for the community of a specific repression, rehabilitation, and secondary prevention policy flow together into the overall benefits of policies aimed at controlling and preventing crimes, and at facilitating the social rehabilitation of the criminal population. In other terms, considering that in both the United States and Sweden drug use and traffic are considered by authorities indictable behaviors, the costs and benefits of a "drug-free society" can hardly be distinguished from those of a "crime-free society."

THE COST OF SOCIAL POLICIES IN SWEDEN

In Sweden, only to some extent is there a specific control, rehabilitation, and prevention policy. Otherwise, police activities are intended to repress criminal behavior in general. The social rehabilitation of the imprisoned population—apart from its possible condition of drug addiction—is the goal of prison policy (Swedish National Institute of Public Health 1995:22). The prevention of criminal deviation is widely entrusted to the welfare services. The control activities carried out by the local, regional, central, and border police authorities are very expensive. This is in part due to the fact that police authorities have formed teams and organizational departments specialized in repressing drug crimes. The activities of the judiciary, which have lately been to a considerable extent oriented to the application of the penal rules that sanction these crimes, are also quite expensive (Swedish National Institute of Public Health 1995:19–20; Swedish Institute 1995).

Nevertheless, the heavily repressive laws against drug sales and use have not led to a particularly high rate of imprisonment in comparison with the other European countries (we will later consider the United States). With 58 imprisoned persons per 100,000 inhabitants, Sweden was in 1990 seventeenth out of twenty-four European countries. In the following year Sweden occupied eighteenth place out of twenty-three European countries (Hagan 1994:162; Von Hofer et al. 1997:65). Despite antidrug laws that are very repressive and resolutely observed, there is in Sweden a relatively small number of convicts, no more than about half of whom are drug abusers (this rate has stabilized in the last ten years) (Swedish National Institute of Public Health 1996:255). A partial explanation of this paradox, to which we will return during the appraisal of the cost-benefit ratio, lies in the strong and continuous commitment displayed by the social services in cooperation with prison and official authorities to the social rehabilitation of imprisoned drug addicts (ibid.:27–28; Swedish Institute 1995).

Like the repressive actions implemented by the police and the official authorities, the rehabilitation and therapeutic interventions for all drug abusers—whether imprisoned or not—are also very expensive. In this regard, official estimates place the total expenditure, including rehabilitation expenses for alcoholics and with considerable differences among the various administration districts, in the range of 2.5 billion Swedish crowns in 1995, equivalent to 1.5 percent of the gross national income. This represents an increase compared to the estimate of 2.3 billion crowns in 1992 (at the current rate of exchange, 1 crown is about $0.095, that is, an expenditure of about $26 per inhabitant in 1995) (National Board of Health and Welfare 1994:43, 1996:107).[2]

Primary prevention activities oriented toward the very ambitious target of limiting as much as possible relative privation, poverty, unemployment, and residential segregation of ethnic groups and classes are very expensive as well. It may be difficult to obtain specific expenditure estimates for single items, such as the expenses for psychological support for families in trouble. However, according to some estimates, in the early 1980s welfare expenditure—including pension, health, education, and family expenses—had grown in two decades from one-sixth to one-third of the gross domestic product (GDP), the highest rate among OECD countries. In spite of cuts in social expenditures, this record continued to be maintained, with welfare expenditures equal to 40 percent of the GDP in 1992, 38 percent in 1994, and 35.6 percent in 1995. This decrease in the percentage of expenditures did not, however, bring Sweden back to the expenditure level of the early 1980s, which was in any case high. There is accordingly no reason so far to see any sign of the dismantling of the Swedish or Scandinavian welfare system in general.

We should, however, bear in mind that meanwhile both individuals and families may have faced a reduction in income (due to sickness, unemployment, or difficulties in entering the labor market) and in welfare services (economic aid and service provision).[3] The reduction in welfare services has particularly affected poor single-parent families. Currently, in low-income cases, the difference in available net income between single parents with one or two children and childless adults or couples with the same number of children is lower in Sweden than the average European rate (based on the same gross income and without deducting home costs) (Bradshaw 1998:113, Tables 6 and 7). The overall public expenditure passed from 25 percent of GDP in the early 1950s to 50 percent in the mid-1970s and to over 70 percent in the early 1990s, ever more diverging since the 1970s from the average rate of European Union and OECD countries.[4]

The costs of social services, which are almost entirely borne by municipalities, after having doubled at constant prices throughout the 1980s (National Board of Health and Welfare 1994:6–7, 62) grew further by 70 percent in only a few years, from 92,312 million crowns in 1991 to 132,509 million crowns in 1995 (1995 prices) (ibid.:62; 1996:27, 179, Table 5), and increased from 6.4 percent of the gross national income at current prices in 1991 to 8.2 percent in 1995. Most of the social expenditure on social security (which is formally separate from expenses on social services) was absorbed by seniority, old age, disability, and disease pensions (Hagemann 1995:36–37, 42).

We can add to these figures further benefits given to families, some of which have in part a social security nature, and are not accordingly completely borne by the municipal or governmental treasury (as is the case for social services in the strict sense of the word). Particularly important are the allowances for children care, which have both a social security and social service nature and claimed in 1993 1.3 percent of the GNP: a higher percentage than in 1990 and double with respect to the first half of the 1980s (Lehto et al. 1999:106–7). These indemnities are granted, together with monetary benefits for maternity, in addition to the overall services for children and other expense items borne by families. Overall, government and the municipalities have made financial transfers to families without distinguishing between welfare expenses and those linked to social security (a distinction might be difficult).[5] In 1991 these financial flows to families amounted to 4.8 percent of the GNP. This percentage was a slight decrease in comparison with the previous year (5.1 percent), but was higher than the percentage that was allocated in the 1980s to families in Sweden, and was almost three times the average rate of European Union countries (1.7 percent) (Hagemann 1995:34; Kamerman and Kahn 1998:89–90).

The expenditure for social services specifically for children has remained almost constant, at about 2.5 percent of the gross national income in the first half of the 1990s (a slightly decreasing rate after the increase, since 1994, in the national income). In buying power units expressed in 1980 dollars, these family allowances for each child under fifteen years kept steady at a high level during the period 1973–84. This level always remained higher than the average family allowances of the other OECD countries, however, increasing during that period to about 37 percent.[6] A considerable part of the social expenditure was, and to some extent continues to be, used for economic aid to families with dependent children. After the increase resulting from the 1991 tax reform (which was aimed at reducing public expenditure), in 1992 the Swedish government and municipalities succeeded in granting families an overall sum for child care equal to 1.4 percent of the GNP (Kvist 1998:11; Hagemann 1995:41). While it is true that in the following years, 1992–96, the importance to family income of governmental cash benefits for children declined fairly heavily, especially for high-income families, the aid specifically provided for children in Sweden still remains high by comparison with other European Union countries (especially for low- and medium-income families). So also does aid provided in general to children in the form of indirect subsidies (Bradshaw 1998:105, 115, 116; Rostgaard and Lehto 2001:152–62).

This considerable absolute and relative growth of welfare and social service costs in Sweden occurred in a five-year period that may be characterized as follows. A decrease of the national income (calculated at constant prices) occurred during the first three years (Economist Intelligence Unit 1996:3), 1991 to 1994, when a conservative government was in power (Gynnerstedt 1997:190; Marklund and Nordlund 1999:49–50). Also during those five years cuts were made in the financing of other welfare sectors. A growth of private and corporate insurance, which was previously very limited, took place, and there was a decrease of governmental financial support to municipalities for social services. The quality standards of the health and social care services have, however, remained very high.[7]

Public expenditure on drug addicts, or on those who in any case abuse drugs, alcoholics included, was estimated—as we previously pointed out—at about 2.3 billion crowns in 1992, and 2.5 billion in 1995 (National Board of Health and Welfare 1994:43, 1996:107). This expenditure is borne by the national budget and most of all by municipalities, and it is jointly directed to care and rehabilitation activities on the one hand, and to secondary prevention activities on the other. Primary prevention expenditures are aimed at limiting

- relative deprivation, and consequently absolute poverty, compared to a conventionally set vital minimum, and relative poverty compared to an acknowledged or estimated average income;
- the rate of unemployment;
- segregation by ethnic groups and social classes, by offering everybody good-quality housing in well-designed neighborhoods provided with

adequate services. Subsidies have been made available to working-class families not only for housing but also for bearing household and maintenance costs ("municipal housing allowances"). These subsidies, despite recent reductions, total over 1 percent of the GNP.

All together, these welfare services are very expensive, and for a long time the Swedish national government and municipalities have allocated a considerable share of their resources to implement them. In 1995, all public expenditure absorbed 64 percent of the gross national income in comparison with 33 percent in the United States. In particular, expenditures for social services alone were over 8 percent of the gross national income, an increase compared to 6.3 percent in 1991, in spite of the economic difficulties of the early 1990s and the consequent efforts the government made to limit their costs.[8]

The government's commitment to limiting relative deprivation involved, first of all, income reallocation measures through the personal income tax, which by itself is almost 30 percent, and together with local taxes about 40 percent of the average gross income. The personal income tax rate has been declining, though in any case it is much higher than in other industrialized countries, and almost double that in the United States. The percentage of gross personal income taken by the income tax in 1980 amounted in fact to one-sixth in the United States and to a little less than one-third in Sweden. The income tax is only a part of the overall tax burden, which during the 1980s absorbed in Sweden one-half of gross personal income, reaching 58 percent in the early 1990s. At 50 percent of income, it continues to remain among the highest, compared to income, in OECD member countries.[9]

Further income support measures through subsidies or services provided to citizens or residents in a proven state of necessity (means-tested benefits) have been implemented and involve allotments of money, assignment of apartments in working-class housing, and fiscal allowances. These social assistance subsidies, which are borne by municipal budgets, have proved increasingly heavy, going from 5.6 billion crowns in 1991 (at 1995 prices) to almost 10.8 billion crowns in 1995, equivalent to about 0.7 percent of the gross national income that year, after having increased sixfold (at 1980 prices) from 1949 to 1991. This amount would be even higher if all the Swedish municipalities, instead of only one-fourth of them, had conformed to the rather liberal recommendations of the National Committee for Health and Social Security (*Socialstyrelsen*).

The burden of the expenditure for assistance is, however, negligible compared to the burden of welfare and social security expenditure, which includes—among the other items—money transfers for seniority, old age, accident and disease pensions, unemployment subsidies, health services, as well as care for children, the elderly, and the disabled. After increasing until 1990 before leveling off, these charges totaled almost 500 billion crowns in 1995, equal to about 30 percent of the gross national income. This percentage approximates the rate of other European Union countries, which is however much higher than the corresponding rate for the United States, which in turn has grown during the 1960s and 1970s.

In detail,

- Health, accident, and disability insurance has absorbed, and continues to absorb, a significant share of the GNP: in 1995, real health service expenditure totaled 7.5 percent of the GNP (Economist Intelligence Unit 1996–1997:23)—a considerable rate but, as we shall later see, much lower than the U.S. one—whereas in the early 1990s the indemnities for accidents and disability involved disbursements for, respectively, 0.8 and 2.1 percent of GNP income. The current tendency to reduce the duration and amount of benefits, and to establish more selective access conditions, does not seem adequate to achieve a substantial reduction in this public expenditure area (Hagemann 1995:40–41).
- The reform of the Swedish pension system was approved by parliament in June 1994, but implementation has been hampered up to now because of uncertainties in interpretation and delays in the issuing of implementation regulations (Palme 1998). In the next decades this reform should gradually change the principles and guidelines of the current pension system. Still, the amount of benefits and the conditions for accessing them should not be substantially reduced (cf. for Denmark, Christoffersen 1997; for Sweden, Gynnerstedt 1997:193, 204; Hagemann 1995; Pierson 1996:36; Stahlberg 1995).[10]
- The cuts made in 1995 in social security expenditure with respect to the 1991–92 budget, equaling 17 billion crowns, did not prevent Sweden from remaining, together with Norway, the country in Europe and throughout the world in which there is the highest public expenditure per child. A part of this expenditure is covered by compulsory social security contributions. Some cuts were decided in 1996: a 15 percent reduction of the basic family allowance for all families with dependent children, and abolition of the supplementary family allowance for families with three children or more, but keeping vested rights unchanged. However, with regard to public expenditure, the enormous increase (which started in the early 1970s but reached 45 percent in the years 1990–97) of the number of children through six years old who have been placed in public or private nursing centers, operating within the National Health Service, balanced these cuts. Families who do not want or cannot (because of lack of places) send their children to these centers usually receive an indemnity for caring for them directly at home, or for paying for their care.[11]
- With regard to labor policies, great importance has been given by the Swedish political authorities to fighting unemployment, and in general to fully injecting the active population into the economic system. As a

consequence, the expenditure for active policies—at least until the early 1990s—was higher, although in decreasing proportion, than the expenditure for passive policies.[12] The full-employment target that Sweden has pursued with consistency and determination since the 1930s has involved a considerable amount of financial obligations. These obligations totaled over 2 percent of GDP in the 1980s, reaching about 5 percent in the first half of the 1990s despite a number of financial straits and the temporary victory of a conservative party coalition. Currently, they amount to 4.5 percent and are equally divided between active and passive interventions (OECD 1997:189).

Even in the worst moments of the economic crisis in Sweden, the same conservative coalition increased in absolute and percentage terms expenditures on both passive and active policies. Passive policies provide subsidies to the unemployed. Their costs rose for the first time to over 3 percent of the GNP, a percentage five times greater than only two years earlier. Currently, Sweden, despite recent cuts in the amount and duration of benefits for the unemployed, still remains, together with some other Scandinavian countries, one of the countries that spends the highest percentage of national income on the unemployed.[13]

The costs for services aimed at preventing inequalities in life opportunities and in social segregation have been high as well. The Swedish government and municipalities have spent non-negligible shares of the national income not only for building working-class housing but also for giving the population an opportunity to live in decent housing without paying excessive rents. Public housing allowances have been in the range of 1–1.5 percent of GNP, and have not undergone important changes in the last twenty-five years (Hagemann 1995:37). The costs of Swedish housing policies are part of the wider costs of social security policies, which are all aimed at preventing a marked inequality in the distribution of income and in general in life opportunities. With the same purpose, non-negligible shares of GNP (about 0.4 percent in 1986–87) have been spent to help the immigrant population in different ways: by setting up first aid and nursing centers for refugees; by encouraging, through economic aid, foreigners and linguistic minorities to learn the national language; and by lavishing funds on immigrant associations and organizations (Friis 1988:106; Zucchini 1994:47, 49–50).

THE COST OF SOCIAL POLICIES IN THE UNITED STATES

For both Sweden and the United States it is almost impossible to make an appraisal of the portion of public expenditure (municipal, state, and national) used to repress drug crimes versus overall expenditure for police, justice, and prison administration. It is, however, possible to assess in which country public expenditure for the repression of crimes is higher in general, and particularly for crimes in connection with the laws on drugs. The public expenditure for crime repression in the United States is very high and continuously growing. This has been so both in absolute terms and as a percentage of the total amount of public expenditure at different administrative levels. This increase has produced a corresponding reduction in welfare expenses, which in any case were dramatically reduced during the 1980s. The proportion of prisoners, both those waiting for trial or convicted, compared to the overall population, is probably the highest all over the world and about nine times higher than in Sweden. The large size of the imprisoned population in the United States, because the U.S. authorities almost exclusively stress the repression of drug traffic and use, has involved enormous direct and indirect costs for the treasury.

Each prisoner is supposed to cost the state on average $22,000 per year, considering direct costs only. The cost of the so-called war on drugs and in general the stress U.S. authorities lay on repression and consequently on imprisonment instead of other ways of social control, totaled $20 billion per year during the first half of the last decade. That amounts to about $3 per thousand of the gross national income, with an upward trend. In 1995, the public expenditure borne at different administrative levels for enforcing the laws on drugs totaled $25 billion. For the about one and one-half million prisoners as of this writing (the rate of prisoners out of the overall population is about 0.5–0.7 percent) the expenditure can be estimated in the range of $33 billion, equivalent to about $5 per thousand of the GNP (Davis and Lurigio 1996:2; Donziger 1996:38; Nadelmann 1998:290–91; Reuter 1998:317). Let us suppose by rough calculation that the yearly expenses per prisoner were the same in the two countries.[14] The approximately 4,000 Swedish persons imprisoned at any given time during the same period (1994) (Swedish National Institute of Public Health 1995:22) correspond to an incarceration rate of less than 0.05 percent (one-tenth the American rate). Their incarceration involved (assuming a rate of exchange of 10.5 crowns per dollar) a yearly expense of about 920 million crowns. This amount represents about 0.5 percent of the Swedish national income of those years, which is one-tenth the corresponding yearly expenditure rate in the United States. The enormous difference in the respective proportion of prisoners involves therefore corresponding differences in the respective shares of national income that are engaged in the repression of crimes through imprisonment.

Among all the crimes involving imprisonment, those related to drug laws are particularly important not only in the United States (about one-third of all new incarcerations), but also in Sweden. Their importance is suggested by the extremely strict Swedish penal laws on this matter, according to which penalties involving imprisonment are often inflicted for crimes in connection with drugs, as well as by the high proportion of habitual users among prisoners and in general among the criminal population in Sweden. This proportion was already on the increase in the early 1980s (Persson 1981:153). More recent information has pointed out a concentration of heavy drug users and sellers within the Swedish criminal class, and particularly in criminals belonging to the extreme right. "Skinhead" organizations claim, however, not to allow their members to use or sell drugs (Loow 1995:144, 159, note 141; Swedish Institute 1995). We can therefore reasonably assume that the same 6:1 ratio may be roughly found in the respective proportions of national income that have been spent for repressing crimes in general, and particularly those concerning the laws on drugs.[15]

Unlike Sweden, in the United States several estimates of the public expenditure just for rehabilitation treatments of drug addicts are available. According to one source, between the late 1980s and the early 1990s this would have totaled $2 billion per year, according to another estimate, $3 billion. This sum corresponds to about 10 percent of the resources allocated during the same period for the repression of drug use and traffic, and to 0.5 percent of the U.S. GNP for the same period. This percentage amounts to about one-third of the corresponding Swedish rate, which however pertains to a much smaller share of individuals, compared to the overall population.[16]

As far as we can tell, estimates are not available on the public expenditure for interventions of secondary prevention for these people, and therefore the financial commitment of the U.S. authorities can be only indirectly and approximately assessed. In particular, according to the American Psychiatric Association, Congress reduced federal support for "research and service on mental disease and addiction troubles" programs (these pathologies being jointly considered by the source): forty federal programs were eliminated and over four hundred reduced—with 30 percent cuts in federal financing and direct savings in public expenditure, for an estimated amount of over $25 billion. In comparison with these savings, however, direct and indirect costs result from the lack of rehabilitation of mental patients and drug or alcoholic addicts. Their amount in 1990 was estimated at over $300 billion (Kornblum and Julian 1995:193; Nahon 1997:42), equal to over 5 percent of the GDP of the United States of that year (Economist Intelligence Unit 1995:3). Similarly, cuts made in the 1980s in federal financing for the rehabilitation of juvenile delinquency amounted to over 50 percent (Kornblum and Julian 1995:193).

Furthermore, there are some indications concerning the lack of commitment of the U.S. authorities for expenditures on interventions aimed at fighting relative and absolute deprivation, and therefore also distribution inequality, poverty, unemployment, and ethnic and social segregation. As a matter of fact (but not intentionally), these interventions might be considered as drug addiction primary prevention activities if they were otherwise conceived, better financed, and implemented in a systematic and continuous way throughout the country. While the effectiveness of specific interventions against some aspects of deprivation will be considered and appraised below, we note the following:

- The share of GNP absorbed by overall social expenditures in the United States (about one-fifth) is in any case significantly lower than in Sweden (over one-third),[17] and consequently—as we have previously pointed out—so also is the relevant share of tax burden.
- The cuts made by the Reagan administration did not involve social security expenses, which on the contrary grew during the early 1980s (despite reductions made in unemployment subsidies) and continued to grow thereafter, being focused, however, on assistance expenses.[18]
- In the United States there are considerable differences between states regarding sums paid for assistance, old age pensions, and unemployment subsidies.
- Quite often these amounts are not enough for raising the personal and family income over the threshold of poverty.
- The federal contribution to social expenditure, and particularly to social assistance expenditure, was heavily affected by political trends of that period. Social assistance expenditure, after having reached its all-time top during the 1960s and 1970s, decreased by about 3 percent in the early 1980s under Reagan's Republican administration.[19] The government preferred to entrust welfare tasks to private charitable associations, based on the illusory assumption that this might reduce the costs borne by the treasury.[20] However, later legislation such as the Tax Reform Act of 1986 and the Family Support Act of 1988 improved the economic conditions of needy families inserted into the labor market (but did not involve those who were not), with a corresponding rise of the federal and state government budgets (Danziger and Gottschalk 1995:23–35).
- The tendency of employers who have provided health insurance to their personnel (which is compulsory, except for part-time and limited-duration jobs) to deduct a share of insurance costs from the salaries of their staff has become increasingly widespread. This tendency has produced the consequence that a growing part of the staff—generally speaking, the poorest—is left without coverage or only with partial coverage. The now prevailing practice of entrusting the management of social insurance funds to external insurance companies has increased this tendency (Clarke 2001:137–40; Iglehart 1999a:70–71; Kuttner 1999b).

In light of the above considerations it is not surprising that the proportion of persons covered by the welfare system and the amount of benefits granted are quite different in Sweden and in the United States, even though the authorities of both countries are institutionally committed to covering the economic and health requirements of the poorest part of the population. A recent comparative survey examined whether there is a relation, in some economically developed countries (such as Sweden and the United States), between the benefits provided by the compulsory social security services (particularly pensions and health coverage) and the degree of income distribution inequality and the diffusion of relative poverty. This survey showed in general that poverty and inequality are more limited by universal welfare systems—such as the Swedish one— than by systems with benefits specifically addressed to the poor. It also provided evidence that these results have been achieved through welfare expenditure that in Sweden has been more than double that of the United States (Korpi and Palme 1998:particularly p. 675, Table 3).

This does not mean, however, that in the United States the overall expenditure aimed at welfare (including housing allowances) is small. On the contrary, welfare expenditure reached in 1980—that is, in the period of expansion preceding expenditure reductions made under Reagan's presidency—about 2 percent of the gross national income (Jencks 1992:76–77). This rate, which considerably further grew from the mid-1980s, is much higher than the corresponding rate allocated by Sweden for the same welfare purposes. In 1980, it totaled a little more than $0.1 per thousand of GNP (Lindahl 1981:512, 1983:494; National Board of Health and Welfare 1994:48). In 1995, Swedish welfare expenditure reached 0.7 percent of the GNP.[21] Therefore, though the United States has an overall social expenditure—and consequently a tax burden—proportionally much smaller than Sweden, it bears a higher charge for social assistance expenditure as a consequence (among other factors) of a greater number of aided individuals in comparison with the overall population. Nevertheless, the meagerness of social assistance subsidies in the United States makes the results different from those of Sweden in terms of income maintenance.

Similarly, despite a relatively high child mortality rate and a low life expectancy rate, the costs of the expenditure for health services in the United States have been extremely high and (until 1996) quickly growing. In 1989, the cost for (public and private) health services was about $2,350 per capita and almost $4,000 dollars in 1997, by far higher than in any other country of the world. Particularly, in 1989 it was higher than the considerable Swedish expenditure for health services by over 70 percent. This expenditure, in turn, was in that period (in absolute terms and with respect to the national income) higher than in the previous decades (Ginsburg 1992:205, Table A.19; Lehto et al. 1999:106, Table 5.1). In the same year, as a percentage of gross national income, the American expenditure for the health services was 12 percent. This gap, in comparison with other developed countries and particularly with Sweden, later grew. In fact, it reached 13.7 percent of GDP in 1995, without any significant decrease in more recent years (it totaled in fact 13.5 percent of GDP in 1997), compared to 7.5 percent of Swedish national income engaged in the expenditure for the health services in 1995.[22] In addition to the high and, until the early 1990s, rapidly growing levels of the fees and salaries of doctors, and the widespread and increasing use of medical technology, other factors have contributed to the rise of the American expenditure for the health service:

1. the relatively high proportion of needy or almost poor persons, who are generally in worse health than the average population,

2. the enormous number of AIDS cases in the United States,

3. the practice—aimed at reducing costs and meeting the requirements of the state and federal authorities—of discharging from hospitals poor patients covered by Medicaid funds before their time (thus allowing an in-patient cost reduction and an increase in the number of stays in hospital).[23]

On the contrary, the overall expenditure for labor policies is currently relatively negligible. This holds true for passive labor policies. In the first five years of the 1990s expenditure ranged between 0.3 and 0.6 percent of GNP, without significant variances in comparison with the previous fifteen years, as opposed to between 2.25 and 2.75 percent in Sweden. The difference was even greater for active policies (in the same period, respectively, 0.25 and 2.25–3 percent, a 1:10 ratio).[24] This comparatively modest U.S. expenditure not only depends on less liberal subsidies (in terms of amount and duration) and their much smaller extent (in terms of proportion of entitled unemployed people—generally, the unemployed belonging to the ghettos do not receive anything). It is also a consequence of the very low share of national income allocated for the training or retraining of young and adult unemployed, for the direct creation of job opportunities for the unemployed, and for the financing of employment in the private sector (in all, during the same period, about $1 per thousand of GNP in the United States versus 1–2 percent in Sweden).[25]

Public expenditures for allowances to families with children under fifteen years old are also relatively modest. In 1984, they amounted to about 40 percent of the average rate of OECD countries, and less than 30 percent compared to Sweden). The share of national income allocated in the form of money subsidies for children and families has also been comparatively low (in 1990, about one-third the share of Sweden and the average share of OECD countries). Furthermore, unlike the other OECD countries and particularly Sweden, the United States does not provide any economic aid to families with dependent children, except in specific forms. Social assistance is provided to needy families, and tax credits are granted when at least one of the parents is regularly employed in the labor market (Kamerman and Kahn 1998:81–84, 91, 94–95).

NOTES

1. The estimates on the costs deriving from the crime produced by drug abuse are very high for the United States (Platt et al. 1998:175). These estimates are in any case very uncertain.

2. For the data on Swedish national income in the period 1991–95 cf. Economist Intelligence Unit (1996:3).

3. Cf. Censis (1998:311), Ginsburg (1992:33–34, 197), Hagemann (1995:32–33), Heikkila et al. (1999:271–72), and Marklund and Nordlund (1999:27–28).

4. Cf. Ginsburg (2001:199–200), Gynnerstedt (1997:192), Hagemann (1995:31–32), Kamerman and Kahn (1998:78–79), and Lachman (1995:1).

5. As a matter of fact, in Sweden all services are financed not only through compulsory contributions but also through money transfers borne by the national and/or municipal budgets (Hagemann 1995:36).

6. Cf. Kamerman and Kahn (1998:80–81), National Board of Health and Welfare (1996:179), and Plough (1999:93).

7. Cf. Gynnerstedt (1997:193, 204), Lehto et al. (1999:112–14), Mullard (1997:36), National Board of Health and Welfare (1996:7), and Plough (1999:100–2).

8. Cf. Economist Intelligence Unit (1996–1997:11), Hagemann (1995:34), Gynnerstedt (1997:194), and National Board of Health and Welfare (1994:13, 15–16, 62, 1996:179, Table 5).

9. Cf. Economist Intelligence Unit (1996–1997:15), Esping-Andersen (1990:183), Ginsburg (1992:102–14, 197–98, 201), Gynnerstedt (1997:201), Jencks (1992:72–79), Kautto (2001:214–44), Mullard (1997:36), and Stein and Doerfer (1992:66).

10. The system in force until 1994 included two kinds of services that could be cumulated. First of all, benefits, in the form of a pension that was almost equal to the total amount of a preestablished basic sum, were paid to anybody sixty-five or older who had lived in Sweden for at least forty years or had paid contributions for thirty years. Second, a supplementary pension corresponding to 60 percent of the average annual amount of the fifteen years of work with the highest salary (up to a preestablished maximum amount) was also granted starting from the age of sixty-five to anybody who had paid thirty years of contributions. The system currently in force involves a basic pension starting from the minimum age of sixty-one, which is proportional to the social security contributions paid, and a supplementary pension having a much lower amount and depending on a pension fund. This pension fund will be managed—as happens with private insurance—based on a capitalization system, but the calculation of the pension will not only consider the inflation rate but also the estimated growth rate of real salaries for the whole duration of the retirement age. During the long transition period between the old and new pension systems, public finance will achieve savings. This will occur to the detriment of the retired, if the actual growth rate of salaries should become higher than the estimated rate, since the amount of the pensions will be partially determined by the estimated growth rate of salaries instead of the actual rate. For further investigations, cf. Hagemann (1995:44–46).

11. Cf. Ginsburg (1992:34, 38–39, 197–200), Halleroed (96:152), Kvist (98:13), Lehto et al. (99:116–18), Mullard (97:36), and National Board of Health and Welfare (94:7, 10–11, 48, 1996:14, 132, 134–35).

12. For an in-depth appraisal of the active labor policies in Sweden and Scandinavia in general, cf. Dropping et al. (99:142–46).

13. Cf. Abrahamson (93:126), Furaker et al. (90:152–60), Ginsburg (92:40–41), Gynnerstedt (97:204), Hagemann (85:36–37), Kvist (98:17–22), OECD (97:189), and Reyneri (96:382).

14. As a matter of fact, we can assume that each imprisoned person is economically more onerous in the United States than in Sweden. In the United States, the

tendency to imprison and to keep in jail for long periods even the perpetrators of minor crimes has proved extraordinarily expensive. In fact, to the direct costs for maintenance and control of prisoners we should add also the indirect costs, such as health service costs for prisoners, social assistance costs for their families, costs for building new prisons, and prisoners' lack of income from a job. Rehabilitation activities implemented in prisons, on which the Swedish authorities insist, are expensive too. We should, however, consider that such activities may help shorten the length of prison stays—either because the penalty has been reduced or is being partially served outside the prison—and may also reduce recidivism (Donziger 1996:19–27, 49, 52–55, 202–4; Swedish Institute 1995).

15. Cf. Donziger (1996:18, 30–37, 47–54, 200–1), Economist Intelligence Unit (1996:3, 1997b:5), Hagan (1994:159–62), and Swedish National Institute of Public Health (1995:19–20, 1996:255).

16. Cf. for Sweden, National Board of Health and Welfare (1994:43, 1996:107); for the United States, Reuter (1998:317–18) and Wilson (1998:309.

17. Cf. on the subject Clarke (2001:144), Colozzi and Bassi (1995:23–4), Danziger and Gottschalk (1995:27, 33–5), Censis (1999:328, Table 44), Ginsberg (1994:111–12), Ginsburg (1992:107–9, 197), Kamerman and Kahn (1998:79), and Kramer (1992:439.

18. Expenditure is growing in all economically developed countries, mainly because of the aging of the population (Pampel and Williamson 1989). Sweden's public social insurance expenditure, in comparison with national income, is almost double that of the United States (in 1989, respectively, 9.7 and 5 percent, disregarding the welfare expenditure for public employees; Esping-Andersen 1990:84, Table 4.2). This difference can be explained, not by the older age of the Swedish population, but by the much higher proportion of the old population covered by public pensions in Sweden (Ginsburg 1992:36, 105–6).

19. This decrease mainly referred to the real social assistance expenditure without taking into account social insurance expenditures and federal contributions for medical care to the elderly and the needy (Danziger and Gottschalk 1995:27; see also Clarke 2001:134). The share of federal budget destined for expenditures in connection with urban problems decreased to a little more than one-third in ten years, dropping from 18 percent in 1980 to 6.4 percent in 1990 (Hollingsworth 1997:146).

20. These organizations cover about one-third of their financial needs through public contributions, whereas only one-fourth are covered by private subventions. Therefore, it is not surprising that in the United States and in Great Britain (which in the 1980s followed the same policy of public service privatization) the direct costs of these services, when they are provided by private associations, have turned out to be the same as (or even higher than) the costs of the corresponding governmental services. To direct costs we should also add indirect costs deriving from nontax receipts that depend on deductions and exemptions of the appropriated amounts to the so-called nonprofit associations that provide assistance and social security services. Cf. Colozzi and Bassi (1995:23–24) and Kramer (1992:459).

21. In this regard, cf. Economist Intelligence Unit (1996:3), Danziger and Gottschalk (1995:24–26), Ginsburg (1992:109), Iglehart (1999c:404), and National Board of Health and Welfare (1996:134). It should be noted that in the United States, in the early 1990s, the federal assistance expenditure for aid to families with dependent children (AFDC) itself absorbed 3–4 percent of the GDP (corresponding to $20–$25 billion) though it represented only a fraction of the overall public social

assistance expenditure. In 1996, about $50 billion, that is, about 7 percent of the national income (equal to the share of Swedish national income destined for the entire welfare expenditure) have been spent only for tax reimbursement to needy workers and families with minor dependent children. In the same year, public health expenditure destined for the economically and/or physically disadvantaged population, granted through the Medicaid program, amounted to 2 percent of the gross national income, a rapid growth in comparison with the previous years (Danziger and Gottschalk 1995:36, 159; Economist Intelligence Unit 1997b:5; Iglehart 1999a:73, 1999c:403–4; Jencks 1992:232).

22. The Swedish governmental authorities, in accordance with the health authorities, have successfully endeavored to prevent reductions in public health expenditure from involving—unlike what happened in the 1980s—a decrease in the amount and quality of those services. Further reductions would, however, call into question the attainment of this purpose (Economist Intelligence Unit 1996–1997:23; Stein and Doerfer 1992:59).

23. Cf. on this subject Angell (1999:48), Bodenheimer (1999b:584), Gortmaker and Wise (1997:149, 158, 161), Horton et al. (1994:213), Iglehart (1999a:70–73, 1999c:403–5), Kornblum and Julian (1995:35, 39, 47), Rose (1993:89–90), and Ruggie (1992:926–27). Expenditure for the Medicaid program has a welfare nature, though the 1996 reform separated the right to access the benefits of this program from the right to public assistance.

24. In Sweden, budget difficulties in the early 1990s ran up against the need to keep and possibly to increase, in a period of economic crisis and rapidly growing unemployment, expenditures for active labor policies. As far as we know, the overall commitment in this area of public expenditure continues, but there have been reductions in the expenditure for encouraging labor mobility (United Nations, Department for Economic and Social Information and Policy Analysis 1997:149).

25. Cf. Danziger and Gottschalk (1995:21, 197, note 24), Ginsburg (1992:110), Kornblum and Julian (1995:434), OECD (1997:189–90), and Pierson (1996:22).

4   Consistency Between Goals and Expected Results

PRELIMINARY CONSIDERATIONS

The consistency between goals and expected results can be ex ante (beforehand) evaluated, that is, before public policies start to go into effect, or at least before they are fully implemented. We refer to the available information on their effects not only on those to whom these policies are addressed, but also on other subjects (e.g., environmental impact evaluations). In expressing a judgment of consistency, concerning most of all ex ante impact appraisals, a public decision-maker can avail him- or herself of the advice of sociologists and other experts on the effects of social policies (Palumbo 1995:329–30). For a preliminary impact evaluation of U.S. and Swedish public policies, either on drugs or in general, a judgment of consistency should mainly refer to the available information produced in the 1980s and early 1990s. That was the period when these policies were initiated and were in any case far from being completely implemented (provided that this may be possible, for public policies referring to drug use and sales). Since these policies are still current, in making an impact evaluation we will take into account the currently available information.

CONSISTENCY BETWEEN GOALS AND EXPECTED RESULTS OF SOCIAL POLICIES IN THE UNITED STATES

As we previously pointed out, during the 1980s, first under the Reagan and then the first Bush administrations, a predominantly repressive instead of a rehabilitative and preventive approach asserted itself with regard to the social problem of drugs and criminality in general (Donziger 1996:115–20; Hagan 1994:156–57). This kind of approach was politically favored in response to the great alarm spread about the (declared more than actual) growth of criminality, and particularly criminality connected to the laws on drugs (Donziger 1996:63–73; Reuter 1998:331). It is possible that because their own neighborhood had become a place in which drugs were sold and used residents may have had an unfavorable image of the neighborhood and have come to consider it as a place of delinquency in general (Hillenbrand and Davis 1993:14, 17). Therefore, authorities and the public opinion believed that a victoriously led "war on drugs" might offer the solution to a wider social problem.

As far as criminology, the repressive approach was legitimated by the "new penology," according to which "drug use is not so much a measure of individual acts of deviance as it is a mechanism for classifying the offender within a risk group" (Feeley and Simon 1992:462). This meant renouncing investigation of the causes of criminal behaviors, and therefore renouncing the search for more efficient policies aimed at preventing those behaviors and at socially rehabilitating their authors. On the contrary, the new penology recommended focusing on the goal of imprisoning subjects belonging to categories considered dangerous, in particular, young blacks of the urban underclass. This goal was seen as particularly important as a means of social control (Feeley and Simon 1992:458, 461–63; cf. also Hagan 1994:163–66).

The premises of the new penology are based on the following assumptions:

1. Some individuals show a tendency, which is not determined or influenced by macrosocial conditions, to commit particular crimes.

2. These individuals form a particular category well known to agents of social control.

3. Their imprisonment is not relevant to their future tendency to commit crimes.

By the 1980s the available body of sociological knowledge had already proved that those theories were groundless. Specifically, the so-called Chicago school had already demonstrated the crime-generating consequences of social disorganization processes in an urban community. Also, the effects of massively resorting to imprisonment had been first appraised in the late 1970s and later confirmed by research (Greenberg and Larkin 1998; Hagan 1994:164, 166–67; Park 1967:105–12).[1]

Throughout the 1980s, major surveys described some interrelated macrosocial conditions that fostered criminal behavior among the ethnic minorities of the urban ghettos: an increase in the cohorts of the younger generations, discrimination in the real estate market, and changes in the labor market to the detriment of those minorities. These factors led to their residential concentration into poor urban areas, which were heavily hit by unemployment and joblessness, mainly involving young people, and therefore contributed to the spread of single-parent families dependent on public assistance, and ultimately to crime.[2] Research done in the 1980s demonstrated, moreover, the causal relation between the high rate of imprisonment among males living in the urban ghettos, their chronic condition of joblessness or unemployment, the consequent difficulty for them to create stable families, and crime (Sampson 1987).

Knowledge produced in that decade had shown, on the one hand, the counterproductive effects of the recommendations of the new penology and, on the other hand, the effectiveness of public policies aimed at changing macrosocial conditions promoting crime. Nevertheless, the political elite, including the last three presidents (with the partial exception of President Clinton), rather than using this body of knowledge to provide the electorate with any other solution to the social problem of drugs, and crime in general, continues to resort to repressive police and judicial measures.[3] The available knowledge concerning the importance and effectiveness of primary prevention has thus been ignored by an elite that has acted under pressure from a frightened and ill-informed public opinion. Therefore, an inconsistency remained between the declared goal of social control and the expected results, which in light of this knowledge experts had proved not to be attainable by simply using repression. Similarly, in the early 1980s the federal administration decided on cuts in social expenditure, based on considerations inspired by the political convenience that prevailed in that period and on conservative principles, rather than on the specialized literature on the subject of welfare policy. A considerable part of the electorate was reluctant, as a matter of fact, to bear what it considered to be too heavy taxes. Furthermore, traditional American ideology was in favor of economic individualism, and was contrary to a heavy tax burden and to public aid to the needy and economically inactive population. Therefore, it negatively judged the effects of welfare services on the basis of elements it considered to be of particular social importance: cohesion of the family institution, control of public expenditure, and an excessive tax burden. The goal of covering the needs of the poorest socioeconomic segments was generally only supported by those who belonged to those segments (Ginsburg 1992:100–2; Hasenfeld and Rafferty 1989; Pierson 1996:26–28). On the other hand, some U.S. social scientists tried to legitimate the cuts in social welfare expenditure, which had already occurred anyway.

The essay *Losing Ground* by Charles Murray, published in 1984, stands out among these attempts. This work soon became well known in conservative political circles, which used it to support their hostility toward welfare programs (Jencks 1992:70–71). Murray's theories can be summarized as follows: welfare services have undermined the willingness to work of the marginal labor forces, particularly black males from the urban ghettos, due to an alleged "culture of dependency on social services" in the ghettos instead of a "labor ethic." Furthermore, aid to mothers with dependent children may have had the perverse effect of making this dependency condition profitable: in order to continue to receive checks from the welfare services, these mothers may have been encouraged not to marry, thus weakening the family institution. Young men, moreover, being kept by a woman as head of family would no longer have had an incentive to find a job. Finally, as a consequence of that perverse effect, welfare services may have contributed to the spreading and deepening of poverty.

Throughout the 1980s and the early 1990s, under the Reagan and first Bush presidencies, despite a political atmosphere unfavorable to a substantial increase in welfare expenditure (Pierson 1996:28–29), Murray's conservative theories were not welcomed by social science circles. On the contrary, they were confuted by the following arguments: first of all, research and experience have shown that both in the United States[4] and in Sweden (Davies and Esseveld 1982:291–92) there is a labor ethic rooted also among the needy and unemployed population. Second, the inclination toward labor among young black males is not affected by the liberality of social assistance services, nor by the proportion of black women who are head of family. On the contrary, it is positively influenced by favorable economic trends and by the job opportunities that may exist for the marginal labor force (Sanders 1990:824–26). This holds true, however, only provided that inequality in the distribution of income does not grow further, as on the contrary happened in the United States during the 1980s (Danziger and Gottschalk 1995:59–61).

Moreover, contrary to Murray's theories, the state of poverty is actually relieved by social assistance services. Available data show that the increase in the extension and amount of welfare services decided in 1965 by Johnson's Democratic presidency were not ineffectual or dangerous. Rather, a significant decrease in the rate of individuals and families with an income below the poverty threshold was achieved in the period 1965–80 (Jencks 1992:72–79). A recent comparative survey carried out in fifteen developed countries, including the United States and Sweden, comes to the same conclusion. The survey concerned the effects of the range and liberality of welfare policies on the share of population living below a conventional rate of poverty (50, 40, 30 percent), before and after having received welfare subsidies (Kenworthy 1999). Moreover, recognized experts, in line with this reasoning, have argued that the reduction of these subsidies during the 1980s in the United States contributed to an increase in the share of population below the poverty threshold (Danziger and Gottschalk 1995:28–29). They have also argued that there is no reason to hope that a reform of the welfare system may be effective in this sense, referring to the reform implemented through the Personal Responsibility and Work Opportunity Reconciliation Act of 1996 and the Temporary Assistance to Needy Families (TANF) program of 1997 (Clarke 2001:141–44; Kenworthy 1999:1135–36).

On the contrary, the condition of poverty is exacerbated by the growing number of mothers who head families and by the decrease in men (needy and belonging to the same black ethnic group) considered "marriageable" (Jencks 1992:87; Sanders 1990; Testa, Astone, Krogh, and Neckermann

1993).[5] Finally, the inclination of needy women who head families to pro-create outside the bound of matrimony does not depend on their wish to maximize welfare benefits, which do not significantly influence the pro-portion of single-parent families with women who head families, and con-sequently the rate of illegitimate births. Rather, out-of-marriage births depend on the low cultural capital, and therefore scanty future income op-portunities, of those women and their possible partners (Jencks 1992:81–83; Lichter, McLaughlin, and Ribar 1997; Testa et al. 1993).

In light of the literature published in the 1980s and in the early 1990s, cutting welfare expenditure would not have achieved these purposes. An inconsistency has accordingly emerged between the goals pursued by Murray (safeguarding the family unit, reducing poverty, and promoting employment while at the same time decreasing public expenditure) and the expected results. Furthermore, a welfare system that provides services to all citizens (like the Swedish one) is more effective in reducing poverty than a system that merely provides social assistance to subjects who are in a demonstrable state of necessity (such as the system in force in the United States). Such has been in any case the conclusions reached by recent liter-ature (Korpi and Palme 1998).

This inconsistency between the goals of social policy and the expected results concerns, in particular, the benefits—or the lack of benefits—for the more disadvantaged part of the population of the United States. The ab-sence of these benefits has derived from recent reform proposals of the pen-sion system, and actions already implemented in public health policy (particularly through the Balanced Budget Act of 1997). While the perverse effects of the health pension systems will be examined in detail below, their evaluation concerns in this case, according to experts, the consistency be-tween aims and expected results. In summary, criticism has pointed out the likely presence of perverse effects not only on the administrative expenses of health organizations, but also on the quality and costs of public health assistance for economically disadvantaged patients. These patients were covered, during the 1970s, by compulsory health insurance if they were el-derly, or by free health service if they were needy. The literature, however, has highlighted that since the 1980s the privatization of the health and wel-fare systems has lowered the quality of the health service provided, and made access to this service more difficult.

The proposed reforms of the pension system, though different, share the purpose of investing part of the national-insurance funds set aside in the financial markets. According to the opinion unanimously expressed by qualified observers with medical and sociological background, the re-quired financial resources are hardly available for the poorest part of the population. Besides, these funds may be mismanaged (as has recently hap-pened in at least one well-known instance; Maggi 2002), and would in any case no longer be available for the assured coverage of the disabled and the elderly. What is more, for the neediest population no private insurance policies are in practice available. In the same way, the recent reform of the program for free health assistance to the elderly with compulsory insurance coverage has offered the insured the opportunity to use a share of these funds for private insurance coverage or for their family doctors. This reform risks, however, crowding the neediest patients into the traditional Medicare program, with the result of lowering its quality (Angell 1999; Quadagno 1999:6–8; Physicians for a National Health Program, no date).

The actual inconsistency between pursued goals and expected results, which had already been partially identified during the 1980s, does not seem, however, to have diminished the renown of Murray's work in U.S. conservative circles. Nor did this inconsistency lead, in the 1980s and 1990s, the executive and legislative branches of government, constrained in any case by the heavy deficit and rigidity of the federal budget, to reconsider the social policies they had wanted and implemented. The case of public policies aimed at reducing unemployment and its relevant financial burden has been somewhat different. As mentioned, Republican public decision-makers were oriented in favor of a policy aimed at cutting unemployment subsidies, within an overall framework of greater flexibility in the labor force and little regulation in the labor market. Though this tendency gained, and continues to gain, the support of influential economists close to the theoretical neoliberal current (cf., for example, Feldstein 1998), economic theorists have long been divided into several currents linked to various authors and research centers (Mullard 1997:56–66).

The ideas produced by social science experts have been selectively used to argue and legitimate decisions and practices in the field of public policies, as happens in other fields as well. The implementation of these ideas has been directed and constrained by interests, ideology, and contingent considerations based on political opportunism (Giddens 1990:40–45; Stehr 1991:93–95). The fact that the implicit or explicit conclusions and recommendations of most experts have not been welcomed by the Republican administrations of the 1980s and early 1990s[6] indicates a chronic tension between intellectuals and established authorities. This tension manifested a long time ago when the intellectuals felt free to express their ideas as they began not to hold offices no longer sanctioned by tradition (Shils 1969:42–43). Nevertheless, recent experience suggests that such tension can be partially overcome. For example, the policy of tax reimbursement to low-income workers is known in the United States as the Earned Income Tax Credit (EITC). This policy has gained the political support of several administrations and congressional majorities, as well as of welfare policy researchers with different ideological orientations, both conservative and progressive.

These researchers have proved that federal or state tax reimbursements aimed at welfare and national income redistribution are able to effectively increase the income of needy workers. The consistency between pursued goals and expected results is, however, jeopardized by the possibility, indicated by U.S. economists and sociologists, that reimbursement may encourage employers to keep salaries at a low level, reimbursement thereby acting as a subsidy to employers. Furthermore, EITC still remains insufficient for solving the problem of officially acknowledged poverty in the United States. Social scientists have proposed further measures: an increase in welfare subsidies to the poor without requiring compulsory work, subsidies to enterprises employing the economically marginal labor force, or offers of public employment. These measures might achieve the expected result of eliminating poverty, provided they are able to build up an organic, rather than desultory set of provisions. However, as these researchers admit, such measures would hardly gain the approval of both Congress and the most conservative segment of public opinion. Implementation is therefore questionable (Danziger and Gottschalk 1995:158–66; Jencks 1992:20, 233; Kornblum and Julian 1995:253).

By way of conclusion, what is authoritatively considered effective in the United States for counteracting relative and absolute deprivation and can be implemented in the political and U.S. ideological context is, however, not enough for achieving this purpose. On the other hand, what is considered effective and, as a whole, sufficient, cannot be implemented in that context. In order to reduce the rate of unemployment, the proportion of the population below the poverty line, and the crime rate, well-known U.S. researchers have recommended higher public investments in education and professional retraining, in the explicit belief that the market alone does not allow these goals to be achieved. They have also recommended public policies aimed at reducing ethnic and social segregation, and at improving the quality and availability of working-class housing and municipal services.

Research has proved that the lack of employment in the legal labor market and the inadequacy of these public benefits highly contribute to a number of effects in some urban areas, among which are residential instability, concentration of poverty, a high proportion of broken families, and finally social disorganization in the area itself and a high rate of delinquency within it. After the 1960s, the necessary support of the legislative branch (and in the 1980s also of the executive branch) for these expensive investments failed. Thus, the current proposals do not seem to have much chance to be supported and implemented by politicians (Danziger and Gottschalk 1995:153–54; Sampson and Wilson 1995; Solow 1994:75).

CONSISTENCY BETWEEN GOALS AND EXPECTED RESULTS OF SOCIAL POLICIES IN SWEDEN

The inconsistency that has been ascertained in the United States between the goals pursued by political authorities and the results expected by specialized researchers cannot be found in Sweden. We will first investigate

this thesis with regard to the goals of rehabilitation and primary prevention policies: this will involve, from the point of view of the achievement
of these aims, an appraisal of the peculiarities of the Swedish welfare mix.
Our argument will later consider what has been done in Sweden about secondary prevention, with reference to the environment of real or potential
drug users. The consistency between goals and expected results, insofar as
the primary and secondary prevention policies implemented in Sweden
are concerned, can be appraised in light of the knowledge of the likely preventive effects of some particular welfare policies. Swedish policymakers
have used this knowledge, provided by social science, either consciously
or thanks to a fortuitous intuition that has often preceded the execution of
such policies.

As a matter of fact, in Sweden, primary and secondary prevention of the
traffic, use, and abuse of drugs is especially the task of the welfare institutions operating in the field of assistance, social security, and social service
provision. In line with the prevailing trend of Swedish public opinion, the
task of containing relative deprivation has been entrusted to these institutions. Furthermore, in Sweden as elsewhere, a welfare mix, that is, a national welfare system inspired by different guiding principles, has been
implemented in recent years. The relevant criterion for an evaluation of the
Swedish welfare mix is the presumed ability to achieve its institutional
goals: this ability can be evaluated according to the principles indicated by
recent U.S. and European literature on the welfare mix.

An evaluation of the effectiveness of the *rehabilitation* policies is uncertain everywhere, due to the methodological inadequacies that have affected research up to now, as well as to different criteria of success to be
used (Anglin and Hser 1990:406–16). An exception is the evaluation of the
effectiveness of methadone rehabilitation treatment. Many U.S. studies on
the subject have pointed out the ability of this treatment to induce most patients to abandon illegal drug abuse and criminal behavior, and to promote
their working and social rehabilitation in general. Nevertheless, widespread heavy resistance to rehabilitation via methadone and a lack of
funds have discouraged a wider use of this substance in the United States.[7]

On the contrary, Swedish authorities have been regularly administering
methadone, under medical control, to chronic drug addicts twenty years
and older. Since 1984, the year in which the use of methadone became an
integral part of official rehabilitation programs, its effectiveness has been
continuously monitored in conjunction with research institutes. Furthermore, this treatment has been suitably financed and integrated, like all the
other rehabilitation treatments in general, by the support provided by psychiatrists and social workers (Swedish Institute 1995; Swedish National Institute of Public Health 1995:24–25). Therefore, there has always been in
Sweden, as recommended by the specialized literature, a continuous interaction between available knowledge on rehabilitation and real thera-

peutic and social rehabilitation activities, which is not generally the case in the United States.[8]

One of the conditions for the effectiveness of the Swedish *primary prevention* policies with respect to drug traffic and abuse is the limitation of relative deprivation and, more generally, the limitation of inequality in income distribution. This has always been an explicit target of the Swedish welfare system. The relatively low rate of poverty, much lower than that of the United States, has been attributed, with compelling argumentation, both to the extent and the universalistic character of the Swedish welfare system, as opposed to the U.S. system (Esping-Andersen 1999:163–64; Kenworthy 1999; Korpi and Palme 1998).[9] According to some U.S. inquiries, the fact of Sweden having achieved—though partially—this redistribution purpose seems to have led to the following—probably unexpected but desirable—effects:

First of all, criminal behavior in general (not only that related to drug traffic and abuse) is not very widespread. As has been noted in this connection, the diffusion and intensity of relative and absolute deprivation, and the absence or weakness of noneconomic institutions that might mitigate it, are causally related to the production of criminal deviance, including drug abuse and traffic.[10] A particular tendency to commit crimes has, however, been found also among young people of privileged socioeconomic background. In this case, they manifest this tendency by a marked inclination to risk-taking, to consider themselves exempt from the legal consequences of committing crimes, and not to feel bound by conventional values (Wright, Caspi, Moffitt, Miech, and Silva 1999).

Second, and more particular, is the relatively modest relevance of criminal behavior of minority ethnic groups. In this connection, the consequences of ethnic inequality leading to crime have been demonstrated.[11] The consequences of social and ethnic inequality are evident in the weakening or even the destruction of the family institution (Blau and Golden 1986; Sampson 1987; Shihadeh and Steffensmeier 1994). Even more than family integrity, the quality of the relations among the family members is important to this effect (Van Voorhis et al. 1998:235–61). We will later discuss the presumable effectiveness of Swedish secondary prevention policies aimed at families with members at risk.

A further condition for the effectiveness of primary drug prevention policies is—according to Swedish policymakers—the limitation of the portion of the active unemployed or jobless population (Swedish National Institute of Public Health 1995:33). From this condition, which is consistent with the results of contemporary criminological research,[12] has followed a particular relevance given to economic and labor policies considered apt for achieving this purpose, and consequently to the opinion of experts in these disciplinary areas. The belief of some U.S. researchers, that greater investments in educational and professional retraining courses are advis-

able, was shared for a long time—and basically continues to be shared—
by the Swedish political elites, whether social-democratic or conservative
(for the limited periods of their political dominance). Since the 1930s, they
have cooperated by mutual consent with university economists for a Keynesian economic policy and a social welfare policy (Weir and Skocpol
1985:129–32, 149), though economists are divided on the effectiveness of
active labor policies.[13]

Finally, primary prevention actions implemented in Swedish schools
conform to the accumulated knowledge of many years of experimentation
not only in that country, but also elsewhere, particularly in the United
States. As a result of this knowledge, schools have abandoned the preventive measures used during the 1960s in the United States, as well as in
Sweden. These methods had proven to be ineffective and often had the opposite effect, such as arousing fear over the consequences of using drugs
or providing information on the characteristics and the psychosocial effects of drugs, but disregarding the context of the information. Instead,
other methods have been adopted, aimed at:

1. promoting an ability to resist the dangerous influence of fellow students or adults;

2. establishing autonomous values and behaviors;

3. increasing personal and social competences.

Furthermore, researchers have not only turned to the school population
and teachers, but also to parents and other adults in contact with young
people because of their professional activity, and to mass media (Swedish
National Institute of Public Health 1995:16; Nersnaes 1998:79–83). These
methods have been successfully implemented, mainly in the United States.
Accordingly, they are now recommended by specialized researchers (Botvin 1990; Hawkins et al. 1995:400–6).

Swedish policies for the *secondary* prevention of criminal deviance, particularly traffic, use, and abuse of drugs, have not only conformed to but
sometimes have even preceded the conclusions and suggestions of the U.S.
researchers. Some of them have examined the experience of "communi-
tarian" prevention programs. These programs are aimed at enabling the local community to prevent and repress illegal activities that are carried out
locally, and at involving citizens, leaders, and associations based in city areas in which illegal behaviors, usually in connection with the buying and
selling of drugs, often occur. Researchers have analyzed the operational
modalities and the permanent success conditions of these programs. They
have agreed that it is necessary to achieve an active individual and collective commitment not only from concerned citizens, who would carry out
an informal control activity, but also from the police, social services, and
other local public authorities. Tasks of formal control are assigned to all
these authorities, and not only is their reciprocal coordination important,
but also their coordinating with that part of the population that cooperates
in prevention and repression programs.[14]

Unlike the United States, in Sweden the whole population has apparently always collaborated with the authorities in the repression of illegal activities without any need of urging by prevention programs. At the end of the 1970s, the use and consequently the likely availability of drugs were higher (Swedish National Institute of Public Health 1995:13–15). Still, even then consumers found it very difficult to maintain contact with drug dealers, and the available quantities of heavy drugs were limited (Persson 1981:151, 155–56). Throughout the 1980s, as we previously noted, very strict laws were promulgated (and are still in force) against dealers and even simple consumers. Close coordination, which continues today, began at the same time among police and prison authorities, courts, and social services. The support of almost the whole population (even the most needy part of it, except for a limited criminal underclass) was always given, as one would expect in a society in which there are no socially disorganized areas in which institutions are hardly present and, as a consequence, there is little social control.

Moreover, as U.S. researchers have pointed out, within the urban area to be socially rehabilitated, there is a need to promote normal operating conditions in the family institution. Hence, the relevance of secondary prevention policies capable of providing families—as a group of criminologists suggests—with "the instrumental and social service supports needed to insure their functional development" (Van Voorhis et al. 1988:258, and in general pp. 235–61). The lack of those supports obliges a number of needy U.S. mothers, mainly young ones with dependent children, to make an unpleasant choice: either work illegally, with the risk of leaving little children unattended and without care, and losing, if they are discovered, their scarcely sufficient but vital welfare benefits, or not to work at all, thus not being in a position to satisfy their own needs or those of their children (Harris 1996:424, and in general pp. 407–26).

Furthermore, the beginning of deviant behavior, including drug use and abuse, is made easier in children coming from families marked by poverty and by poor interfamily relations. This is indicated by the presence of conflicts and violence and by a lack of domestic tranquility, love, and control of children (Gorman 1996:511–12; Nurco and Lerner 1996; Van Voorhis et al. 1998; cf. also, among the Italian studies, the remarkable research of Baraldi 1994a). While the variables related to interfamily relationships seem to have a direct effect on children's behavior, the effect of poverty is indirect: poverty seriously prejudices the possibility of success in school (Duncan, Yeung, Brooks-Gunn, and Smith 1998), which in turn, together with broken families (or with single parents) and a conflictual atmosphere, starts young people off on a working future characterized by long and frequent unemployment periods (Caspi, Wright, Moffitt, and Silva 1998). Finally, unemployment, particularly when it is accompanied by economic and social deprivation, has a mutual causal relation with law-violating behaviors (Thornberry and Christensen 1984).

These illegal behaviors, including the use of drugs, are made possible by the availability of a large amount of "unstructured" time. By this, we mean time not involved with organizations, particularly companies and schools, and out of the control of adults invested with power, such as parents or teachers (Mazerolle, Kadleck, and Roehl 1998; Osgood et al. 1996). The negative effects on children in situations of poor interfamily relations are made worse if (as usually happens in the United States) little or no support is provided by the social services. This support may be psychological/psychiatric, or may take the form of advice on problems concerning the family or other subjects (Chavis, Speer, Resnick, and Zippay 1993:263).

Swedish political authorities and social service providers have implemented for many years a combination of preventive interventions, organized and carried out by the local authorities on which these services depend. This seems to have worked (Hawkins et al. 1995:402–5). These interventions are particularly addressed to subjects at risk of deviance, particularly for drug use and abuse. Political authorities have striven hard to reduce juvenile unemployment as much as possible. Social services have in turn provided needy families with what is necessary to make steady progress out of poverty. Also, they have offered psychological and information support to parents who are unable to maintain a good relationship with their children, and school and psychiatric help to children and young people in trouble. If deemed necessary, they have been entrusted to other families or to foster homes. Nonetheless, social services usually try not to keep children, especially those of preschool age, away from their families. Particular attention is paid to the children of alcoholics or drug addicts (National Board of Health and Welfare 1994:52–55, 1996:74). The level of the support provided by social services is considered insufficient even by the Swedish authorities (National Board of Health and Welfare 1994:54). However, Sweden remains one of the countries that spends the most per child throughout the world. Moreover, the professional training degree of social workers operating in the field of child and family services is considered very high (Lehto et al. 1999:128; National Board of Health and Welfare 1996:129).

It is easier to control and inhibit local drug dealing than any other criminal activity. However, poorly functioning families and local institutions— particularly schools—make it very difficult—according to U.S. surveys— for local residents to informally control their children and the groups of neighborhood youth in general, and both families and school have a strategic importance in preventing them from keeping bad company.[15] In fact, according to the conclusion of a comparative survey on the means and causes of heroin diffusion in Holland, Great Britain, and the United States (Grund 1998:251), all organizations that are in contact with groups of young people who may be at risk for drugs are capable of performing a secondary prevention activity.

Furthermore, according to an overview of some recent U.S. inquiries into different explanations for the use of drugs, all these inquiries agree on the fact that the use of drugs seems to depend largely on the encouragement received from schoolmates who use them (White 1996:284). This reinforcement effect, though, grows as drug users move toward drug addiction, which probably happens because they progressively limit the circle of their relationships to other drug users, to the exclusion of others. An effective secondary prevention activity should therefore intervene before young people begin to choose their own friends (Krohn, Lizotte, Thornberry, Smith, and McDowall 1996:423–24). It seems, therefore, that the Swedish authorities have been right in addressing their prevention efforts to the goal of enabling families, schools, and youth organizations to inculcate conventional behaviors and rules, and thus to control, in cooperation with authorities, juvenile deviance (Swedish National Institute of Public Health 1995:16–17, 35).

Moreover, the effectiveness of secondary prevention policies seems to be augmented by primary prevention policies aimed at preventing both the existence of strong relative deprivation and its concentration within some urban areas or particular ethnic groups. In one of the few extant comparative studies on U.S. and northern European welfare policies, differences in the respective crime rates were attributed to the considerable differences in the degrees of relative and absolute deprivation of the poor urban neighborhoods in the United States and in Scandinavia (Abrahamson 1998:34–35). In Sweden, public aid to families with troubles, in terms of economic assistance and psychological advice, has gone hand in hand with a public housing policy. This policy has met in general the demand for good-quality working-class housing. In any case it has avoided the creation of urban areas characterized—as we can infer from the U.S. literature—by a number of unfavorable living conditions: poverty, social disorganization, marked socioeconomic and ethnic isolation of the minorities living there, and consequently crime and a high rate of drug selling and use.[16]

Secondary prevention (involving families, school, other organizations in touch with young people, and the young people themselves), primary prevention (concerning labor and housing), and rehabilitation activities have strengthened one another. This has been done, probably unintentionally, in compliance with the recommendations of U.S. researchers on youth deviance, and in particular on drug use and abuse prevention policies. U.S. heroin addicts constitute a very neglected population that is mainly concentrated in urban ghettos. According to some experts, their terrible living conditions can be mainly attributed to the drastic federal and local cuts during the 1980s in the public financing of welfare services, particularly social assistance services for needy people and rehabilitation services for drug addicts. Usually, these people are not only needy indi-

viduals, but they also like other ghetto inhabitants belong to socioeco-
nomically disadvantaged ethnic groups. They tend to be even more iso-
lated socially than other residents of the ghettos (Inciardi et al. 1998:36–37,
46–47).

While Swedish public policies in favor of needy people and immigrants
have lessened (though not eliminated) their relative deprivation, the systematic and widespread efforts for the rehabilitation of drug addicts have
resulted for the most part in their successful reinsertion into society. In
conclusion, the political and administrative authorities of Sweden have
conceived and put into practice to a great extent, with constant and considerable (also financial) commitment, an overall public policy aimed at
primary and secondary prevention as well as rehabilitation. This policy in
fact anticipated the lessons that U.S. experts drew some years later from
the disastrous experience of poverty, ethnic discrimination, crime, and the
spread of drugs in urban ghettos, and in general in the United States.

The difficulties in financing welfare expenditure and the notion that the
provision of public services should also depend on the needs and wishes
of the beneficiaries and not only on those of the government are present
both outside and inside Scandinavia (Gynnerstedt 1997:202–3; Kramer
1992:438–39). In Sweden, they have contributed to legitimate in public
opinion and in the Swedish political elites, whether social-democratic or
conservative, a partial withdrawal from the universalistic welfare pattern
that had dominated until the 1970s. In its place, a peculiar Scandinavian
welfare mix has been favored, which is characterized by a combination,
different from any other welfare mix, of "solidaristic components, public
investments and competitive orientation" (Evers 1997:19), in which the importance of local and national government investments has not decreased.
This particular type of welfare pattern was regulated by the reform of 1992.

The complex relation among institutions (public, volunteer, and nonprofit ones) based on work division characterizing the Scandinavian welfare mix pattern is aimed at achieving "wide consent" through "a process
of institutional cooperation with decisions having a public character"
(Klausen and Selle 1997:172). An agreement on specific interventions presupposes in fact a general consent by public and private organizations and
public opinion in Sweden on the need for services to be provided and traditional solidarity values respected. This consent has been maintained continuously despite the economic problems of the early 1980s. Generally,
however, the upper classes seem to prefer welfare programs distributed to
all citizens and residents, such as health services and pensions, rather than
programs such as unemployment subsidies, social assistance, and allowances for household expenses, which favor economically and socially
weak classes. Using a procedure that has been consolidated for many years
throughout Scandinavia, executive authorities consult experts and include

them in deliberative committees. Such committees advise on individual problems—in this way, in particular, the problem of the spread of drugs was confronted in 1977—for the solution of which private organizations offer their services. Experts are no longer consulted, as they were in the past, for their advice on the consistency of welfare aims with ideological principles and with the real possibility of achieving them.[17]

Swedish service organizations have brought about some changes in favor of a more pragmatic orientation, a greater amount of professionalism, and more cooperation with the governmental organizations. These organizations in turn have opened to cooperative relations with volunteer personnel (Klausen and Selle 1997:156–70; National Board of Health and Welfare 1996:127–29). As a consequence, a particular "principle of subsidiarity" has been implemented in Sweden. Generally speaking, this principle is characterized by a "mutual adaptation" between public (particularly governmental) organizations and private associations. Through a "subsidiary" intervention with respect to the activities of general interest carried out by these associations, the public authority evidences a twofold commitment: on the one hand, to "support the autonomy of civil society," and on the other hand, to "significantly limit its own decisional competences." Nonetheless, the authority still keeps "not only juridical competences or initiative rights," but also "the financial and administrative resources that are required for organizing and concretely exerting this power" (Colozzi 1997:27).

Some researchers have maintained, however, that the subsidiary principle could not be applied in Sweden, because—even after the reform of 1992—there are still some constitutive elements of the previous welfare pattern. First of all, the agreements between authorities and private associations are signed on terms established by the authorities themselves, whose regulating function is generally acknowledged. Furthermore, in case these bodies are cooperative associations they are considered also by their members as mere executive instruments of decisions made by the public organizations. Finally, public opinion continues to favor a uniformity of treatment that can be realized only by the social-democratic universalistic welfare pattern. The subsidiary model has been viewed as an alternative to this pattern. The Dutch welfare model, which has been considered a good approximation to the subsidiary model, distinguishes between services leading to "a regulated, controlled and financed system at national level," and services "placed under the responsibility of local public administrations which organize them autonomously to some extent" (Colozzi and Bassi 1996:51), and transfer the provision of services to volunteer organizations. These organizations operate locally, are self-managed, and "hold almost a monopoly position" (ibid.:59).

Each characteristic of the subsidiary pattern can also be found in the

Swedish system in the same way as it is incorporated in the Dutch welfare system; it seems therefore reasonable to consider this pattern compatible with the social-democratic model. Useful information on this subject can be found in a Swedish governmental source that—referring to the innovations introduced by the reform of 1992, by comparison with the previous regulations on social services (1982)—declares that in many municipalities social services are undergoing a reorganization process. Some forty of them—according to this source—have already introduced, or are planning to introduce, a service buying and selling system through which welfare services are let out on contract to a municipal or private supplier. Three-quarters of all municipalities have decentralized their own competences by establishing (autonomous) cost centers that depend on organization units—for example a daytime service center—which are fully responsible for the management of their activities, their personnel, and their resources. It has become increasingly common that a function, or a part of it, is let out on contract by a municipality to a private enterprise, a charity society, an association, or a cooperative. The municipality continues, however, to be responsible by law. The government document indicates in addition that the reform has involved all the main functions of the social services, and particularly "clinics for alcoholics and drug addicts." Finally, the government has reduced financing to municipalities and the relevant controls on them, but it carries out in return a supervisory activity on municipalities. Accordingly, they may provide the political authorities with information on the life conditions of the population. Also, they may follow the provisions of the reform of 1992, their own administrative targets, and the expenditure limits established by the budget (National Board of Health and Welfare 1994:6–7, 13, 54; cf. Klausen and Selle 1997:167; Lehto et al. 1999:110, 113).

As in Holland, the Swedish government also transfers public services to private organizations. These organizations operate with a great deal of decisional independence but under the responsibility and control of local administrations, and with governmental financing and supervision. Complete independence from the control of the public authority over private organizations providing social services would be in contrast with the widespread aversion of Swedish public opinion to any welfare system entrusting private organizations, particularly market-oriented organizations, with the distribution of public services. The public authority remains therefore clearly responsible, both politically and legally, for their operations. Furthermore, a double control activity—of local administrations over private organizations and of the government over local administrations—may obviate, at least to some extent, some difficulties of the public body, such as exerting appropriate supervision over the management and accountability of private service contractor organizations.[18]

The self-management of service cooperatives may be limited, thus infringing the reform law of 1992. It is, however, difficult to believe that institutions, such as churches and schools, that have taken upon themselves welfare tasks may accept becoming merely an executive instrument for decisions taken by the public authority. The operating independence of volunteer organizations, whose possible limitation troubles the researchers of the "third sector" (DeHoog 1993:121), seems sufficiently guaranteed in Sweden. In fact, this autonomy is not only established by law, but in all Scandinavian countries there is a tradition of noninterference of the public bodies in the activities of organizations belonging to the service area, with which they keep on the contrary relations of "integrated cooperation." As a consequence, it does not make any sense to speak about a government colonizing the third sector in Scandinavia (Klausen and Selle 1997:171, 173). The Dutch government also shares with the Scandinavian governments "an egalitarian tradition" and the control on "the contractual modalities in service awarding." Moreover, as in Sweden, also in Holland "their financing is made through money transfers from the national budget" to local organizations (Colozzi and Bassi 1996:51–53).

A comparison between Scandinavian countries "marked by a traditionally strong and pervasive public intervention" and Holland, with a "by far dominating" private sector (Pasquinelli 1999:99–100), belongs therefore to the past. Accordingly, Sweden, Norway, and Denmark can be considered as approximations to a single "Scandinavian pattern" of welfare state.[19] It is not then surprising that the authors of a typology of relations between government and the third sector have considered both Holland and a Scandinavian country, Norway, as examples of "integrated dependency," and have placed them in the same relationship class. Together with Germany, Holland and Norway are, in fact, characterized by the following three aspects:

1. "Private assistance provision is integrated in the overall governmental welfare system."

2. Volunteer organizations "financially depend on the Government."

3. The degree of autonomy of these organizations "may be relatively high" (Kuhnle and Selle 1993:196–98).

The literature on welfare mix points out some risks that are peculiar to it, and maintains that the "subsidiary principle" may avoid those risks, provided that "an incentive . . . to a welfare-friendly mentality" is avoided. This mentality may prevail when a welfare system based on state institutions asserts itself. In this connection, it is also important not "to lose sight of its solidarity tasks, thus promoting social disintegration" (Colozzi 1997:28–31). This may happen when a market-oriented tendency prevails, since "the limit of welfare produced by the market is that we get only what we can pay" (Rose 1993:92).

Among the inherent risks of any welfare mix, there is a possible "lack of equity and an insufficient safeguard of the entitled persons." Some of them are well safeguarded, whereas others might receive less than their due and/or might not have the actual possibility to access public services. In addition to this risk of lack of equity and disregard of legal entitlements in the services provided through volunteer organizations, there are other risks as well. Paternalism and amateurism are cases in point. Also, these services may prove inadequate in comparison with the real needs of the actual and potential users (Colozzi and Bassi 1995:63–64; cf. also Donati 1997:282; Evers 1993:110, 113, 1997:21; Kramer 1992:459).

A number of factors make some of these risks particularly unlikely. First, there is the social-democratic tradition of the Swedish government rewarding distributive equality, and hence the overall access of all citizens to public services. Second, there is "close cooperation with public authorities" (Klausen and Selle 1997:171) of the organizations belonging to the third sector. Finally, the Swedish government carries out monitoring on their activity. The peculiar welfare mix implemented, or to be implemented, in Sweden seems, in the light of the available knowledge and appraisals, very promising, for it has the chance to diminish or cancel the distance between citizen and service providers. The literature considers this distance as a problem in state-oriented welfare states in general (De Leonardis 1996:58–59), and particularly in the Swedish one (Gynnerstedt 1997:203; Svallfors 1991:613).

A preliminary evaluation of the impact of the Swedish social policies, either on drugs or in general, seems therefore favorable. Specialized researchers do expect significant benefits not only from a welfare mix in general, but also—and most of all—from a welfare mix that regulates the relations between public bodies and private welfare organizations according to a subsidiary principle. The Swedish welfare system currently is so characterized. From the peculiar Swedish—and Scandinavian in general —welfare mix we can therefore expect that "new forms of integration or social solidarity" may be actually created through welfare activities carried out by the third sector. As a consequence, "intermediate social bodies between the single individual and the state" may thus be established to further the development of the civil society (Donati 1996:17–19, 1997:277–79). In this way, "the institutional conditions that favor the learning and the actual exercise of citizenship" would be implemented (De Leonardis 1996:70). However, some doubts remain on the actual ability of the government and the municipalities to manage relations with contractor companies in order to substantially reduce service costs, while maintaining a high degree of quality (DeHoog:125–27). These costs, in fact, have continued to be high despite, as we previously noted, the fact that they were reduced in the early 1990s to some extent. Experts fear however that a further reduction would affect the future quality of these services, which is currently very high (Economist Intelligence Unit 1996–1997:23).[20]

NOTES

1. Greenberg and Larkin (1998), in particular, have demonstrated that (a) predictions of future criminal behavior of heroin users with particular sociodemographic and biographical characteristics supporting these predictions are able to identify a significant number of future criminals, but they also identify as criminals subjects who have shown a lower tendency toward crimes or have refrained from them (and would therefore be imprisoned without any reason); (b) even when predictions identify future criminals, since they are generally individuals who exhibit a number of licit and illicit behaviors with a low degree of specialization in peculiar crimes, their preventive imprisonment, as a preventive strategy for particular crimes, would be ineffective.

2. Cf. Chavis, Speer, Resnick, and Zippay (1993:252–53), Kasarda (1985), Massey, Condran, and Denton (1987), and Wilson (1985).

3. Cf. Donziger (1996:79–81), Kornblum and Julian (1995:189, 193), and Reuter (1998:331–32).

4. Cf. Danziger and Gottschalk (1995:133–34, 171), Kornblum and Julian (1995:241–42), and Solow (1994:28–32).

5. The survey by Testa et al. (1993) was originally published in 1989 in the *Annals of the American Academy of Political and Social Science.*

6. For example, on the failure to bring research on the causes of child poverty in the United States to the attention of public officials in a position to intervene in them, cf. Lichter (1997:141).

7. Cf. Deschenes and Greenwood (1994:266–68), Dole and Nyswander (1998), Anglin and Hser (1990:417–21), and Platt et al. (1998:particularly pp. 178–81).

8. Swedish municipal social services have systematically tried in various ways since the 1980s with great commitment to identify and then to assist all drug addicts or subjects at risk. For some years now, they have also introduced, on a limited scale, an experimental damage reduction program through the supply of sterile syringes. This program remains, however, subordinate to drug use prevention programs (Swedish National Institute of Public Health 1995:24–25). Similar programs for risk reduction have been started in the United States, though also on a limited scale, but they depend entirely on local initiative (whereas in Sweden all the policies aimed at prevention and risk reduction are decided by central authorities, though their implementation is entrusted to local social services). Furthermore, only during the 1990s have programs aimed at identifying, studying, and assisting the "hidden" population of drug addicts been implemented in the United States with federal financial support. Despite a quantitative expansion, these programs still only exist in a very small number of places (Kornblum and Julian 1995:59; Singer and Needle 1996).

9. As evidence of the importance of complying with a universalistic principle in the distribution of welfare benefits in order to achieve an income redistribution

(Korpi and Palme 1998) we should note that the benefits that have less support from Swedish public opinion are precisely those aimed at exclusively benefiting particular categories of the population (Andersen et al. 1999:249).

10. Cf. Chamlin and Cochran (1995), Parker (1989), Patterson (1991), and Rosenfeld (1986:117–19).

11. Cf. Krivo and Peterson (1996), Liska and Bellair (1995), Messner (1989), and Peterson and Krivo (1993).

12. More precisely, criminological research has highlighted the mutual causal relation between unemployment and criminal deviance in general (Thornberry and Christenson 1984), as well as the causal relation between lack of employment availability and quality on the one hand, and juvenile criminality on the other hand (Allan and Steffensmeier 1989). With reference to drug consumption, it has also been pointed out that there is on the one hand a causal relation between belonging to families in economically and socially deprived areas and the quantity of available nonstructured time (which is inversely related to the fact of having a job), and on the other hand the pursuit of deviant activities (Cook and Roehl 1993:252–53; Osgood et al. 1996). Finally, as underscored by the U.S. and European literatures, there is a particular willingness of unemployed or jobless persons who are not in the legal labor market, belong to disadvantaged ethnic groups, and live in deprived urban areas to participate in the drug traffic taking place in those areas either as dealers (Fagan 1996:55–68; Grund 1998:230–31; Jankowski 1995:82–85; Johnson et al. 1999:30–31) or as users (Brunswick and Titus 1998:93–96, 102; Inciardi et al. 1998:36–37; Kinlock et al. 1998:14–15).

13. Econometric literature on this subject has not come to univocal conclusions either in general or with regard to Scandinavia. According to a group of U.S. economists, the low rate of unemployment in Sweden during the years preceding the 1990s cannot be attributed to active labor policies. Some other U.S. and Scandinavian economists have nonetheless asserted the effectiveness, though partial, of these policies and have recommended their implementation in the United States (Danziger and Gottschalk 1995:168–74; Dropping et al. 1999:157–58; Gynnerstedt 1997:200).

14. Cf. Chavis et al. (1993:266–67), Mazerolle et al. (1998), Smith and Davis (1993:123–25, 135–37), Weingart (1993), and Wikstroem (1995:461–62).

15. Cf. Botvin (1990:510), Chavis et al. (1993:252–53), Davis et al. (1993b:xii–xiii, xv), Elliott, Huizinga, and Ageton (1985:150–51), Liska and Reed (1985), and Wiatrowski, Griswold, and Roberts (1981).

16. Cf. Massey (1990), Mazerolle et al. (1998), Sampson (1987), Shihadeh and Flynn (1996), Tigges et al. (1998), and Wacquant and Wilson (1993).

17. Cf. on the subject Andersen et al. (1999:245–46, 249, 254), Klausen and Selle (1997:167–69, 172), National Board of Health and Welfare (1994:6–7), Svallfors (1991:611–15), and Swedish National Institute of Public Health (1995:9–10). Foreigners living in Sweden in the second half of the 1980s and in the first half of the 1990s constituted about 5 percent of the population, in comparison with about 7 percent in France and Germany. Almost one-half of the persons of foreign origin living in Sweden came from another northern country (Censis 1990:82, Table 8; Martens 1997:186–89; Zucchini 1994:41, 43). The relative ethnic homogeneity of the Swedish population did not prevent a considerable development of the third sector, although a theoretical current relates this development to the heterogeneity of the population (Barbetta 1993:66–68).

18. Cf. DeHoog (1993:121–22, 127–28), Klausen and Selle (1997:167), Svallfors (1991:613–14). The relevance of control and supervision exerted by Scandinavian governmental authorities on third sector organizations can be appraised through the isomorphism (structural similarity) these organizations have taken upon themselves in order to conform to the instructions given by the authorities, as happened in Norway (Kuhnle and Selle 1993:186).

19. Cf. Klausen and Selle (1997:157–59); cf. also Kautto et al. (1999a:10–14) and Kramer (1992:454–58).

20. The reduction of governmental financing to municipalities for covering service costs led some Swedish municipalities to make drastic cuts. As a result, there was a disproportion among users for accessing services and the actual quantity of received services, especially regarding public assistance (National Board of Health and Welfare 1994:7, 46). These disadvantages did not, however, result from service contracting procedures or from the peculiar Swedish welfare mix, but rather from the economic crisis and the consequent budget deficit of the early 1990s. The difficulty in reducing public service costs derives not only from the continuous and strong popular approval of public support for social services, which are distributed to the whole resident population with universalistic criteria (Svallfors 1991:612), and from the opposition of trade unions to a squeezing of their financing (Mullard 1997:36). It perhaps also derives from a possible "limitation of competition in the organizational environment and in public contracting procedures" (DeHoog 1993:125). As a matter of fact, Swedish authorities often sign contract agreements with "institutionalised volunteer structures," which assume therefore a semipublic juridical status (Klausen and Selle 1997:169), with the consequent restriction of the organizational environment and of the enterprises with which transactions are handled.

5   Perverse Effects

PRELIMINARY CONSIDERATIONS

As we already noted, by perverse effects we mean effects that contrast with the defined goals and the expected results of public policies. We shall present and appraise in this chapter the effects (achieved results, effects on policy beneficiaries, overall social consequences) that can be considered perverse in this sense and that literature attributes to the public policies implemented in the United States and in Sweden.

PERVERSE EFFECTS OF PUBLIC POLICIES ON DRUG USE AND TRAFFIC IN THE UNITED STATES

We examine in order the perverse effects of repressive policies, those involving rehabilitation, and then preventive policies.

Repressive Policies

The almost exclusively repressive orientation of authorities had counterproductive effects, even from the point of view of the authorities themselves. Their policies affected the ability to limit drug traffic and use, the cohesion of urban subclass families, the spread of criminal deviance in general, and finally the crime-generating consequences of cuts in financial support for prevention programs. The cuts came as a direct result of the heavy financial burden of imprisonment costs borne by the public treasury. The negative effects of this orientation were not restricted to the actual and potential public of drug users, but rather involved all of society. Further relevant perverse effects on the spread of drug sales and use have resulted from the public housing policies implemented in the United States.

The almost exclusively repressive orientation of the U.S. authorities, far from reducing drug traffic and use, has increased them, as several elements suggest. First, repression does not address the social causes of drug traffic and use, but merely attempts to eliminate their symptoms (Chavis et al. 1993:252–53). Second, the effects produced by the imprisonment of pushers are thwarted when it is easy for criminal organizations to find new dealers, or to displace their market areas (Davis and Lurigio 1996:112–14, 126–27; Donziger 1996:61; Smith and Davis 1993:137). The counterproductive consequences of a mainly repressive orientation appear evident in the light of the following considerations. Due to this orientation, and not to a significant growth of crimes involving the sale and possession of drugs, an increasing number of persons has been condemned and imprisoned. Since 1991, more than one-half of the prisoners in the federal prison system and more than one-fourth of the prisoners in state prisons have been sentenced for drug-related crimes. The proportion was much smaller in the previous decade (Donziger 1996:16, 18–19; Hagan 1994:161). This trend has had considerable perverse effects:

1. In the short term, the massive imprisonment of young men from urban ghettos, against whom police and judicial authorities often behave in a discriminatory way, decreases the number of persons whose biographic course might allow them to create a family and to obtain a regular job. This number is already low among the members of underprivileged ethnic minorities. As noted by some studies done in the United States, young women from the ghettos look for "marriage-suitable" men in terms of quality and type of job and curriculum vitae (especially, the absence of a criminal background). Moreover, the business world is still extremely reluctant to employ, even if only temporarily, young people from the ghettos who have spent time in prison, because this confers on them the public image of criminal. Finally, their extensive contact with other convicts and with prison personnel gives them a definite criminal identity.[1]

2. As a medium-term consequence, there has been a decrease in the urban ghettos of families headed by a man who has a regular job. A further impoverishment of families belonging to the black urban underclass—with a woman head of family who depends on public assistance—has resulted, along with an even higher diffusion of such families (McLanahan 1985; McLanahan and Garfinkel 1993; Neckerman et al. 1988:406–14). The consequent disintegration of conventional interpersonal relationships and the social disorganization deriving from these circumstances make it usually more difficult, if not impossible, for the adult inhabitants of these urban areas to informally control the activity of the young people who live or gather there. As shown by empirical research in the United States, low-income and disorganized communities are lacking in informal social control. This social condition contributes to producing criminal behaviors, and therefore all attempts made to fight crime not involving the population have had effects that are only temporary, although they cannot be precisely evaluated.[2]

In particular, regarding the struggle against local drug traffic and use, these attempts—even if made by a small number of persons—have achieved some results only within the local neighborhood, provided that certain conditions have been met. First of all, residents willing to exert informal control should be seriously committed, suitably financed, and supported by public institutions (such as the police, social workers, and political authorities). Second, these institutions should be acting in concert.[3] In the United States, all these conditions cannot be easily found operating in conjunction, and their effects are in any case restricted to local areas. More significant results would require a massive participation of the neighborhood's inhabitants and organizations to the reconstruction of community life. According to qualified observers, this has so far proved almost impossible in low-income areas in the United States (Chavis et al. 1993:256–66).

3. The U.S. authorities, at different administrative levels, have shown a strong tendency to confront the problem of criminality, and particularly drug pushing, through a massive resort to imprisonment of those considered socially dangerous. In the long term and as a consequence, this has given a powerful impulse to the creation and maintenance of socially disorganized areas. Not only is imprisonment not an effective social control instrument, as it is easy for criminal groups to replace their imprisoned members, but this policy of social control has other perverse effects:

a. The breakup of families.

b. Economic difficulties for these families resulting from the imprisonment of members who were previously economically active. In a typical situation of scarce or low-paying legal jobs, mostly among the young population in U.S. urban ghettos, imprisonment increases the already heavy burden of finding legal and steady work, as opposed to the relatively easy access to more lucrative illegal markets.

c. The prevalence, among needy families from the black minority, of unemployed or jobless women as head of family.

Because noneconomic institutions—such as families and political or religious organizations—are absent or weak within these areas and have inadequate public financing, they are not in a position to significantly counteract the crime-generating effect of relative deprivation. This holds true in spite of the efforts of many private organizations, often having a religious character, in different social areas (education, health, and welfare). Socially and economically disadvantaged urban areas have in turn promoted crime, particularly the traffic and use of drugs. Authorities try to suppress this activity by massively resorting to the imprisonment of young males living in the urban ghettos. Many judges seem receptive to the prejudices of public opinion. They have accordingly followed the widespread and still existing practice of handing out—for the same indictment, previous offense record, and other relevant variables for judgment formulation—particularly long sentences for subjects considered socially dangerous, such as blacks, males, and the young.[4]

As a consequence, these almost exclusively repressive tendencies have produced serious, lasting, and considerable perverse effects not only on the young inhabitants of the ghettos, but also on U.S. society as a whole. A particular tendency to use and sell drugs is a priori attributed to ethnic minorities because of their physical aspect and previous offenses, and of the bad reputation of the area. Resorting to the imprisonment of young people belonging to these minorities produces another perverse effect. The frequent arrests and subsequent imprisonment of "suspicious" young people as a social control instrument contribute to maintaining a particular diffusion of drug use and sales in the area, especially among those young people. Police forces, courts, and public opinion are wont to predict a marked tendency to crime (not only to drug-related crime) in these young people and in general in the population of that area. This attitude leads to the almost exclusive use of repressive interventions for the purpose of exerting social control, and tends therefore, in conjunction with other circumstances, to be a self-fulfilling prophecy (Hagan 1994:168–70; Hagan and Peterson 1995).

The widespread existence of criminal deviance in the United States, particularly in connection with drug use and sales, can be attributed to these crime-generating conditions, which are mainly present in urban areas characterized by poverty and social disorganization. Among these conditions, we previously noted the inability of U.S. welfare organizations, due to a lack of funds and organizational fragmentation, to make sufficient provisions in terms of amount, temporal continuity, and extension in a number of welfare areas. Social assistance measures for income support in case of unemployment, mainly long-term unemployment, and public housing are cases in point. This insufficiency was worsened by cuts in federal social expenditures, which were made in the 1980s because of, among other circumstances, the very heavy financial burden of prison expenditures (Donziger 1996:48). The almost exclusively repressive response to the social problem of criminal deviance has therefore contributed to reproduce this very social problem through an abatement of welfare services.

Rehabilitation Policies

U.S. drug policies in the 1980s caused heavy cuts in public expenditures for drug addict rehabilitation. Their paradoxical effect has been to force on those willing to detoxify themselves and who do not have the financial resources to pay for treatment the alternative of procuring the resources illegally or doing without the treatment. In the former case, crime increases as a consequence. In the latter case, the use of heavy drugs has been maintained in just those persons who would be otherwise prepared to give them up (Hunt and Rosenbaum 1998:196–99, 206–7; Knight et al. 1996). The second alternative surely does not coincide with the goals of U.S. policies of simultaneously repressing criminality and drug sales. It cannot be considered an expected result, and hence a perverse effect, however, since the decrease of public financing for the rehabilitation of drug addicts would presumably have prevented some of them from access to those services. It is likely that the first alternative, where social rehabilitation is rewarded with criminal activities, had not been foreseen, becoming in this way a true perverse effect.

Prevention Policies

Public policies at different (federal, state, and local) levels have not had the goal of preventing or reducing ethnic and social segregation, which has been one of the causes of relative deprivation and social disorganization. Furthermore, active interventions in the labor market—which are instrumental for preventing unemployment and limiting its economic and social consequences—have been almost completely lacking. Therefore, the very high amount of drug abuse and sales among young people from the urban ghettos originates not only from hostile labeling on the part of the authorities and public opinion. It also results from the absence, in the goals of public policies, of the purpose of preventing relative deprivation.

This absence is the result of a strong presence in U.S. public opinion and the political elites of an individualistic culture of competition in the market, and social life in general (Hagan, Hefler, Classen, Boehnke, and Merkens 1998:311–17; Lewis 1993). This culture conforms to a widespread dislike on the part of public opinion and of the whole population in general—except the more disadvantaged part of it—for governmental interventions in the social area (Ginsburg 1992:100–2; Hasenfeld and Rafferty 1989). By contrast, the majority of the Swedish population has evidenced a strong adhesion to redistributive welfare measures (Heikkila et al. 1999:270–71; Svallfors 1991:611–12). The culture of competition involves an acceptance of inequality and the diffusion in a non-negligible part of the population of a criminal "anomic morality," which is not sufficiently offset by families, schools, and other noneconomic organizations. It also involves a rejection of social groups that are felt as external bodies, not socially integrated and therefore undesirable (Chamlin and Cochran 1995; Hagan et al. 1998). The classical (Cloward 1960:179–86) and contemporary (Fagan 1996:48–49) criminological literature on the subject has shown that many young "anomic" criminal bands reject and hold drug addicts in contempt. Their members do not accept such conventional values as honesty and respect for legality, but do believe in the value of economic success. Accordingly, drug addicts suffer, in addition to negative labeling by the nondeviant majority, also from negative labeling by young criminals. In this way, their condition of deprivation and isolation is enhanced, whereas their steady social rehabilitation becomes more difficult.

In the provision of welfare services, there is, however, a specific sector—public housing policies—that has directly enhanced ethnic and social segregation. Indirectly, by way of its contribution to the creation of socially disorganized areas, it has also strengthened relative deprivation. The public housing policies implemented in the United States have turned mainly to the benefit of privileged classes (gentrification), while proving harmful, or of limited benefit, to the needy population that previously lived in housing projects. While limited benefit has been the result of the quantitative and qualitative inadequacies of public housing policies, harm has been done to those who are not in a position to afford the high rentals of the "reclaimed" areas, and have been forced to move elsewhere. This gentrification effect has been the result of the federal or governmental support granted to urban renewal programs (Hodos 1997:12–3; Horton et al. 1994:309), for the authorities have favored private economic interests. As a rule, such interests do not find it profitable to meet the requirements of people with limited purchasing power (Weber 1974:volume I, p. 59). The efforts to offset this effect through alternative housing policies have failed to produce a greater amount of housing in good condition at reasonable rents. According to some observers, this policy has actually decreased the amount of such housing and led to endless waiting lists in all large cities (Handler 1979:495; Horton et al. 1994:272, 309–10; Jencks 1992:219; Kornblum and Julian 1995:460–61).

The gentrification effect produced by public housing policies, however, cannot be considered a perverse effect in the restricted sense of the term used here. U.S. authorities have not usually pursued the goal of reducing the territorial segregation of underprivileged classes and ethnic groups, or their concentration into specific residential areas. On the contrary, they have encouraged the opposite tendency. Until the 1970s, many municipal authorities, with the support of the Federal Housing Administration, implemented a policy that regulated the use of building land and provided, in addition to public services, subsidies for buying houses or apartments. This policy prevented—probably on purpose—the neediest part of the population, which continues to coincide with the most disadvantaged part of the black population, from having access to the new neighborhoods in the suburbs. In fact, if not intentionally, the federal financial support increased the segregation and concentration of poor black people in housing projects of inferior quality, situated in dilapidated areas (Farley and Frey 1994:25–26; Shihadeh and Ousey 1996:653–54; Somma 1991:65–67, 75–132; Stahura 1986:132–33, note 1).

The federal law against discrimination in the real estate market (Fair Housing Act of 1968), and the subsequent enactment provisions, have reduced residential segregation in the United States. Contributing to this has also been an attitude in the white majority, particularly the younger part of it, of progressively accepting opening the possibility of living together with ethnic minorities. This reduction in residential segregation has, however, proved appreciable only in some regions and urban centers, those characterized by a small black population, by military settlements, or by strong economic development and consequently by new buildings (Farley and Frey 1994; Steeh and Schuman 1992). Outside those areas, segregation—mainly to the detriment of the poorest segment of the black population—is still very strong (Massey and Denton 1988; South and Crowder 1998), and is still affected by a discriminatory approach—either voluntary or involuntary—in public housing policies.

The federal laws of 1995 and 1996 changed public housing regulations in two ways. First, they abrogated the 1937 proviso not to decrease the overall available quantity of working-class housing. Second, they ordered city authorities to demolish within ten years all state-owned residential buildings that were damaged to such a degree that they could no longer conform to the regulations in force. The new areas built with public funds avoid the overcrowding and concentration of disadvantaged economic strata and ethnic groups (usually needy and black), at the cost, however, of increasing the demand for housing of individuals and families belonging to those strata and groups (Gotham 1998:12–13; Howlett 1998).

Nonetheless, political interests continue to operate in favor of residential segregation. The authorities of the centers adjacent to the neighborhoods of the needy ethnic minorities still avail themselves of their power in order to prevent these unwelcome minorities—both because of their ethnic diversity and their poverty—from "invading" their territory. They do so with the support of locally based insurance companies, banks, and real estate agencies. This coalition of political and economic interests is sustained by the will of the majority of the white population, which prefers to live in white or even mixed neighborhoods, but almost never likes to live in mostly nonwhite areas, particularly if the majority of residents is black.[5] It would not have been easy, at any rate, to oppose with adequate public policies the processes of residential segregation and the concentration of unemployment, joblessness, and poverty within black and, to a smaller extent, Hispanic populations. The territorial concentration of relative and absolute poverty has interacted, to the detriment of these groups, with economic discrimination in the housing and labor markets and with social discrimination from the white ethnic group. These two processes have thereby strengthened each other (Massey 1990; Massey and Eggers 1990).

Within the housing and areas built with public subsidies, and in general within these poor and ethnically segregated neighborhoods, activities promoting relationships based on conventional values ("seeding" activities) have been hardly relevant in comparison with those repressing crimes related to drug traffic and use ("uprooting" activities) (Davis and Lurigio 1996). This has happened not only because seeding activities are in contrast with the stress laid by authorities and public opinion on repression, but also because it is very difficult to promote nondeviant behavior and relationships in ethnically segregated and socially disintegrated urban environments. Urban environments with these characteristics have been produced, as we previously argued, by public opinion and a political orientation rooted in all administrative levels, which generally used to be and still are hostile to primary prevention programs concerning relative deprivation, social disorganization, and ethnic segregation.

These circumstances have thus been responsible for creating the social conditions that in turn produce crime in general, and heavy drug use and traffic in particular. The most deprived population living in poor urban areas has been most affected by such conditions, and most involved in these activities (Gorman 1996:513; Krivo and Peterson 1996; Shihadeh and Flynn 1996; Shihadeh and Ousey 1996). The almost exclusively repressive character of social control interventions has further exacerbated these conditions. Municipal and also, until recent times, federal housing policies aimed at segregating the poorest segments of the black ethnic group have proved successful, in the sense that there has been a consistency between the goal of ethnic segregation, and both the expected and achieved results. This "success," favored by strong and widespread feelings of ethnic prejudice (though less than in the past) among the white population, has been so great that it has paradoxically contributed to make it difficult and limited to achieve racial integration. Officially, but perhaps not in fact, this constitutes the new and opposite goal of federal policies (Farley and Frey 1994:26–27). The results achieved by the "segregating" housing policy of the past have therefore proved inconsistent with the expected results (which have been only partially achieved) of the new housing policy, thus producing a peculiar perverse effect.

A further perverse effect marks the U.S. policies of income maintenance, and consequently of primary prevention. The goal and the expected result have been to limit the costs of social services (social assistance and social security) through a reduction in the duration, extension, and amount of the subsidies granted to the needy and unemployed. In contrast, the achieved result has been highly increased costs of social assistance, and higher economic and social inequality (currently, considerably higher than in Western Europe), without obtaining significant reductions in the percentage of GNP engaged in income transfers in favor of the unemployed. The growing number of needy people and a longer average period of poverty, which have resulted from the cuts made in federal social expenditures during the early 1980s, have contributed to this undesirable effect.

The reductions made in federal expenditures have in fact increased the number of needy people, since a greater number of unemployed people have been left with no or insufficient subsidies. Moreover, the reductions have extended the average period of poverty, due to increased difficulty in getting out of the condition of poverty, and finally increased inequality in the income distribution. These effects have not been amended in successive years, despite an extension during the early 1990s (under the Republican presidency of the first Bush) of the period in which unemployment subsidies are granted, and despite an increase in the minimum wage. As a matter of fact, the minimum wage still remains insufficient for raising many families, particularly those with single parents, over the poverty line. Inequality in the distribution of income, furthermore, has not decreased since the early 1980s. Finally, the growing proportion of the marginal labor force with temporary and/or part-time jobs is not entitled to receive unemployment subsidies (Danziger and Gottschalk 1995:35, 47–54, 91, 93–110, 114–18: Esping-Andersen 1999:181; Keister and Moller 2000:67–69; Kenworthy 1999:1135–36; Lichter 1997:135–37; O'Connor 2000; Small and Newman 2001).

The reform of the U.S. welfare system has encouraged many former aid beneficiaries to enter the labor market through the Personal Responsibility and Work Opportunity Act of 1996. It has also put an end to the previous welfare program (Aid to Families with Dependent Children, AFDC) through the Temporary Assistance to Needy Families Act (TANF) of 1997. This reform has had two further perverse effects. First of all, the strong incentive to enter the labor market and the insufficiency of wages have caused a growth, or at least a nonreduction, in the proportion of needy families. Second, the introduction of a separation between the right of the needy to medical assistance on the one hand, and the right to economic aid on the other hand, has complicated the regulations for benefiting from all social assistance programs. The undesired consequence has been, in the last analysis, to discourage a considerable proportion of potential beneficiaries—usually the more economically disadvantaged—from registering in the program of free or semifree medical assistance to the needy (Medicaid). This would at least partly explain why, among entitled persons, about 40 percent of the children are not registered in this program (Iglehart 1999a:72, 1999c:405–6; Kuttner 1999a:163–65; O'Connor 2000:549–52).

Within the U.S. system of coverage of health service requirements, the reforms of Medicaid, which has a social assistance character, and Medicare, whose benefits are reserved for elderly people and which belongs to the social security system, have caused additional perverse effects. The overall tendency to entrust the management of funds for Medicaid and Medicare to private companies has involved pressure on doctors to reduce the costs of their services, and therefore also the attention and time they can give to each patient, with the consequence of lowering the quality of this service (Bodenheimer 1999a:491, 1999b:586; Iglehart 1999a:73). Particularly regarding the Medicaid program, the management of federal funds

by private companies was introduced in the 1980s with the purpose of
bringing greater efficiency to the implementation of this assistance program. The reform has failed to achieve its expected results. Costs rapidly
grew until 1997, and their subsequent limitation has damaged those who
were entitled to receive social assistance. Many of them, especially children, no longer have health service coverage, and have therefore been
forced to turn to emergency rooms in hospitals in order to receive medical
services. The reform has had in addition the undesirable effect of limiting
the available benefits for needy patients requiring expensive care (Iglehart
1999c:403, 407; Kuttner 1999a:163, 165).

Somewhat similar effects have resulted from the innovations introduced into Medicare. As regards the compulsory pension plans that enterprises structure for their employees, there has been a gradual transition
from pension plans with defined benefits to plans with defined contributions. The latter plans have become prevalent since the 1980s, partly because they have been promoted since the 1970s by the federal government.
Companies and single individuals covered by Medicare also have the possibility of turning to private organizations (health maintenance organizations, or HMOs) for their health coverage. This allows users to receive
greater benefits, as compared to those that would be available through the
traditional refund system for health services paid by users. The costs of
the traditional refund system have been borne by the state or national budgets. Each private pension scheme with a definite contribution does not
guarantee a minimum amount of benefits, which on the contrary are subject to the hazards of the financial market. Moreover, employees with low
wages are particularly penalized by these hazards. This innovation in the
management of Medicare may therefore increase inequality in the social
distribution of insurance coverage. A growing proportion of persons has
in fact "decided" to come out of the pension scheme provided by their employers, mostly because insurance costs (which employers increasingly
tend to charge to their employees) are too heavy for them. Generally, these
persons are not in a position to autonomously sign insurance policies and
do not have any right to the medical assistance provided by Medicaid, and
therefore are left without any pension or health assistance. The latter, in particular, in 1993 was extended only to 27 percent (as against 40 percent in
1979) of the most economically disadvantaged citizens, that is, persons
whose income is in the lowest quintile of the income distribution. Furthermore, in recent years different HMOs have signed contracts with Medicare
aimed at reducing costs. The competition among them has involved a limitation in the amount of health services expenses subject to refund, and a se-
lection of participants to the detriment (as in the case of persons who are no
longer covered by Medicaid) of those requiring expensive care.

This perverse effect has become more likely since the recent (1997) reform of Medicare. The introduction of the opportunity for private insur-

ance companies instead of public welfare services to decide had the explicit purpose for the future beneficiaries of Medicare of increasing the choice among the available pension plans. This increased opportunity has turned advantageous for those who can pay an insurance premium, and have personal characteristics (such as income, age, health conditions) that make policies profitable for companies and medical associations operating in the insurance business. The majority of citizens who are more at risk from the point of view of insurance companies are still included in Medicare, whose costs per patient consequently increase, while the quality of service deteriorates. These undesirable consequences intensify as soon as HMOs operating in agreement with Medicare announce their withdrawal from the agreement, and there are no other HMOs in the area to which one can turn. In this case, previously insured persons are compelled to face the unpleasant alternative of either contenting themselves with the relatively limited benefits offered by the traditional Medicare program, or signing expensive policies with organizations that do not cooperate with Medicare.[6]

PERVERSE EFFECTS OF PUBLIC POLICIES ON DRUG USE AND TRAFFIC IN SWEDEN

Perverse effects, as mentioned, indicate a discrepancy between, on the one hand, explicit goals and expected results of public policies, and on the other hand, the results actually achieved. With reference to Sweden, perverse effects have been particularly stressed by a literature with conservative tendencies, and therefore hostile to the political and ideological hegemony of social democracy on the Swedish public policies.[7] Referring to these perverse effects, this literature maintains that any social democracy would produce serious inefficiencies in the production of goods and services, and therefore public policies would achieve results contrary to those pursued and expected by the decision-makers. In particular, it makes the following claims (Stein and Doerfer 1992:56–62):

1. With regard to the production of private goods and services, a "welfare policy based on ideas inspiring to socialism" would have been responsible for the prevailing egalitarian income redistribution tendency. Such a tendency would account for the heavy tax burden borne by individual taxpayers, the protection of jobs, and the equalization of wages. Accordingly, a host of undesirable consequences would ensue. A drop would have occurred in the propensity to work, and more in general a reduction in supply and demand for the labor force, and hence in the formation of savings and wealth. The final consequence would be stagnation in productivity and economic development.

2. With regard to the production of collective goods, public services in particular, some experts maintain that "a public sector based on monopoly

produces lack of competition and waste of resources," and consequently high costs and low productivity. They also maintain that, due to the uniformity of public services provided below cost at almost monopoly conditions to all residents, benefits would be paradoxically granted to the more advantaged socioeconomic segments. They can divert to the treasury—so the argument goes—the access costs to services such as free high school education from which, as a matter of fact, the other segments are excluded.[8]

These theses on the affirmed perverse effects of the Swedish welfare system should be separately and carefully considered. Their correctness would in fact involve, in the short term, the inefficiency of prevention activities—particularly insofar as drug use and abuse are concerned—as a consequence of low productivity and high costs of public services. In the long term, it would involve the ineffectiveness of these activities, because of the growing social inequality in access to these services and the consequent increase in relative deprivation. The correctness of such theses would also involve the final abandonment or radical reduction of prevention activities, because of their unbearable costs in a context of economic decline.

The alleged negative effects on the propensity to work have been imputed to the ideological and political hegemony of social democracy. A number of consequences would follow because of this hegemony. A heavy tax burden would be instrumental to bear the high social expenditure. Also, a tendency to income redistribution and rigidity in the labor market would prevail. The objections that may be raised concerning this line of reasoning call into question the conclusions, but not, however, the premises, which are apparently correct. In particular, so far as wage differentials are concerned, Sweden is the most egalitarian country among the developed countries, and few changes have occurred in the last fifteen years in this respect. The United States is instead the least egalitarian country, with a tendency toward growing inequality (Danziger and Gottschalk 1995:118–20; Gustafsson et al. 1999; Keister and Moller 2000:63–69; Ramaswamy 1995:16; United Nations, Department for Economic and Social Information and Policy Analysis 1997:137).

The above-indicated conclusions are then questionable. First of all, it is difficult to establish a causal relation between a decrease in tax burden and social expenditure on the one hand, and higher propensity to work on the other (United Nations, Department for Economic and Social Information and Policy Analysis 1997:149). However, it does not seem that there is an appreciably negative relation between the amount of public expenditure (in relation to the GNP) and propensity to work (indicated by the average number of work hours per person). At an aggregate level, we might argue that the heavy reductions made during the 1980s in the public expenditures of the United States did not correspond to a proportional increase in the annual work hours. The former decreased by 20 percent in relation to the GNP, while the latter only grew by 2 percent. In Great Britain, also during the 1980s, the Thatcher government cut off social expenditure and tried hard to reduce the tax burden, but the average number of annual work hours decreased by about 3 percent.[9]

If we consider another indicator of propensity to work, the participation of the active population in the labor market continued to grow in Sweden during the thirty years of social democratic political hegemony (with the exception of the years 1976–82), reaching in 1990 the historical peak of 84.5 percent.[10] During the heavy unemployment period of the early 1990s, unemployed people had, on the contrary, the opportunity to receive economic benefits without a termination date, by alternating temporary jobs provided by the government with liberally subsidized unemployment periods. This might have involved a lower propensity to work to the detriment of the national economy (Ramaswamy 1995:13–14). However, experience showed that despite this institutional incentive not to work, the average number of work hours did not decrease in Sweden during the years of crisis (1990–93). On the contrary, it slightly increased in both periods (OECD 1997:179, Table g).

The thesis according to which a higher inequality in income distribution, particularly earned income, would promote a greater propensity to work is equally disputable. In Great Britain, the labor policy implemented by the Thatcher government showed the negative effects that the introduction of individual wage incentives, aimed at increasing the productivity of the labor supply, produced on employees' morale and their capacity to do teamwork (Graham 1997:128–30). On the contrary, as the U.S. and Swedish experiences have pointed out, income maintenance policies (having either assistance or a social security character) usually promote the participation of the labor force in the labor market, particularly regarding needy women with dependent children. In contrast, reductions in money transfers to the detriment of these needy women are related (and this is probably a causal relation) to a marked tendency to withdrawal from the labor market.

In Sweden, during the 1980s, the increase in the already liberal income support to parents with dependent children, most of all if needy, went along with a considerable increase in their participation in the labor market as part of the employed labor force. This participation later slightly decreased, due to subsequent cuts in this subsidy. In Sweden, public employment, where there is a strong concentration of women, offers lower average wages than the private sector. Still, the massive participation of Swedish women in the labor market achieves an income redistribution effect not only between men and women, but also between different social classes, since employment—usually in the regular labor market—allows needy Swedish women with dependent children to keep out of poverty. In the United States, on the contrary, the working participation of fathers, in the case of two-parent families, and mothers, in the case of single-parent families, has become lower in correspondence with cuts in money transfers to needy families with dependent children. It is noteworthy, finally, that Swedish workers have a very low propensity to strike, in the last years perhaps the lowest among developed countries. The number of working days lost on strikes per thousand workers in Sweden was on average, in 1999–2000, less than 4 percent of the corresponding number in the United States.[11]

A relative equality in income distribution, instead of a marked inequality, seems therefore to encourage propensity to work, both in general and particularly as regards the more disadvantaged socioeconomic stratum.[12] A greater participation in the labor market allows the economically marginal population to contribute to the national income and to the tax receipts. It also allows governmental administrations and local organizations to limit public expenditure on social assistance and crime control, for there is a relationship between relative and absolute poverty on one hand, and crime and an increase of drug use among the population on the other hand. In conditions of efficiency in public administration, money transfers and public services tend, at least in part, to pay for themselves.

Finally, in recent years researchers have shown the unemployment rate and hence the demand for labor do not seem to be strictly dependent on the rigidity of offer. A growth of labor market flexibility, following deregulation, has gone along with a lower unemployment rate in the United States, but with an increasing rate in Great Britain. Furthermore, total and long-term unemployment rates in Sweden until the end of the 1980s were lower than the U.S. rates. The Swedish labor market has been, however, subject to much greater regulation, in comparison with the labor market of the United States (OECD 1997:181, Table 1; United Nations, Department for Economic and Social Information and Policy Analysis 1997:134–35). It may be argued, in any case, that in the United States the socioeconomic policy of wage inequality and labor market deregulation has caused a decrease in social protection, and put a large amount of workers below the threshold of poverty. This amount has been estimated as 15 percent of the overall labor force. On the other hand, in Sweden, and in Scandinavia as a whole, women's participation in the labor market has been very strong, and therefore families with a double income are particularly widespread.[13]

These families not only provide a barrier against poverty, but also create jobs. This has been so because, thanks to their relatively high income, they are able to satisfy their requirements for services by buying them on the market, and also because their requirements can be satisfied by an active, employment-producing welfare state (Esping-Andersen 1997:38–39, 32–35, 1999:103–16). Moreover, a different diffusion of part-time jobs has at least partly balanced the possible negative consequences on employment produced by the greater rigidity of the labor market in Sweden. In fact, part-time jobs, either voluntary or involuntary, which were and still are more widespread in Sweden than in the United States, provide flexibility to the labor market (Mullard 1997:55; OECD 1997:178; United Nations, Department for Economic and Social Information and Policy Analysis 1997:143–47).

A literature with liberal-conservative orientation has maintained, as previously noted, that the long permanence in power of the social democratic party may have resulted in smaller growth of productivity, loss of international competitiveness, and stagnation in economic development and the creation of national wealth. This would be a consequence of the "welfare state mechanism," which undermines—so it has been contended—the very process of wealth creation, although it needs constant economic growth (Stein and Doerfer 1992:62). Social democracy would therefore produce a discrepancy between goals and expected results on the one hand, and on the other hand the overall perverse effects or impact. The goals and expected results regard safeguard of employment and income maintenance for the nonprivileged segments. The perverse effects or impact would consist in carrying out social and economic policies that destroy the national wealth, and consequently fail to achieve any of these goals and results.

Has, as a matter of fact, an economic failure of social democracy occurred in Sweden, and would it be in this case an indicator of an overall failure of social democracy? The economic difficulties of Sweden during the 1980s and mostly during the early 1990s are: first, a lower increase in productivity and national income (both as from the 1970s); second, a higher inflation rate compared to the average increase rate in OECD countries; third, a decrease in the real national income during the years 1991–93; fourth, a flight of capital toward other EEC countries; and finally, an increase in national debt and balance deficit.[14]

We could, however, raise two objections against these statements. Both objections concern the causes of recession in the early 1990s, and the possible responsibility of Swedish social democracy. First of all, a survey carried out by the International Monetary Fund (IMF)—an authoritative economic and financial international organization with theoretical neoclassical and liberal tendencies—excluded any causal connection between the decrease in international competitiveness of the Swedish economy during the 1980s and the economic crisis of the early 1990s. The contribution of exports to income production had in fact grown at the beginning of the recession, in 1990, and was determining, three years later, for an economic recovery. Rather, the experts of the IMF point to different immediate causes of recession:

1. A drop in consumption and investments following (paradoxically, from a liberal point of view) the liberalization of the financial markets in 1985;

2. A subsequent (1985–90) very rapid expansion of consumption and investments, which affected private savings (Ramaswamy, Green 1995).

Some other experts agree, at least in part, with this diagnosis (Economist Intelligence Unit 1998–99:13).

Second, it is not plausible, for many reasons, to simply attribute to social democracy or to the welfare policies implemented and managed by Swedish social democracy the economic difficulties of the 1980s and the early 1990s. Some objections would be as follows: first of all, if social democratic governments and the welfare organizations that are their expression produce detrimental economic effects, why did these effects reveal themselves only after many decades in power? In fact, the Swedish welfare system was not a creation of the 1980s and 1990s, and went along—as previously noted—with unemployment rates that until recent times were lower than the corresponding U.S. ones. Also, it did not prevent Sweden from having rates of national income growth that were in line (with slight upward or downward variances) with the average growth rate of OECD countries in the 1980s, namely, the period of greatest development of the Swedish welfare system (Marklund and Nordlund 1999:21–22).

Furthermore, a higher national debt may be the result of economic policies implemented by conservative instead of social democratic governments. In the United States the economic-fiscal policies implemented by President Reagan produced such a deficit in the federal balance that "since then it became very difficult to finance further expansions of the social programs" (Danziger and Gottschalk 1995:24). In Sweden, the "bourgeois" government of the 1976–82 period accumulated "an enormous deficit" (Pontusson 1997:67) equal to 70 percent of the gross national income (Green 1995:26). In the United States, the balance deficit served to finance increasing military expenditures. In Sweden, on the other hand, it was the result—as acknowledged by the liberal-conservative observers themselves—of a "growing intervention of the government." This growing intervention, however, had not been brought about by the social democrats, but by precisely that "bourgeois" government, particularly through the nationalization of the naval and textile industries as well as of the major steel mills (Stein and Doerfer 1992:56–57; cf. also Hernes 1991:256).

It was, on the contrary, the social democratic government, after its return to power in 1982, that squeezed public expenditure and reduced subsidies to industry and agriculture. It also liberalized the financial market, rationalized the public sector and the tax burden, introduced payment for public services, trying at the same time not to affect the extension and liberality of welfare services. Finally, it reduced the percentage of national debt to gross national income from 70 to 45 percent in only eight years

(1982–90). This is much lower than the average of all OECD countries (60 percent in 1990) (Green 1995:26–27; Pontusson 1997:58–59). From 1991 to 1994, there was again a conservative government in Sweden, which accumulated an enormous balance deficit in 1993 (among the OECD countries it was the second highest after Greece as a proportion of gross national income). In contrast, successive social democratic governments managed first to reduce this deficit and then, in 1998, to achieve a surplus.[15]

Scandinavian social democracies, particularly in Sweden, never had such economic difficulties that might force them to substantially reform their welfare organizations, though in Sweden—as previously noted—there were some restrictions in welfare services with respect to unemployment, sickness, accidents, disability, and pensions. Moreover, the huge capital flow from Sweden to other European countries during the 1980s could be partly attributed to the fact that Sweden did not yet belong to the European Union, that is, to reasons that did not depend on the social democratic regime. The undeniable decrease in productivity that occurred in Sweden during the 1970s and 1980s (Pontusson 1997:67, 70, note 3; Ramaswamy 1995:18–19; United Nations, Department for Economic and Social Information and Policy Analysis 1997:134) should be to some extent considered within its overall context. There has been a smaller growth of productivity in all developed countries since the early 1970s. Accordingly, the decrease in productivity in Sweden could hardly be attributed fully to the economic and industrial policy implemented by the social democratic and conservative governments, which alternated in those years.

The Swedish economy lost competitiveness in the 1980s. This drop could be hardly attributed to the social policies implemented by the social democratic governments, in power during most of that decade, for following reasons:

1. From 1980 to 1989, the contribution of exports to the Swedish national income grew significantly (from one-fifth to one-third) (Pontusson 1997:70, note 2), though by then the economy was in an expansion stage. Accordingly, the relatively lower growth of productivity in comparison with the average rate of the European Union countries did not risk jeopardizing Sweden's international competitiveness. As in 1992 the conservative government had been forced to devaluate the crown (the national currency), the economic competitiveness of the country, and consequently its exports, grew. The contribution of the international economic sector to national income remained high, despite some fluctuations, throughout the 1990s (Economist Intelligence Unit 1998–99:14 19, 1998c:17–18).

2. The relative decline (in terms of a smaller rate of growth) of Swedish productivity during the 1980s cannot be accounted for by specifically social democratic labor policies. According to the experts of the IMF, a competitive disadvantage would have derived to Sweden because of the limited flexibility (numerical, functional, and temporal)[16] of its domestic

labor market. As they have maintained, its allocation inefficiency would in fact have resulted from the stiff regulation that trade unions and government applied to wages (through centralized collective bargaining), and qualifications of the labor force (through professional retraining courses that do not take into account the specific requirements of companies). To some extent, allocation inefficiency would also ensue from the regulation of the recruiting system (through subsidies granted to companies engaging personnel) (Ramaswamy 1995:15–20).[17]

The stiff regulation of the labor market has, however, characterized, rather than Sweden in particular, in general all the countries that have approached the so-called neocorporative model of labor market regulation. Therefore, there is no reason to believe that there is necessarily a relation between northern social democracies, with their income redistribution policies and their universalistic welfare systems, and the fact that Scandinavian labor market regulation approximates to this neocorporative model.

In fact, the social democratic government as well as the conservative government during the short period in which it was in power in Sweden (1976–82) before the 1990s committed itself to keeping the neocorporative model. During the six years of conservative government the lesser relevance of this model followed from the "unheard-of resistances to the establishment of the yearly wage settlement" from a part of the labor force. It did not ensue, on the other hand, from governmental decisions to this effect (Carrieri, Donolo 1983:478; cf. also Martini 1981:302). That resistance, though perhaps "unheard of" with regard to its intensity, was not, however, new for Sweden (Martin 1981:318–24) and occurred again later on, when the social democrats returned to power (Hernes 1991:246–50). On the other hand, Austria, with its coverage policy of needs and interests, is considered nearer to a model that emphasizes "occupationally segregated social-insurance programs" (Esping-Andersen 1990:32) than to the pure universalistic model that characterizes Sweden. Austria, then, turns out to be more neocorporative than Sweden if we assume organizational centralization and associative monopoly of the representation bodies as indicators of neocorporatism (Schmitter 1983:428–30).[18]

Accordingly, the causes of the economic crisis in Sweden during the early 1990s and of the lower growth rate of productivity in the previous decade have nothing to do with the Swedish welfare system. Even currently, perverse effects on the economy cannot be attributed to this welfare system. The present overall economic condition of Sweden and Denmark, which are both still ruled by social democratic governments, is considered satisfactory with reference to the well-known "parameters of Maastricht." In particular, with regard to Sweden, the economic difficulties of the early 1990s seem to have been overcome:

1. The national income calculated at constant prices, after having

dropped during the first three years of the previous decade, later increased every year between 1.3 and almost 4 percent.

2. The ratio between the budget deficit and the gross national income, which in fiscal 1992–93 was over 13 percent, decreased to 1.3 percent in 1997. In 1998, there was a credit in the public budget despite a growth in public expenditures, and most likely this credit trend will continue.

3. Inflation—which in 1993 totaled 4.5 percent—was in 1997, with a rate of 0.5 percent, among the lowest in Europe and all over the world, and has remained so also in the following years.[19]

4. The 65.5 percent ratio between national debt and gross national income in 1999 was higher than the established limit of 60 percent. Still this ratio was in any case much lower than the almost 90 percent rate reached in 1995, and also lower than the arithmetic average of this rate among the European Union countries (67.6 percent in 1999). The ratio foreseen for 2001 (55.4 percent) would place Sweden in a relatively privileged position among these countries (*Corriere della Sera,* 22 April 2000, p. 23).

5. The present social democratic government, in power since 1994 after a short period (1991–94) of conservative power, has continued for some years the policy of cuts in public expenditures, especially social expenditures, that the previous government had carried out. The welfare system has not been substantially changed and remains—like the other northern European systems—particularly liberal with regard to services provided. The growth of national income after 1993 has allowed a reduction in the share that has been absorbed by the expenditure for social protection (from 38.5 to 34.8 percent during the period 1993–96). However, it has also allowed a considerable increase in the per capita expenditure, which in 1996 exceeded (in terms of the European currency) the corresponding expenditure per head of all the other countries of the European Union, except Denmark and Luxembourg. By the same token, the share of national income spent for education decreased from 7.7 percent in 1993 to 6.6 percent in 1995. Yet, Sweden spent in the same years a much higher average amount per student (expressed in U.S. dollars, the purchasing power being the same) than any other OECD country, except the United States and Switzerland. Moreover, since 1997–98, the growth of the national balance has permitted the cancellation of some cuts in welfare expenditure that had been made in the immediately preceding years. In particular, the replacement rate of unemployment subsidies was brought back in 1997 to 80 percent of one's most recent wages, for a maximum period of 800 days. In this way, authorities succeeded in going back to the replacement rate established in 1993, after the rate had been reduced in 1996 to 75 percent. Furthermore, the 1998 balance allocated a higher amount of public expenditure for social and health services and assigned greater financial resources to local institutions, thus marking a reversal of trend in comparison with the previous balances.

6. After the entry of Sweden into the European Union in 1995, EU au-

thorities did not object to its forthcoming participation in the European monetary system. However, a referendum held in Sweden in September 2003 decided against it. Moreover, in the second part of the previous decade the Swedish economy showed a growing productivity and greater international competitiveness, evidenced by an increasing surplus in the trade balance, as well as an overall growth in the volume of the exports.[20]

Regarding the production of public services we should consider the two alleged perverse effects separately. The first one alleges, in terms of the relation between costs and benefits, a lack of efficiency of public services provided under a regime of monopoly (as is the case of Swedish services). The second perverse effect concerns the social class that is more advantaged by these services. Since these services are provided free, or at almost no cost to users, they would have a uniform and poor quality from which the privileged classes, presumably because of their higher cultural capital, would particularly benefit. The efficiency of the Swedish public services (evaluated in terms of the cost/benefit ratio for the most disadvantaged socioeconomic segment), seems very high, and higher than the efficiency of the U.S. public services, in contrast to the previously mentioned theses.

We wish to dwell here particularly upon education and health services, which everywhere absorb a large share of public expenditures and national income (United Nations, Department for Economic and Social Information and Policy Analysis 1997:27, 49). Both countries spend considerably for education and health services. The expenditure for education in 1994 amounted to 5.5 percent of the gross national income in the United States, more or less the rate of other advanced countries such as France, Germany, Great Britain, and Italy. In Sweden, this expenditure rate was 8.4 percent, one of the highest rates all over the world (UNESCO, Reference Tables 1–5, column 15 and 1–9, column 15). As for health services, as previously noted, in 1989 the public health service absorbed in the United States 12 percent of the gross national income, against 7.5 percent in Sweden in 1995). Nevertheless, the percentage of adults provided only with basic educational competence was in 1995 almost three times higher in the United States (20.7 percent) than in Sweden (7.5 percent). These were, respectively, the highest and the lowest rates within a group of countries with an established rate of economical development (United Nations, Department for Economic and Social Information and Policy Analysis 1997:57). Similarly, according to recent official sources, in the United States child mortality is 33 percent higher, the probability of death within the first four years of life 50 percent higher, and life expectancy 3 percent lower than in Sweden. Child mortality is much more prevalent in the more disadvantaged socioeconomic segments. This occurs to a very small extent in Sweden, but to a much greater extent in the United States.[21]

The decision to prefer either state or market for the provision of these public services has then involved different efficiency degrees. This seems to contrast with the liberalist thesis according to which more market and less state would promote greater efficiency. These terms seem, however, quite inaccurate, since in Sweden it is possible to turn to the market in order to procure these very same services, while in the United States these services are also provided by public organizations. Furthermore, in both countries great importance is given to voluntary associations, which, however, receive public financing for the provision of some services, in particular the physical and social rehabilitation of drug addicts. From the point of view of the least favored socioeconomic strata, the Swedish welfare system, which entrusts to the government and local institutions the provision of public services, has proven more advantageous than the U.S. system. On the other hand, any public welfare system must be able to satisfy the requirements of more privileged strata, for they always have the opportunity to turn to the market. To this end, it should be prepared to meet their growing requirements for service quality and variety. This holds true, in particular, for the Swedish welfare system, which is still mostly public, in contrast to the U.S. system (cf. Esping-Andersen 1990:3.1, column 5; Gynnerstedt 1997:203–4; Rose 1993:88–91).[22]

This would be, however, possible only on condition that governments are prepared to bear the high costs of market competition. The current constrained balance conditions do not allow governments to completely bear this financial effort. The so-called welfare mix indicates a mutual adaptation of several alternative welfare principles, such as state, market, and third sector. The actual tendency toward a welfare mix in Sweden, as well as in other European countries, has involved a "limited acknowledgement of third sector organizations," and hence—as regards Sweden—a partial removal from its "heritage of state control."[23] The coverage of social needs through business firms still has a limited importance in Sweden in this area regarding their use and expenditure share. Rather, "social markets with suppliers competing among themselves" have been added to public services, have been coordinated with them, and placed under their financial and operating control (Evers 1997:16; cf. also Klausen and Selle 1997:170–73).

In the integration process between the state sector, or rather between services provided by public institutions, and the so-called private social sector, Sweden has been committed for some ten or fifteen years to finding a solution to a number of problems related to the Scandinavian welfare systems. Among such problems are safeguarding the quality of some public services and their availability to the more disadvantaged socioeconomic segment, decreasing the difference in decisional power between those who provide and those who receive these services, and complying at the same time with the stiff constraints of public expenditure.[24] The beneficiaries of these services always have in any case the right to the option of turning to companies operating on the market for a profit. In Sweden, as elsewhere, social needs, and particularly public services, are covered through a welfare mix (Gynnerstedt 1997:204). Within this welfare mix, in Sweden the market functions only residually, whereas the third sector, which has a long tradition throughout Scandinavia, "has always operated side by side with the Government and has always filled its gaps" (Klausen and Selle 1997:173).[25] The difficulty, since the 1980s, in limiting public-service costs by keeping their quality and by making them available to anybody seems in the process of being overcome through this hybrid solution, which, however, conforms to the Scandinavian welfare pattern (ibid.).

The perverse effect noted by a literature hostile to social democracy, according to which benefits provided would not be compatible with pertinent costs, has not revealed itself so far, despite cuts made in public expenditure. Further, given its progressive readjustment, there are no signs that this undesired effect might reveal itself in the near future. As for the provision of public services, the peculiar welfare mix implemented in Sweden, which we previously examined, has oriented the public production of services (or the portion under public control) toward some specific goals. The goals that have been pursued and achieved are "balancing income inequality by turning to the most needy persons," of "promoting equality through an offer of assistance without any economic compensation" (Rose 1993:92–93). The market has been accordingly kept in a subordinate position. This has been the consequence of a number of factors. Governmental control has been maintained over the provision of services considered of a collective interest. Private companies operating for a profit on the market have had relatively little relevance. And finally, use has been continuously made, in the provision of public services, of nonremunerated or only partially remunerated personnel belonging to nonprofit volunteer or cooperative associations, which in this way assume the status of semipublic institutions (Klausen and Selle 1997:166–70).

As mentioned, the second alleged perverse effect would consist in granting an undesired benefit to the upper class and in general to privileged classes, including those of employees and professionals who are already privileged in terms of division of labor and cultural capital (Esping-Andersen 1993a:18–26). This effect would be the result of a gratuitous or semigratuitous provision of public services, such as, in particular, education. In countries with a social democratic tradition, such as Sweden, education is borne by the public budget and therefore at zero direct cost for users. Those classes would particularly benefit, for nonexplicit reasons but likely because of their greater cultural capital, from the consequent uniformity and mediocrity of teaching. The achieved result of favoring already advantaged classes would contrast with the expected goal and result of providing a good education, in terms of quality and amount, also to nonprivileged classes. These statements are, however, in contrast with what empirical comparative research has found about mobility opportunities for those who do not have means of production, and educational opportunities for those who have a nonprivileged family background.

In comparison with other advanced countries, among which the United States, Sweden is together with Holland the only one in which "the effects of the paternal job and education on the starting and intermediate transitions [of the school career] decrease as time goes by." This has been attributed to "a comprehensive policy aimed at equality in life conditions" (Blossfeld and Shavit 1992:173). Furthermore, in Scandinavian countries such as Sweden and Norway the barrier to vertical mobility constituted by property is less relevant than elsewhere. Its importance is similar to the barrier constituted by educational qualification or by other qualifications appreciated by the labor market (expertise), whereas in the United States property is a much more significant obstacle to mobility. The lesser weight of this obstacle to mobility has been attributed to the ability of the Scandinavian social democracies to lower social inequality by origin (Western and Wright 1994:particularly pp. 620–21, 623, 626). Moreover, the educational opportunities for those without benefits of family background are greater in Sweden than in any other developed country, and the educational opportunities of those subjects reveal—unlike anywhere else—a convergence with the corresponding opportunities of those who have a more privileged origin. The smaller disadvantage in Sweden for persons with low social origins in achieving high educational qualifications has been attributed to the life opportunities promoted by the social democratic regime. Of particular relevance is the relatively high certainty of jobs—and consequently of income—produced by the Swedish social and labor policies (Erikson and Goldthorpe 1993:164–65, 177–78; Goldthorpe 1996:498–99).

So, in comparison with the United States, the lack of property and disadvantaged social origins seem less likely to prevent people in Sweden from rising to a higher class and from achieving a higher level of education. This tendency may be attributed to the social policies implemented by social democracy. Far from producing the perverse effects of benefiting already advantaged socioeconomic classes, these policies have then attained their goals of redistributing income and improving opportunities for educational and social mobility. Hence, the peculiar Swedish—and Scandinavian—welfare mix displays neither the perverse effects of granting benefits that are incompatible with related costs, nor of favoring already privileged classes. The literature hostile to social democracy also pointed to a second alleged perverse effect, namely, that economic and social policies inspiring to social democracy would produce a lowering of investments, productivity, propensity to work, and therefore a decrease in international competitiveness and national wealth. It has been here argued, however, that this state of affairs cannot be attributed to the social democratic governments of the 1970s and 1980s.

The considerable economic and financial results achieved by the current social democratic majority through a progressive rebalancing of budget deficit and national debt, the growth of national income, and the remarkable growth of productivity show that this success is compatible with social democracy and economic efficiency. The ability to avoid perverse effects, which is an indicator of the external effectiveness of social policies, thus characterizes the Swedish universalistic policies rather than the "residual" policies of the United States. This holds true in general, as well as in particular, insofar as it concerns the repression of drug traffic and use, the rehabilitation of drug addicts, and the prevention of the use and abuse of those substances.

NOTES

1. Cf. Anderson (1993:78–81), Bridges and Steen (1998), Donziger (1996:47, 125–26), Hagan (1992:9–11, 1994:147–58, 166–67), Hester and Eglin (1992:251–57), Kornblum and Julian (1995:279–80), Sampson (1987:378), and Testa et al. (1993).

2. Cf. Donziger (1996:175–76, 178–79), Miethe and Meier (1994:121–40), Sampson and Groves (1989), and Uchida and Forst (1994:84).

3. Cf. Chavis et al. (1993:259), Davis and Lurigio (1996:124–25), Davis, Lurigio, and Rosenbaum (1993b:xii–xiii, xv), and Smith and Davis (1993:124–25, 135–37).

4. In this regard, see Allan and Steffensmeier (1989), Chamlin and Cochran (1995), Fagan (1996:51–68), Ginsburg (1992:102–3), Lichter (1988), Rose and Clear (1998), Sampson (1987), Sampson and Groves (1989), Steffensmeier, Ulmer, and Kramer (1998), Thornberry and Christenson (1984), and Wilson (1997:392).

5. In this regard, cf. Bobo and Zubrinsky (1996), DeSena (1994), Gotham (1998:17–21), Jargowsky (1996), Nelson and Milgroom 1995:33–35, and South and Crowder (1998).

6. In this regard, cf. Busana Banterle (1993:255–62), Iglehart (1999b:329), Kuttner (1999b, 1999c:666), Quadagno (1999:7–8), and Social Security Administration (1996:13–14).

7. The Marxist literature emphasizes, by way of contrast, the insufficiency and discriminating character of the benefits provided by the Swedish social policies, insofar as not only women, but also disadvantaged classes and ethnic groups are concerned (Ginsburg 1992:Chapter 2).

8. This objection according to which universalistic welfare services become particularly profitable to already advantaged socioeconomic segments becomes paradoxical if stated by authors with a free-market orientation. A welfare system complying with this orientation would even further increase inequality in accessing social services. Therefore, it is not surprising that some members and representatives of the Swedish working class have made this objection (Ginsburg 1992:65). Moreover, here we leave out of consideration objections concerning the competence of public service users in making their choice when public services are provided by companies operating in competitive market conditions (Barbetta 1993:69–70; Coppini 1994:211; DiMaggio and Anheier 1993:38). That users are competent has been implied or suggested by the *public choice* approach, to which the above-mentioned critics of Swedish social democracy seem to adhere. Finally, we shall not dwell upon the thesis according to which the Swedish welfare state finds political support, and therefore the possibility of self-perpetuation, from that "over

40 percent share of the electorate" that "directly or indirectly depends on public sector subsidies" (Stein and Doerfer 1992:59). It seems that the authors are not familiar with the empirical research on the sources of electoral support of Swedish social democracy. This research highlights an inverse relation between, on one hand, income and other dimensions of class and, on the other hand, support for welfare measures. Further variables, particularly a distinction between public and private sector employees, are unimportant. Cf. Svallfors (1991:623–27).

9. Available data show that in Sweden the average number of work hours per head remained almost constant, with few fluctuations, from 1973 until 1996. From 1973 to 1993, when the governments in power would have ignored "the negative consequences of redistribution policies in the long term" (Stein and Doerfer 1992:55–57), the average number of working hours decreased by about 3 percent only (OECD 1997:179).

10. Cf. Ginsburg (1992:34, 143–44), Graham (1997:119), OECD (1997:179), National Board of Health and Welfare (1996:177), and Pontusson (1997:60). Other sources report a lower participation rate in the Swedish labor market. This would still be high (about 81 percent of the male labor force), however, and without significant variations until 1990. The economic difficulties of 1991–93 led to a decrease in employment and partly, due to a discouragement effect, in the participation share of the active population as well. However, the latter only slightly decreased between 1991 and 1995 (by about 5 percent), stabilizing at about 78 percent of the overall population. This rate is higher than the rate achieved by most European Union countries (Hvinden et al. 2001:179, Table 8.1; National Board of Health and Welfare 1996:12, 177; OECD Statistics Directorate 1997:76–77; United Nations, Department for Economic and Social Information and Policy Analysis 1997:141). Only women contributed to the growth or maintenance of the participation share during the 1970s and 1980s, while the male participation share dropped—as in almost all developed countries—during those years, though only slightly (by about 2 percent of the active male population). In Sweden, women have increasingly found job opportunities in public welfare services, usually in nonskilled and less well paying jobs. A great deal of the creation of new jobs in Sweden during the 1980s can be attributed to public welfare services (Esping-Andersen et al. 1993:43–47; Ginsburg 1992:87, 203; Kjelstad 2001:91–93; Sorensen 2001:106–10; Tahlin 1993:83–84, United Nations, Department for Economic and Social Information and Policy Analysis 1997:140–41).

11. Cf. Bradshaw (1998:116), Gornick and Jacobs (1998:707), Harris (1996:424), Jaentti and Danziger (1994:52–53), Jencks (1992:98), *La Stampa,* 6 May 2002, p. 23), Marklund and Nordlund (1999:35), and Sanders (1990:824).

12. We leave aside in this case general criticism of the theory of wage efficiency, to which those who attribute to egalitarian wage redistribution the effect of diminishing work propensity seem to adhere, at least implicitly. According to this criticism, propensity to work is widely determined by extrawage considerations of equity in the relationships with employers and other workers. For theories of wage efficiency, cf. Akerlof (1982:particularly pp. 545–58, 563–68) and Solow (1994:42–44, 76–78). For Italy in particular, cf. Reyneri (1996:26–28).

13. Estimates of the proportion of the overall employed labor force with part-time jobs vary considerably, according to the particular source. However, they agree in indicating a higher proportion in Sweden than in the United States. This

variation is due to the stronger participation of women in the Swedish labor market, and to women's widespread preference for part-time jobs (Jaentti and Danziger 1994:53, Table 2; OECD 1997:178; United Nations, Department for Economic and Social Information and Policy Analysis 1997:142).

14. Cf. Economist Intelligence Unit (1996–97:12, 17–18, 1998–99:13–15, 1994b:10, 12–13, 18, 1996:3), and Pontusson (1997:67, 70, note 3).

15. Cf. Economist Intelligence Unit (1998–99:14, 1998b:12–13, 1998c:13–14).

16. Concerning the different meanings of the word "flexibility" applied to the labor market, cf. Regini (1996:185).

17. The importance of flexibility in the labor market for creating and keeping employment was recently underlined again by a survey of the IMF. Temporal (meant as a massive resort to part-time jobs) and numerical (meant as facility to hire and fire workers) flexibility would account for the considerable ability of, respectively, Holland and United States, during the years 1980–97, to create more employment opportunities than those that had been lost through reorganization processes. The opposite case, which mainly characterizes Sweden and Finland, would be a consequence of the rigidity with which those labor markets depend on an excessive amount of legal and trade union regulations (*La Stampa*, 2 November 1999, p. 3). We can, however, raise some objections against these theories: (1) Denmark and Norway, Scandinavian countries, are characterized by economic and social policies similar to those implemented in Sweden and Finland. The IMF points out in the same context that in Denmark and Norway more jobs have been created than those that have been destroyed. This trend calls into question the thesis of a "structural" tendency in northern countries toward job destruction because of an extreme rigidity in the labor market. (2) In contrast with the same thesis, we may remark that, still according to the IMF, the loss of job opportunities was concentrated in Sweden during the 1990s. That occurred when the economic-political authorities began to orient themselves—though very cautiously—toward greater flexibility, aiming at diminishing the amount and duration of unemployment subsidies, and making the conditions on benefits more restrictive (Plough 1999:100–1). (3) In Sweden, the tendency toward a debit balance between the creation and destruction of jobs apparently came to a halt during the second half of the 1990s. This is indicated by the growth of the share of the active population, and the decrease in the unemployment rate, after the crisis of the years 1990–94 (Marklund and Nordlund 1999:34–36, cf. also Note 24). The emphasis placed on an active labor market policy counteract recession, and unemployment in particular, seems then to have achieved some results (Dropping et al. 1999:143–44, 157–58). Nevertheless, these policies are in debt for their inspiration and continuation precisely to those trade union forces that the IMF considers jointly responsible for the loss of jobs (Gynnerstedt 1997:192). (4) Job opportunities created in a country with a great numerical flexibility such as the United States are not equivalent to those created in continental Europe, particularly in Scandinavia. They are, on the contrary, worse on the average in terms of wages, stability, and skills (Esping-Andersen 1997:35–36; Gallino 1999). An in-depth discussion on the relation between flexibility and employment can be found in Esping-Andersen (1999:150–60).

18. Also with regard to Austria, as in general, any social policy model may be only approximated by real social policies. Concerning "Austrian neocorporatism" and the limits of Austria's application of the "neocorporative" model in labor market regulations, cf. Pappalardo (1993:232–43).

19. With a 0.2 percent rate in July 1999, Sweden—along with Luxembourg—had the lowest rate of inflation among the fifteen countries of the European Union, confirming in this way a trend that had already been noticed in 1997 (Economist Intelligence Unit 1998–99:12, 18; *La Stampa*, 24 August 1999, p. 3).

20. For all this information, cf. Censis (1998:171, Table 56, 1999:164, Table 65, 328, Table 44), Economist Intelligence Unit (1994b:19, 12, 1996:10, 1997a:7–9, 24, 1998a:5, 1998b:12–13, 1998c:5, 13–21), ISFOL (1999:134), *La Stampa*, 2 February 1998, p. 14), Marklund and Nordlund (1999:47–51), Mullard (1997:69), OECD (1999:119–21), Pierson (1996:35), Plough (1999:100–3), and Pontusson (1997:38).

21. Cf. WHO (1996:A-5, A-7, A-12, A-13); also Ginsburg (1992:63) and Kornblum and Julian (1995:29, 32–33).

22. Providing services of sufficiently good quality to the most privileged and demanding categories among the service recipients without cutting off the support granted to the most disadvantaged categories is a problem that may prove difficult to overcome. This problem, in particular, affects the large Swedish trade unions, as they strive to represent all of their heterogeneous members (Hernes 1991:246–50).

23. The "state-oriented" tradition of the Scandinavian welfare system has not prevented the establishment and consolidation of a cooperative relationship between public organizations and volunteer associations. It has consequently limited the tendency "to develop a bureaucratic structure and a decisional apparatus ruled by professionals" (Pasquinelli 1999:101). Therefore, this tradition has not brought about welfare system bureaucratization.

24. These arguments were in part discussed in the recent successful book by R. Dahrendorf, *Quadrare il cerchio* (English ed., 1996) (1995:particularly pp. 66–67).

25. For example, nonprofit organizations have massively operated in an area—public housing—in which public authorities have not succeeded in fully meeting people's requirements, providing only "40 percent out of all the houses built or restored in Sweden" (Anheier and Salomon 1997:299).

6 The Social Policies on Drugs Implemented in Italy

PRELIMINARY CONSIDERATIONS

This chapter provides a description and an evaluation of Italian policies on drugs, bearing in mind similar policies implemented in Sweden and in the United States. This description will highlight the ambivalence between a repressive and a rehabilitating approach, and will discuss what has been done with regard to secondary and primary prevention. The latter point will involve a short presentation of Italian public policies aimed at limiting relative deprivation, with particular reference to poverty, unemployment, housing inadequacies, and the health conditions of the most economically disadvantaged population. Conforming to the same criteria we previously used in evaluating the effectiveness and efficiency of public policies, we shall provide some indications of the ability of the Italian welfare state to implement effective rehabilitation and prevention activities, as well as of the prevalence of drugs in Italy. We shall compare, as usual, the costs of social policies to those borne in Sweden and in the United States. We shall also discuss the costs of assistance, social insurance, and social security activities, when the actual expenditure borne to rehabilitate drug addicts and prevent drug use is not known and cannot be easily appraised. The consistency between goals and expected results involves an evaluation of the effectiveness of rehabilitation policies (which in any case we shall attempt though it is particularly uncertain in Italy). It also involves an evaluation of the effectiveness of policies related to primary and secondary prevention. While primary prevention particularly regards labor policies, secondary prevention is addressed to a youth public of potential users. Finally, as for the perverse effects of these social policies (in terms of discrepancy among goals, expected results, and results achieved) we shall mention labor policies and policies explicitly aimed at limiting drug use and abuse.

THE SOCIAL POLICIES ENACTED IN ITALY,
WITH PARTICULAR REFERENCE TO
THOSE CONCERNING DRUGS

Drug selling—including so-called soft drugs—is considered a crime in Italy. However, the ambivalence between a repressive approach on the one hand, and a rehabilitative and preventive approach on the other hand, has involved serious uncertainties in the legislative trend on this matter, and in the implementation of the regulations in force. The abrogation referendum of 18 April 1993 decriminalized drug purchase and possession for personal use (but not drug selling), which are nonetheless considered administrative offenses, and gave authority to organizations other than the public services also to supply methadone.

In spring 1999, the government evaluated the possibility of decriminalizing shared use and domestic growing of hashish and marijuana for personal use, which, however, still remain serious criminal offenses. In fact, law 162/1990, subsumed under the Consolidated Act of laws concerning the control of drugs and psychotropic substances, the prevention of drug addiction, and the care and rehabilitation of drug addicts, which was approved by presidential decree 309 of 9 October 1990, is still in force. This law involves several provisions, such as:

1. Establishment and management of the National Fund for Interventions Aimed at Fighting Drugs within the Presidency of the Council of Ministers, Department for Social Affairs, integrated by further law decrees that have been renewed several times. This fund provides financial support to projects drafted by the administrations of the state, the regions, local authorities, local health organizations (Aziende Sanitarie Locali, ASL), and private nonprofit organizations, in order

- to rationalize the survey and evaluation systems of the different interventions, linking government measures with other community measures, and to carry out primary prevention activities, particularly in schools (state administration);
- to carry out secondary prevention activities, namely addressed to some borderline categories, such as marginal young people, and activities for the rehabilitation of drug addicts (local authorities and local health organizations);
- to pursue the recovery and the social and professional reinsertion of drug addicts (private nonprofit organizations, particularly therapeutic communities, which receive public acknowledgment as auxiliary bodies of the public administration and have to be put on the regional registers);
- to provide personnel training for social-health assistance to drug ad-

dicts and for checking and evaluating interventions (state and regional administrations).

2. The establishment, always within the Presidency of the Council of Ministers, of a National Committee for the Coordination of Antidrug Actions. This committee is entrusted with the overall management and the intervention policy on this matter. Further, the establishment of a commission for the preliminary examination of intervention projects, and of an operating team for the evaluation of the procedures used in developing these projects.

3. Finally, the creation at the Ministry of the Interior of a permanent board on the phenomenon of drugs, which is charged with monitoring the spread of drugs and all actions implemented to fight it (Corte dei Conti 1996:16–17; Negri and Saraceno 1996:265–66).

Law decree 130/1996, article 4, prescribes the transfer to the regions of a 75 percent share of the National Fund for Interventions Aimed at Fighting Drugs. It also charges the regions with the task of preparing criteria and procedures for the allocation of the financial funds, as well as of checking the effectiveness of these interventions (cf. *Forum*, 1996, 12:6, 11). Moreover, in March 1997, the Chamber of Deputies approved an amnesty for the effects of the adopted law decrees on the prevention of drug addiction and drug addict rehabilitation and the operations of the Drug Addict Recovery Services (Servizi Recupero Tossicodipendenze, SERT) (*Forum*, 1997, 4:8–11). SERTs have the task of providing drug addicts and their families with psychological, pharmaceutical, and social rehabilitation treatments (Arzuffi 1991:303).

In addition, further motions were approved authorizing the government:

1. To intensify in schools and in other places where young people meet the so-called education to health (educazione alla salute) primary and secondary prevention activities (addressed in general to young people who might run the risk of using heavy drugs). It is, in the words of the former minister for social solidarity, an "information and sensitization activity addressed to young people, mainly activated through school and media" (Turco 1998:8–9, 13). In some cases these activities led schools or groups of teachers to draft projects on drug prevention, which received public financing (Negri and Saraceno 1996:213–14).
2. To provide, within primary and secondary prevention programs, through a free telephone service called Drogatel, "psychological support and . . . behavioral advice also addressed to non-drug addict young people and to their families" (Turco 1998:9).
3. To take care of the professional training of those who work in nonprofit organizations that carry out prevention and rehabilitation activities.

4. To coordinate intervention methods and aims between public—either national or local—and private nonprofit organizations.
5. To improve interventions aimed at socially rehabilitating imprisoned drug addicts (ibid.:8–11).

Furthermore, several activities concerning primary and secondary prevention and social rehabilitation have been started by many municipalities, mainly in the center-north of the country, often within the framework of projects addressed to young people. These projects have tried to establish a connection between local authorities (municipalities, provinces, regions) and other public organizations, such as education offices and local health organizations, as well as youth associations and groups. Besides an attempt at making a joint organizational effort, these local "projects for the young" are characterized by an integrated social policy, in the sense that they aim at providing services able to cover different needs of youth, such as education, entry in the labor market, and structure of leisure time. These programs, as well as others with similar purposes, do not specifically aim at preventing drug use and abuse, but in general at preventing and overcoming in local contexts a youth condition qualified as "uneasiness."[1] Youth policies have been and still are implemented by the local authorities, while in this context some experts claim that the "state is in hiding" (Neresini and Ranci 1994:94–97, 101–5). The term "in hiding" in this case means the inability of the state administrations to directly draft and manage prevention projects. The Italian government, however, is indirectly involved in this sense, since it provides to local authorities and to private nonprofit organizations and associations the necessary legal and financial tools for prevention activities.

In this connection, particularly relevant are law 266/1991 (outline law on voluntary service), law 381/1991 (law on social cooperatives), and more recently, law decree 460/1997 on nonprofit social utility organizations (ONLUS). Law 266/1991 states the criteria for determining a voluntary activity (it should be gratuitous, free, spontaneous, and aiming at the provision of aid), and establishes regional registers of the volunteer organizations having the required characteristics. Law 381/1991 specifies the social aims of cooperatives (depending on the type of cooperative, these aims may be of public interest or of working aid to their members) and the roles of their operators (ordinary members, voluntary members, and employees). In the case of "integrated" cooperatives, operators should at least include a 30 percent share of disadvantaged persons (from a family, psychiatric, social, economic point of view). Moreover, law 381/1991 provides for the creation of regional registers of social cooperatives interested in establishing agreements with public authorities. Finally, law decree 460/1997 states the necessary requirements, premises, and specific activities of the organizations that pursue social solidarity purposes, by granting them fiscal franchises and the possibility to access public financing.[2]

These laws, like those that provide for and rule the recourse of public organizations to private associations providing services of public interest,[3] have involved some consequences, probably depending on the institutional acknowledgment of the organizations of the so-called third sector. Some of these consequences are noteworthy: (a) development of their organizational structure; (b) greater professional expertise within this structure; (c) more frequent resort to external professional collaboration.

By way of contrast, voluntary activities not included in the regional registers have been marginalized, for they receive neither subsidies nor any other kind of public acknowledgment (Rei 1997:136, 143–45).

As previously mentioned, therapeutic communities for drug addicts have also been institutionally acknowledged through the Consolidated Act of the laws on drugs. The National Fund for Interventions Aimed at Fighting Drugs, regulated by article 127 of the Consolidated Act, provides for an allocation of funds to projects drafted by nonprofit organizations aiming at the rehabilitation and at the social and professional reinsertion of drug addicts. The cooperation between public authorities (regions and drug addict recovery services) and the so-called social private area, however, has not involved a univocal definition of their relationships, nor of the therapy and prevention methods (Prina 1999:156).

Within secondary prevention programs having a general nature (that is, those not specifically aimed at preventing drug addiction), the new Department for Social Affairs collaborates with municipalities, private associations, and volunteer teams in order to implement law 216/1991. This law allocates governmental funds for drafting and implementing local programs for the prevention of juvenile delinquency. These projects are mostly aimed at introducing or reintroducing "borderline" young people into formal relationships (school and work) and informal networks (noncriminal peer groups). Nonetheless, the sometimes-present goal of checking general conditions favoring deviance, such as the untimely abandonment of school and a condition of marginality or exclusion relative to the labor market, has a primary prevention character (Rei 1997:109, 111; Segre 1998:308–12).

The same primary and secondary prevention purpose characterizes the program for "juvenile socialization and creativity," drafted by the Department for Social Affairs in agreement with the minister of labor. This program is cofinanced by the European Social Fund and its implementation is entrusted to local authorities. The major aim of this program is the introduction of marginal young people into the labor market, particularly those who live "in areas where uneasiness is more widespread" (*Forum*, 1998, 11:11–12). Similar programs, which foresee the collaboration of municipalities with some specific governmental bodies, have been added to the prevention programs planned and managed by municipalities (*Forum*, 1997, 6/7:27–31).

In Italy, like elsewhere, primary prevention of drug use and abuse and of all deviant behaviors in general implies—as we shall later see when checking the consistency between goals and expected results—a limitation of relative and absolute deprivation. While the latter can be faced within the framework of assistance activities through income support measures, relative deprivation can be reduced through suitable social security policies involving labor and housing market, school, and health services. These policies can be specifically addressed to Italian subjects or those from other countries of the European Union who have paid compulsory social insurance contributions for social protection services, such as retirement pensions and indemnities for temporary disease, accidents, unemployment and (until recent times) maternity. Presently, maternity gives one the right to receive an indemnity, which is granted as a citizenship right. So also are the services institutionally provided within the school and, partly, within the health services. All citizens are entitled to receive this kind of service.

In Italy, like elsewhere, many primary prevention policies provide for an intervention of nonprofit organizations. The contribution of the third sector or social private area to the Italian welfare mix varies according to the kind of services provided. It is in any case very relevant, and usually it even replaces public interventions in the field of assistance and special social services (such as rehabilitation of drug addicts or assistance and protection of the disabled). Therefore, public organizations (often the regions) allocate funds—generally through agreements—as an acknowledgment of the social utility of those activities (Ranci 1992:495–99). This acknowledgment is only implicit, since in fact a public body does not usually consult private organizations when it drafts intervention programs. There are, furthermore, some private nonprofit organizations operating in the field of education and health services that also receive public funds and acknowledgment. But in this case the public authority keeps a strong control on expenditure procedures and service management, since they are granted in principle to all citizens (Barbetta and Ranci 1997:197–203).

Currently, there are in Italy *income support or assistance measures* in a variety of forms and for a plurality of recipients. Assistance measures that could guarantee a minimum income—the so-called vital minimum—were discussed for a long time during the 1980s and 1990s. As a consequence of this debate, in 1995 the Inquiry Commission on Poverty and Social Marginalization made an authoritative "proposal on the vital minimum," as it was called, which was later implemented. Until 1997, these proposals had the characteristic of not helping the major part of the needy population (citizens and residents) but only those in specific categories.

The financial law of 1997 established an annual fund of 1,500 billion lire (roughly $750 million) destined—in the words of the minister for social solidarity—"to the poor and the needy" (*La Stampa*, 19 July 1999, p. 6). The financial law of 1998 introduced on an experimental basis a minimum guaranteed income, 90 percent to be borne by the national budget and 10 percent by municipal budgets, as an "active" assistance measure. This should not be considered merely a way to provide income integration to working-age adults who are in a recognized condition of poverty and do not have serious physical or mental impairments. It is also a way to put these persons and their families in a position to overcome those conditions, and enter the labor market. The persons entitled to this assistance service are those who have an income below the official poverty line, and show their willingness to attend training courses and to work.[4] The minimum guaranteed income—which is similar to an income support measure implemented in France since the 1980s—currently amounts to about 270 Euros (about $300) monthly. It has been put into effect experimentally, first in thirty-nine and then in three hundred cities (Coluzzi and Palmieri 2001:168; Saraceno 2002:90). Furthermore, as the minister for social solidarity declared, other reforms concerning assistance and social policies are on their way to being discussed or approved.

First of all, the "outline law for the reform of welfare and social policies" (law 328/2000) has established a National Social Fund, initially endowed with 40 billion lire (about $18 million), in addition to sums already allocated to services to children, disabled people, and their families. It is aimed at

(a) allocating the necessary funds and establishing "the services and opportunities to be granted throughout the national territory";

(b) establishing "the planning and control functions of the public institutions";

(c) exploiting the tasks of nonprofit organizations (Turco 1999; see also Coluzzi and Palmieri 2001:169–70; Gori 2002:99–100).

Second, the former executive examined the possibility of creating a "single Ministry for Welfare gathering all the competencies that are now divided among the Ministries of Health, Labor and Social Policies" (Turco 1999).

Among the services—having partly a welfare nature—that are financed by the national budget there are (disregarding the amounts for contributions paid by private subjects, such as individual persons and companies):

1. Family allowances. "Families of workers or retired persons who find themselves in particular economic conditions" are entitled to receive family allowances. Nevertheless, the level of the maximum income threshold giving the right to receive these benefits (which have a hybrid character of assistance and social insurance at the same time) is low. Moreover, this income is provided exclusively to families with adults with regular jobs. As a consequence, as will be shown later in the discussion on benefits, many

needy families have not been entitled to receive them, whereas other entitled families have gained meager benefits due to the scantiness of allocations.[5] Although "family as such [is] rarely the object of explicit policies" (Saraceno 1995:46), family allowances—despite the previously mentioned quantitative and entitlement limits—have become an exception in this sense. The increase of family allowances provided for by financial law 448/1998 (article 3, clause 2) to families with income and property conditions below the preestablished threshold has mitigated the quantitative insufficiency of these allowances. It has also extended the number of entitled persons not only—as previously—to those who have regular employment, but also—through article 66—to all Italian women who do not benefit from any other maternity indemnities (Coluzzi and Palmieri 2001: 168–69; *La Stampa,* supplement "Tutto Soldi," 2 July 1999, p. 2; Turco 1998:12). Other exceptions are represented by (a) public services to children, which are, however, borne by municipal budgets; (b) financial aid to women having a precarious position in the labor market (law 488/1999); (c) paid leave for working parents who wish to take care of infant children (law 53/2000) (Coluzzi and Palmieri 2001:169).

2. Supplements to the minimum old age pensions for retired persons who, at the moment of their retirement, are not entitled to receive the foreseen minimum pension and do not have a minimum income (Negri and Saraceno 1996:40–44).

3. Civil disability pensions, which are in fact often granted for assistance purposes, but are formally allocated as a citizenship right to those who cannot work because of physical inability (ibid.).

4. The ordinary (CIG) and extraordinary (CIGS) Redundancy Fund (which is currently regulated by laws 223/1991 and 226/1993). CIG intervenes in favor of all employees of companies that are going through a temporary period of crisis. CIGS provides unemployment benefits to the workers employed in industrial concerns with a staff totaling over fifteen persons and to those employed in commercial companies with a staff of over two hundred persons, if these companies are in a lasting period of crisis or are undergoing a reorganization. The allowance totals 80 percent of the last wage up to a ceiling—for most workers—of about 650 Euros, which is formally paid for twelve months but is extended in many cases (CIGS almost without limits). However, CIG and CIGS represent an income protection tool for the portion of unemployed who succeed in getting them. This percentage is rapidly decreasing, as we shall later see when discussing the benefits granted by the Italian welfare system. For the rest of the unemployed, unemployment benefits—which currently total 30 percent of the most recent wage for a maximum period of six months—are absolutely inadequate in terms of income protection (ibid.:62–65; Reyneri 1996:192, 196–97).

5. Finally, the social pension is separated from the previously mentioned

income support measures due to its exclusively welfare character, but is equally selective with regard to recipients. Those who are entitled to receive it are all citizens over sixty-five, with an income below an established threshold, who are not entitled to receive an old age pension tied to the minimum floor. In comparison with the latter, which is very scarce anyway, the amounts granted by the social pension are considerably smaller (Negri and Saraceno 1996:50–51).

A great deal of the welfare expenditure is borne by the budgets of local authorities. Regions are entrusted with tasks concerning the direction, coordination, and allocation of funds for social services to local authorities. Municipalities and local health organizations (ASL), which inherited the public functions of the former USL (Unità Sanitarie Locali, local health units), are entrusted with the provision and management of social-welfare services, either directly or through agreements with private nonprofit and profit organizations. In this regard, municipalities have already enacted some regulations—in conformity with the law in force (particularly law 142/1990) and the municipal statute—concerning economic aid to persons who are needy or at risk of social marginalization (cf. *Forum,* 1997, 10:13–16).

Regional and municipal interventions are mainly focused on the elderly, minors, and the disabled, thus penalizing "the new categories that appear on the welfare scene," such as in particular drug addicts (Commissione d'indagine sulla povertà e l'emarginazione 1992:145). Therefore, they carry out primary prevention measures through services addressed to minors (to all of them or to those deemed worthy of attention), to the detriment of interventions aimed at rehabilitation. Within municipal services, nursery schools for children of preschool age essentially provide social services, since they are in principle available to all citizens and residents. On the contrary, day nurseries for children up to the age of three years (established by law 1044/1971) have a prevalently social welfare character. They are by priority reserved for children from families who cannot take full-time care of them, due to different and often preceding circumstances (socioeconomic disadvantage and working, separated, divorced, or unmarried mothers) (David 1984:197; Saraceno 1995:49–50).

Nonprofit organizations since the 1970s have increasingly received public financing in exchange for the management of welfare services (David 1992:479). They deal—as the major area of their activity—with social services, which have involved over one-third of their staff and volunteers, and benefit more than other areas from public subsidies (Barbetta and Ranci 1997:187–90). Among them, particularly important are religious organizations, and namely the Public Institutes for Welfare and Charity (IPAB) (Berzano 1991:166–67; Censis 1994:366, Table 53), which was given a clearly private juridical status only in 1988, through a decision of the Constitutional Court (Rei 1997:110).

Labor policies should be considered as preventing deviant activities, particularly the use and abuse of drugs. This is so to the extent to which they attempt to relieve the economic consequences of unemployment or job-lessness (especially of youth), to protect the employment of those who already work (passive and defensive policies), or to help those who are in these conditions in finding an employment (active policies). As for Italy,[6] passive and defensive labor policies have involved a number of interventions in favor of employment and income protection for the unemployed:

1. The creation of employment lists for the unemployed. For companies, nonetheless, the compulsory employment of persons from these lists fails in the case of small concerns (up to fifteen workers) and in the case of personal employment requests and direct transfers.

2. The establishment of highly restrictive prescriptive bounds to collective dismissals, whereas individual dismissals are only admitted in the cases provided for by the Workers' Statute of Rights.

3. The ordinary and extraordinary Redundancy Fund (CIG and CIGS), which, as previously noted, is in fact more aimed at welfare than at income maintenance for the unemployed. Law 223/1991 tried, however, to bring the institution of CIG and CIGS back to its "natural sphere of temporary support in corporate reorganization or changeover processes" (CNEL 1994:78–79).

4. The solidarity contracts for the income maintenance of workers who are not entitled to the Redundancy Fund: the economic damage workers suffer due to the reduction of work hours is partly balanced through public governmental and community funds.

5. The severance pay or unemployment subsidy in case of individual dismissals without just cause, and in case of collective dismissals for redundancies for workers who do not have any other income protection tool. Currently, this subsidy (from which only subordinated workers are entitled to benefit) totals 30 percent of the most recent gross wage and is granted only for a maximum period of six months. However, a bill of enabling act provides for an increase to 40 percent of the most recent gross wage for a maximum period of nine months in case beneficiaries are over fifty years old (*Corriere della Sera*, 5 February 2000, p. 2).

6. Early retirement for redundant workers with a contribution of not less than thirty years, or in some cases only up to fifteen years (for workers who accept part-time jobs offered by companies that have been under an extraordinary Redundancy Fund regime for over two years). Laws 223/1991 and 406/1992 currently regulate early retirement.

7. The regulations concerning the labor of immigrants, particularly with reference to the so-called Martelli Law (law 943/1986), law 39/1990 (urgent regulations concerning political asylum, entry, and stay of non–European Union citizens), and law 40/1998. All these regulations have in fact a defensive character, as they also aim, in addition to other goals, to protect Italian workers from the nonregulated competitiveness of foreign workers

coming from countries outside the European Union. However, law 40/1998 aims at providing "a greater support to integration programs for regularly resident foreigners" (Censis 1998:283).

Active policies provide for different tools to enter the labor market:

1. Time contracts, such as in-service training contracts (laws 863/1984, 451/1994) addressed to young people within the sixteen to thirty-two age segment. These contracts aim at favoring, through a reduction of the contributions borne by companies, the entry of the young into the labor market with intermediate/high, or low, qualification, depending on the kind of contract. Financing weighs upon the budgets of the Italian government, the regions, and the European Union. Furthermore, a forthcoming law decree should grant some contribution relief to companies that employ people with part-time open-end contracts. The contracts for workers in mobility are time contracts: law 451/1994 provides for reduced contributions to be paid by companies that employ actually unemployed workers who are registered in the mobility lists.

2. Placement without a contract and particularly placement into "socially useful" jobs for young unemployed, long-term unemployed workers in mobility, or those under the regime of extraordinary redundancy funds (laws 236/1993 and 451/1994). Also, placement into "special projects" reserved for nineteen- to thirty-two-year-old unemployed youth who live in high-unemployment-rate areas (law 236/1993).

3. Part-time jobs regulated by laws 863/1984 and 451/1994, involving a contribution relief. This law incentive is a consequence of the will to promote new jobs (as regards part-time contracts signed from the beginning of the job relationship) and to reduce unemployment rates for formerly employed workers (when full-time contracts are transformed into part-time contracts).

4. Incentives to open-end employment. These incentives consist of a reduction in social insurance contributions for companies, and mainly concern workers who are formally employed, but are actually under the regime of extraordinary redundancy funds (law 236/1993) or in mobility (law 223/1991), or unemployed for over two years (law 407/1990). Law 489/1994, however, establishes a tax credit for employers who employ subjects (usually young people) in search of their first job, in addition to workers belonging to the above-mentioned categories.

5. The financial support granted to placement cooperatives (law 381/1991) through tax relief and provisions to ease accounting regulations. This law, previously mentioned, is aimed (depending on the kind of cooperative) at introducing into the labor market and society both the users of the services offered by the cooperatives, and members themselves if they are considered disadvantaged persons from the point of view of job opportunities. In this case, the law is particularly relevant, since among those disadvantaged persons drug addicts are explicitly mentioned. Regarding

their introduction into the labor market, the Consolidated Act of laws concerning regulations on drugs provides for financial support to be borne by the National Fund for Interventions Aimed at Fighting Drugs (Fondo nazionale di intervento per la lotta alla droga). Legislators tried in this way to fight the marginalization or exclusion of drug addicts from the labor market by helping—through a reduction in social contributions and the provision of financial support—organizations, especially cooperatives, that agree to employ these persons.

6. The financial support granted by the regions to new entrepreneurial activities in favor of unemployed youth (law 44/1986). This law provides for economic support to entrepreneurial projects involving a given percentage of young people as new entrepreneurs, to members of associations, or to cooperatives. The regions carry out evaluation and financing of these projects.

7. The encouragement of independent work contracts through the legal acknowledgment (law 196/1997) of temporary work agencies, aimed at favoring employment and at also meeting corporate requirements for flexibility in the labor market (Censis 1998:193).

8. The end of the public monopoly on employment offices (which had already been introduced by law 196/1997) and the management of public employment offices on a regional, instead of national scale were enacted by law decree 469/1997 and by subsequent regulations. The new provisions, which conform to the directions of the European Commission, have radically changed the previous guidelines concerning active labor policies (ISFOL 1999:150–55).

9. The "upgrading of human resources" through professional training courses. These are financed by the European Social Fund (ESF), and are targeted (among other recipients) at long-term unemployed young people and at persons considered "at risk of social exclusion" (such as the physical and mentally disabled, the imprisoned, non–European Union immigrants, and drug addicts) (ibid.:396–400).

10. The pursuit of "social equity" through support actions aimed at an introduction or reintroduction in the labor market. These interventions, too, are financed by the ESF, and are targeted at the same recipients indicated in the previous point (ibid.:402–9).

In addition to these labor policy measures, there are further measures that are simultaneously active and passive, because they aim both at protecting the income of the unemployed and at facilitating their reemployment. We refer in this case to the mobility lists, foreseen and regulated by several laws (223/1991, 236/1993, 56/1994, 451/1994), which are supposed to provide protection to workers of companies forced to cease their activities or reduce the personnel who are protected neither by the Redundancy Fund nor by solidarity contracts. Benefits vary depending on whether these persons previously worked in companies under an Extraordinary

Redundancy Fund regime in small concerns, or those near the retirement age and with a minimum period of contribution.

The policies concerning the *housing market* are different as well, but are usually characterized by the dual purpose of encouraging property ownership (instead of tenancy) and meeting the housing requirements of citizens (and sometimes of foreign residents) in a state of poverty and/or other kinds of difficulty.[7] Accordingly, law 457/1978 has provided for and regulated the concession of (a) public financing, in the form of low-interest loans for the purchase of a first house to families with a given income; (b) financial assistance to construction enterprises that turn to purchasers with scarce funds at their disposal; (c) public housing, which is owned by the Autonomous Institute of Public Housing (IACP) and by municipalities, and which is offered at reduced rentals, according to complex priority criteria, to persons and families meeting the (nonexclusively economic) prerequisites required by the public authority.

Subsidized public housing has a distribution goal. Facilitated housing also aims at favoring access to property and at increasing the number of existing houses.[8] Nevertheless, through law 560/1993, IACP has been allowed to sell up to three-fourths of the real estate it owns, giving priority to the current tenants. The distributive goal has been therefore jeopardized. On the contrary, the law on rent control (392/1978) was completely distributive in its purposes, in favor of tenants and to the detriment of proprietors. The law on rent control regulated the rent market (determined by law in terms of amount and duration), until the introduction of derogatory clauses substantially modified it (laws 359/1992, 431/1998, and the law decree of 22 February 2000). It also established a social fund for the provision of subsidies to those who could not afford a rent (Testa 1987:14). Currently, through law 431/1998, the law decrees of 20 July 1999 and 22 February 2000, the government has reestablished this social fund. The fund has been made available to all those who have signed rent contracts with private proprietors, and whose income is sufficiently low to be included in the categories the law provides for (Gentilini 1999; *La Stampa,* supplement "Tutto Soldi," 6 March 2000, p. 4).

Some provisions, which come at the expense of municipalities, have a distribution and assistance nature, and provide for

(a) subsidies for rents and other housekeeping expenses to needy persons, who would otherwise be forced to turn to the housing market;

(b) temporary shelter in boarding houses or in free hostels. For non–European Union citizens, the Martelli Law provides for reception centers financed by the regions, and subsidized by the government (ISMU 1995:228–30).

Besides these distribution measures, which often have a social assistance nature, the Italian housing market has not been changed until recent times by "any organic policy aimed at urban requalification" (Negri and

Saraceno 1996:176). Law 266/1998 and the relevant enforcement rules (decree 225 of 1 June 1998) were therefore intended to start, in agreement with municipalities and if necessary with other subjects, an organic policy in this area. The policy is aimed at interventions and recovery of dilapidated urban areas, by allocating, together with concerned local authorities, financial support to programs directed at these targets.

Education policies are marked by the purpose of providing everybody with a basic education, and all citizens with equal opportunities to a high school education. Both targets have been primarily pursued through public education, which begins in nursery schools, and becomes dominant in elementary and secondary schools. This involves a corresponding proportionate reduction in the number of private—either profit or nonprofit—schools and in the number of their students and teachers (Barbetta, Ranci 1997:195–96; Censis 1998:108–9). The age of compulsory education, which until recently had been fourteen, and was raised to fifteen during the school year 1999–2000 (law 9/1999), suits the first target. So do a number of other policies, such as

(a) the principle of free compulsory education;

(b) the establishment (in 1962) of unified secondary schools;

(c) facilitated attendance at school for disabled children, through transport services and support teachers, both financed by the municipalities (laws 517/1977 and 104/1992);

(d) public financing of nursery schools;

(e) compulsory education extended to all non–European Union minors, even if they do not have legal immigration status.

The second target has determined up to now (disregarding the comprehensive school reform that the current government is determined to carry out, despite opposition from many quarters; *La Stampa,* 2 February 2002, p. 5; 8 April 2002, p. 11; 11 April 2002, p. 15):

(a) Governmental financing of high schools, both public and private nonprofit schools.

(b) Regional financing and management of professional training courses, which are carried out either directly by the regions, or in agreement with other public or private organizations. As of school year 2000–2001 these training courses have become compulsory for the young up to the age of eighteen years who do not attend high school.

(c) The provision, since the 1980s, of school orientation services financed and managed by a growing number of local authorities. The integration between school and professional training has been entrusted to regional initiatives, which must, however, conform to the targets set by the ESF if they intend to avail themselves of the resources provided for by the fund (Censis 1998:132).

(d) An effort to bring young people who have dropped out of school or those with learning difficulties back into the compulsory education system by means of new forms of control and recovery courses. The past government committed itself to seeing that everyone up to eighteen receives a diploma or a professional qualification.[9] In addition to the financing of the right to study already provided for by the financial law of 1999, since the school year 2000–2001 the law has provided for economic support to students whose families have an income below an established threshold. The goal has been to enable them to have access to public and private education.[10]

Italian *health policy* has been historically characterized by a peculiar mix of public and private medicine, with "a progressive inclusion of health services into the public system" (Vicarelli, 1992:461) until the creation in 1978 of the National Health Service (SSN; law 833/1978). The National Health Service was established in order to provide coverage for medical care requirements, but

(a) It is not complete with regard to service provision and financing;

(b) With the exception of emergencies, it does not extend to those non–European Union citizens without a residence permit who have not applied for it;

(c) It allows users the possibility to resort to private health services for payment;

(d) It is not only financed by the national tax system,[11] but also by compulsory social insurance contributions, which are deducted directly from employees' wages, and which other taxpayers pay proportionally to their declared income (Arzuffi 1991:255–57; Negri and Saraceno 1996:187–88, 192–93; Nonis 1989:363).

On the other hand, in the course of the 1980s, user charges were introduced (in the form of the "ticket") for the provision of health services and medicines, thus deviating from the principle of free health care (Negri and Saraceno 1996:190–91). Furthermore, several associations of service users developed between the 1980s and the 1990s, and thus led health organizations to pay more attention to them. In addition, a partial reform of the SSN was approved during the early 1990s (law 421/1992 and law decrees 502/1992 and 417/1993), and was later implemented by enabling act 419/1998. Some important innovations derived from it are:

(a) The distribution of administrative, legislative, organizational, and control functions to the regions;

(b) The allocation to the regions of financial resources, which are borne by the Health Fund established by a National Health Program;

(c) The transformation of the former USL (Local Health Units), renamed ASL [Local Health Organizations (Aziende)], and of the large hospitals into autonomous organizations from the financial, organizational, technical, management, and accountancy point of view, with the responsibility for balanced budgets;

(d) The introduction of targets such as efficiency and quality in health services, considered from the standpoint of users.

Further health service legislative has been enacted. The law decrees of

15 April 1994 set the overall criteria for fixing the rates of hospital health services. The law decree of 14 December 1994 established these rates. Finally, the ministerial guidelines 1/1995 provided direction on how this decree should be put into effect. These legislative measures have kept the targets of efficiency and quality in health services by establishing

(a) quality and efficiency indicators;

(b) evaluation criteria to be used;

(c) minimum equipment level for public and private health organizations.

Regions can establish further requirements, provided that they comply with the regulations in force (cf. Campari and De Negri 1999:77–79; Censis 1994:281–90; Coppini 1994:206–7; De Masi and Grossi 1997; Vanara 1997; Vicarelli 1992:466–69).

Management and financial control activities on all public, private, profit, or nonprofit organizations were strengthened by the Decree on the Reorganization of the National Health Service (SSN), approved by the council of ministers on 18 June 1999. By means of this decree, regions must commit themselves to

(a) contribute to the definition of the National Health Program; determine the overall requirements of the SSN;

(b) grant authorizations to health organizations, according to quality and safety standards;

(c) concur with the planning, evaluation, and control of services, along with municipalities, user associations, and volunteer organizations (*La Stampa*, 19 June 1999, p. 3).

Finally, regarding policies enacted on drugs and the pathologies that may derive from drug use, it is worth noting what law 135/1990 provides for. The legislative text aims at preventing AIDS infections, at taking care of those who fall ill, at training medical staff, and at planning and providing the necessary organization to carry out all these tasks. The elaboration of the intervention programs for implementing law 135/1990 has been entrusted to the regions (Arzuffi 1991:330–31).

THE SOCIAL POLICIES ENACTED IN ITALY,
IN COMPARISON WITH THE CORRESPONDING POLICIES
IN THE UNITED STATES AND IN SWEDEN

This comparison involves only the enacted policies, leaving aside implementation procedures and consequences. We shall first deal with the legislative acts directly concerning drugs (repression and secondary prevention of drug use and abuse, rehabilitation of drug addicts), then upon the primary prevention policies enacted (public assistance and social services).

Italy shares with Sweden and the United States, as well as with many other countries, an intransigent and repressive approach against drug selling, including soft drugs, though in Italy drug purchase and possession for personal use have been decriminalized. Furthermore, all three countries entrust prevention and rehabilitation activities to local administrations, often in cooperation with private organizations (many of which are nonprofit), though these activities are at least partly financed by the central administration. On the other hand, Italian enacted policies (but not necessarily implemented policies, which will be later examined) are similar in some aspects to the corresponding Swedish policies, while different from the U.S. policies:

1. As previously mentioned, a National Intervention Fund aimed at fighting drugs was established in 1990, with the task of financing projects and primary and secondary prevention activities, as well as drug addict rehabilitation. The coordination of the related activities was entrusted to a special permanent board. Like in Sweden, although much later, also in Italy the parliament and central government authorities have committed themselves to conduct an overall policy of "fighting drugs." This policy, which accordingly includes repression, rehabilitation, and primary and secondary prevention, should be coordinated, centralized, and addressed to all actual and potential consumers. By way of contrast, a similar coordination and centralization of policies enacted on this matter having a non-repressive character have never taken place in the United States.

2. In the United States, but not in Italy and Sweden, a steady commitment to rehabilitation has always been almost exclusively addressed to drug addicts who wish to detoxify. However, authorities have limited themselves in fact to the free (in most cases) supply of methadone for a limited period. Different local authorities (individual states, municipalities, school authorities) have made secondary prevention efforts, sometimes with federal financial support. Yet, at least until recent times, unlike Swedish and Italian authorities, U.S. authorities have not sought to coordinate their efforts for the purpose of conducting a systematic and centralized evaluation of results, nor have they committed themselves to this effect.

3. In Italy and Sweden, the parliament and the government have decreed several provisions that should, in the aims of the legislation, reduce relative deprivation through

- assistance measures, in order to grant an adequate income to all citizens (in Sweden also to residents) who have an income below the official threshold of poverty. In Italy, however, measures intended for all needy citizens have only recently been introduced, and still have an experimental character;
- active and passive labor policies provided for and financed by the central government;
- housing policies aimed at offering decent housing to the needy resi-

dential population through subsidized public housing, and consequently, the building of public houses at reduced rents. In Italy, there are also different forms of subsidized housing;

- education policies established with the aim of granting to all citizens equal opportunities to have access to a basic primary and secondary education, and therefore focused on the public control (carried out by the state administration or by local authorities) of school institutions;
- health policies carried out by pursuing the goal of ensuring access to adequate medical treatment to all citizens and foreign residents. This service may be either public or operate within the National Health Service, and is partly financed by compulsory insurance contributions and for the remaining part by the public budgets of local and national authorities.

In all three countries, some forms of welfare mix have been established. Accordingly, particular social services may be provided either by a public authority, by a nonprofit association, or by companies operating in the market. Nevertheless, the U.S. social policies that aim at relieving the condition of relative and absolute privation have pursued egalitarian purposes in the distribution of life chances with much less determination and consistency. Considering their enactment (but not their implementation), they are therefore in marked contrast to the corresponding Italian and Swedish policies. In fact, U.S. social assistance policies—although they vary in terms of liberality and other characteristics from state to state—are only aimed at relieving, not canceling, the condition of deprivation. Labor policies have almost exclusively a passive character, and unemployment benefits have been restricted to the fraction of workers who belong to the regular labor market. Locally implemented public housing policies for the benefit of low-income persons have availed themselves of some forms of subsidies. However, they have quantitatively been so limited, especially during the last two decades, that it is questionable if they have actually been intended to be redistributive for the entire entitled population, or even for its majority. In addition, recent federal provisions have further decreased the relevance of this aim.

By the same token, public education policy in the United States has only partially aimed at equalizing the opportunities for lower-class students to have equal access to qualified educational degrees and services. On the other hand, the strong quantitative and qualitative relevance of private schools and universities operating in the market, and competing among themselves and with public institutions, would not have allowed in any case this purpose to be achieved as a matter of principle. With regard to health services, this equalizing goal has been formally (rather than actually) pursued through the federal medical assistance program for the needy (Medicaid), despite the lack of compulsory social insurance coverage in case of illness.

THE BENEFITS OF THE ITALIAN SOCIAL POLICIES

The Ability to Implement Rehabilitation and Prevention Measures

Within the Italian welfare state, there has been a considerable, although variable, discrepancy between declared and achieved goals in conformity with the "Latin model" (Abrahamson 1991:257–58). This discrepancy will be evaluated by individual areas of intervention. We shall briefly mention here the benefits that, according to the specialized literature, Italian policies have brought about in rehabilitation, the primary and secondary prevention of drug use and abuse, and limiting relative deprivation. Concerning rehabilitation and prevention, the evaluation of benefits is however hampered by

1. the impossibility, for public services, to "follow up their patients after the end of the therapeutic program" (Turco 1998:10);

2. the nonestablishment, through 1995, of the goals and programs of the intervention projects to fight drug addiction;

3. the nonfulfillment, for most regions, of the obligation to prepare reports on the implementation of the projects;

4. the nonacquisition, for the administration of the Department of Social Affairs, of evaluations and results of inspections concerning these projects;

5. "the failure to perform controls under the direct responsibility of the Administration," according to the State Audit Court (Corte dei Conti 1996).Difficulties, negligence, and delays in the implementation of law 306/1990 have prevented—as the State Audit Court remarked—"the actual start of most of the approved projects." The Department of Social Affairs administration has distinguished itself for "the absence of significant information regarding inspections" during the entire five-year period 1990–95 (Corte dei Conti 1996:22–23, 28–29; cf. also Negri and Saraceno 1996:265). In this regard, the then minister declared in February 1998 that "all the projects submitted by public and non-profit organizations for the financial years 1994 and 1995" had been evaluated and that "the relevant financial support had been provided for." Therefore, in 1996 "the mentioned delays would have been made up, and no further delays" would have occurred (Turco 1998:12).

Assuming that this is true and also that the delays prior to 1994 were made up, an evaluation of the benefits is in any case premature. Law 306/1990 is still relatively new. This law, as mentioned, established the National Intervention Fund for Fighting Drugs and defined its management criteria. Also, more than six years after the establishment of the fund, in February 1997, the department's administration had not yet made a comprehensive and systematic evaluation of the rehabilitation and prevention projects. This was so by explicit admission of the minister for social solidarity (Turco 1998:13), and according to other sources as well (Springer 1998:32). An evaluation might have concerned all these projects, or some specific categories of them (for example, the reintroduction of drug addicts into society and the labor market). Furthermore, it should have dwelt on

1. the outcomes of these projects, bearing in mind "the preestablished goals and the expected results"; and

2. their impact, meant as "the whole amount of the (wanted, foreseen, or not foreseen) effects actually produced by the enacted policy" (Palumbo 1995:322).[12]

There is, however, reason to believe that the results have proved at least unsatisfactory, since the spread or the prevalence of drugs seems to be growing in Italy (as we shall later see). Below we shall examine the failings of the so-called nonprofit organizations or third sector as well as those of the national and regional public administrations, regarding the implementation of enacted policies on rehabilitation or prevention. Concerning the failings (or "difficulties" as they have been called) of the third sector, the specialized literature has often noted the scant effectiveness of interventions. This has been imputed to insufficient professional training and updating of the personnel, its "slowness in understanding phenomena of uneasiness" (Albanesi 1999:283), and its inability to consider specific requirements when it cares for the service users, each of whom needs particular goals and intervention procedures.

The public administrations themselves have increased these difficulties. In their relation with the third sector, they have displayed serious deficiencies, including (1) an absence of planning with regard to intervention requests addressed to the organizations of the third sector (the irregularity of requests produces improvised responses), (2) insufficient financial support, which is often diverted from other destinations; (3) a lack of systematic supervision and control regarding the procedures, the effectiveness, and the efficiency of the interventions of these private organizations. Accordingly, even barely or not at all qualified organizations are entitled to receive financial support (Albanesi 1999:281–84; cf. also Barbetta, Ranci 1997:202–3). The deficiencies of the Italian welfare system have enhanced its arbitrariness, in comparison with a universalistic principle, in the definition of public intervention priorities and requirements for having access to services (Censis 1998:253–54).

We now examine more in detail the individual areas in which welfare activities are operating.

Rehabilitation has been carried out by three kinds of organizations: Public Services for Drug Addiction (SERTs), residential and semiresidential communities, and private nonresidential services. The share of drug addicts undergoing treatment provided by public services has grown, in comparison with those who are undergoing treatment carried out by social-rehabilitating organizations different from SERTs, whether public or private. There were about 20,000 drug addicts connected with the SERTs in 1986, 50,000 in 1991, and about 95,000 in 1997. After a rapid growth during the second half of the 1980s, the number of therapeutic community users, totaling 12,000–16,000 persons, has on the contrary stabilized since the early 1990s. Many drug addicts undergoing treatment in organizations other than SERTs place their trust in communities of a residential or semi-residential nature rather than in private nonresidential services. As a consequence, in the 1990s, the overall number of users of rehabilitation services provided by organizations different from SERTs also stabilized. During the previous decade, less than 30,000 drug addicts turned to these services, considered as a whole, and their number has stabilized since 1994 to about 22,000 persons, that is, less than one-fourth of SERT users. All the organizations providing services to drug addicts offer a variety of programs: support interviews, guidance and consultancy services for users and families, information campaigns, prevention and damage reduction projects, and experimental interventions. Programs aimed more at providing psychological and social support to drug users and their families are, on the contrary, more frequently found in particular kinds of organizations. SERTs are characterized by the prescription and the supply of medicines replacing drugs, such as methadone (widely used by SERT users) and antagonist medicines (less widespread, however). SERTs also frequently provide individual and family psychotherapy services. The other types of organizations, particularly communities, make psychotherapy services for groups more easily available.

Social and labor market reintroduction projects, though found in about half of the public services, are not privileged in comparison with other activities addressed to users, such as prearrangement of therapeutic programs, support interviews, guidance and advice, diagnostics, prescription of pharmacological therapies, and administration of medicines. Personnel carrying out these activities tend to work in conditions of isolation from other informal institutions or associations, and often have not attended training courses (Bagozzi 1999:22; Labos 1993:45).

In contrast, communities and other private organizations more and more frequently manage the "numerous recovery and labor market reintroduction projects implemented through the available funds of the National Intervention Fund for Fighting Drugs" (Turco 1998:10). An increasingly smaller minority of drug addicts has turned to these private organizations. Most addicts seem to be inclined—rather than to a more ambitious program of social rehabilitation—to a detoxification or substitution treatment (through the administration of methadone), which is more frequently available at the SERTs than elsewhere.

As previously mentioned, there is not yet any institutional evaluation on the effectiveness and impact of the services provided by the SERTs and the communities. Still, many indicators show the slight impact of these rehabilitation projects. In particular, there is an increasing consumption of both soft and heavy drugs, and most drug addicts do not opt for full rehabilitation, and therefore for social and job introduction, despite the fact that the SERTs and communities frequently provide support, guidance, and advice. Activities in workshops and social and job reintroduction projects are, in fact, particularly relevant only within semiresidential communities and nonresidential private services, to which only a minority of Italian drug addicts turn.[13]

In light of the available information (as we shall later see), the lack in Italy of a systematic commitment to social and job reintroduction of drug addicts risks reducing the effectiveness and impact of rehabilitation activities. Evidence of this risk is "the presence of a high number of chronic users" among the drug addicts who have turned to the SERTs, thus inducing a sense of discouragement and uselessness in many service operators (Labos 1993:45). In particular, drug addicts who submit to restrictive measures of their personal freedom need to be reeducated and socially rehabilitated. This need has not been suitably satisfied so far, either in prison or outside (in case of alternative measures to imprisonment).[14] The use of alternative substances to drugs, such as methadone, has proved useful to keep some nonimprisoned drug addicts from criminal behaviors and to detoxify other imprisoned addicts (currently about 30 percent of the jailed population) (Colombo and Merlo 1986:115–19; Turco 1998:11). The insufficient commitment to social and particularly job reintroduction limits, however, the benefits of rehabilitation.

An evaluation of efficiency and impact involves considering the benefits that exclusively rehabilitative policies, and those aimed at *primary and secondary prevention*, may possibly provide. Primary prevention is carried out through assistance, social insurance, and social security policies (such as the policies of interventions in the labor market, education, and health). The implementation of social insurance policies is entrusted to the National Institute for Social Insurance (INPS), which, with over thirty-four million members, includes over two-thirds of the entire Italian adult population (*La Stampa,* "Tutto Soldi," 1 November 1999, p. 1; Censis 1998:Table 14, 299.)

Secondary prevention is, on the contrary, carried out through measures addressed to young persons considered at risk of deviance. This latter form of prevention, to the extent to which it has been implemented in Italy, is mentioned here only within the overall framework of primary prevention policies. As should be preliminarily noted, the following factors have hampered the implementation of all prevention measures, and welfare activities in general:

1. problems of competence among national, regional, and local administrations;

2. a lack of clarity of regulations, with a consequent operational uncertainty for administrators. Lack of clarity has been due to the absence until 1999 of an outline law, which has provided the guiding principles con-

cerning assistance, and to continuous legislative innovation at different levels of the public administration (Albanesi 1999:283–84; Turco 1999).

As for *assistance,* some researchers have authoritatively stated that up to now a minimum income is guaranteed only to some particular protected categories, such as "elderly citizens or disabled persons with physical and mental disabilities, if they do not have adequate economic resources" (Negri and Saraceno 1996:113). This is so despite the intentions of the executive branch to guarantee coverage of needs to all citizens, and will remain so until the new experimental law provisions on the minimum guaranteed income become fully operational. These categories receive pensions and other money transfers through "a complicated and erratic overlapping of social insurance and assistance" (ibid.:55), which enjoys a well-established tradition in Italy (Ascoli 1984:43–45). A "definitely limited," and even decreasing, share of the overall assistance expenditure and of the gross national product is allocated for "subjects who need assistance interventions" (Censis 1994:304–6; cf. also Turco 1999). Furthermore, "protection becomes increasingly provisional and weak as soon as the noncentral sectors of the labor market are affected" (Negri and Saraceno 1996:113).

A number of interconnected causes produce and maintain the condition of poverty. Usually, deprived subjects do not have the support of family or friend resources, current employment, or a previous permanent job complying with social insurance regulations. On the other hand, the public institutions that should help deprived and needy persons often fail to do so. In fact, "services are provided only to those who require them" (Pieretti 1991:179). For all the others access is difficult "due to the rigidity of services" and "to a nonawareness of their rights" (ibid.:189). There are also gaps in the assistance laws, particularly to the detriment of nonregular immigrants or homeless people (Albanesi 1999:284). Not surprisingly, then, a high share (42 percent) of the homeless interviewed for an inquiry declared that "they had no contacts with public services," whereas the majority (77 percent) of them stated that "they were assisted by private structures." Among them, those of a religious nature were predominant (Berzano 1991:166–67; cf. also Barbetta, Ranci 1997:196–97).

Some nonprofit organizations too, which are usually connected with the Church and avail themselves of volunteers, operate for all the homeless, as well as for many immigrants often living in conditions of extreme poverty. These organizations offer hot meals and other services, which sometimes include a shelter for the night [*Scarp de' Tenis,* 1994:1(1):4]. Once an individual is on his or her way to pauperization, with respect to the labor market, social relations with friends and family, and the Italian public welfare institutions, often these organizations do not seem in a position to stop, much less reverse this process. The result is "a social drift that makes the conditions of need chronic" (Kazepov 1999:115; cf. also Kazepov 1995). Up to now, Italian institutions have been lacking in the purpose and ability to

(1) economically and socially reintroduce people who find themselves outside the system, particularly if they are homeless (De Bernart 1991:210–12;
Negri and Saraceno 1996:171); (2) allocate assistance subsidies sufficient in
amount and coverage (cf. Saraceno 2002). Regarding the latter aspect, the
"outline law for the reform of assistance and social policies" included in
the financial law of 1999 should—in the aims of those who introduced the
law—improve the effectiveness of assistance measures (Saraceno 1995:48–
49; Turco 1999).

   Therefore, the share of families with an income below the poverty line
(measuring relative poverty) remains high. After having grown during the
1980s, this share remained substantially steady (around 10–12 percent)
during the early 1990s. The decrease that took place in 1993–94 seems to
have depended, for 1993, on the lower income of families who were previously placed over this line, and, for 1994, on the improvement of the
economic conditions of families who were previously needy. This was,
however, achieved in conjunction with a worsening of the income of other
already needy families. More than 7 percent of the population is in absolute
poverty, without the possibility of covering its needs without assistance
from the authorities (as happens in the case of health services and education). The percentage of the population living in relative poverty does not
seem to have significantly changed in the last decade, and now amounts
to some 12–14 percent, according to different estimates. The following factors are of the utmost importance in producing and consolidating a condition of poverty: the inadequacy of assistance and welfare institutions, a
large number of family members, in particular the young and the elderly,
and the educational level of the family head. These disadvantages can be
found with particular frequency, and often all combined, in the south of
the country. A minority of the population lives there, but two-thirds of the
families who reside there have an income below the official poverty line.
Therefore, a primary prevention policy also involves effective labor and
education policies.[15]

   Active and passive *labor* policy means, on the one hand, the introduction into and retraining for the labor market, and income support on the
other hand. The benefits actually granted have favored the same core sectors, characterized by full-time and permanent jobs, that are covered by the
public social insurance system and possibly also by private insurance.
These policies have been detrimental, however, to the unprotected unemployed who have lost their job, and even more to "those who are looking
for their first job, especially if they are young and poorly educated." Finally, "those who are out of the labor market" (Negri and Saraceno
1996:105–6), particularly socially marginal drug addicts, "find it hard to
enter or reenter it" (ibid.:109). Due to the lack of unemployment benefits
(of a social insurance nature) and a minimum guaranteed income (of an assistance nature), it is easy to understand why there is in Italy "extended

economic poverty" affecting the unemployed and the jobless (ibid.:118). Accordingly, passive labor policies have not succeeded in safeguarding the income of most of the unemployed.

Active policies have generally had a very limited effectiveness in fighting juvenile and overall unemployment. The total unemployment rate, after having reached about 12 percent in 1987, has remained in recent years at that level (Censis 1990:275, Table 31, 1994:256, Table 17, 1998:232, Table 19; *La Stampa,* 11 May 1999, p. 17). The rate of youth unemployment went on increasing throughout the 1980s (including persons looking for their first job), and stabilized in the 1990s at about one-fourth of those fifteen to twenty-nine and one-third of those fifteen to twenty-four.[16] The spread in the 1980s and 1990s of "anomalous" job contracts, which, however, are provided for and regulated by the laws in force, does not seem in most cases to have effectively counteracted unemployment. Anomalous jobs are those in-service training, part-time, and limited-time forms of collaboration that are uninterrupted during a given time span and occur in one particular firm. Also included are temporary jobs, telemarketing contracts, and jobs without a contract, particularly through the formula of "social utility jobs" (Censis 1990:287, Table 51, 1998:239, Table 30, 1999:213–14, 230, Table 34; ISFOL 1999:75–95, 138–44, 150–55). In this regard, some researchers have authoritatively noted that "there exists not an assistance network of last resort, aimed at introducing and reintroducing the unemployed into the labor market, and provided with active measures, particularly with an efficient network of employment services" (ISFOL 1999:136).

This conclusion is strengthened if we consider the dramatic decrease in the period 1997–98 in the number of the unemployed introduced or reintroduced as employed labor force through the mechanism of social utility jobs. This number declined sharply, from about 120,000 to about 86,000 persons (Censis 1998:239, Table 30; *La Stampa,* 7 November 1999, p. 17). Some other active policies have also proved rather ineffective. In-service training contracts, in particular, were considered in the past as "a privileged way for youth to enter the labor market" (CNEL 1994:86), after having introduced about half a million young people into the labor market in the period 1987–89. Yet, in the following decade their effectiveness as an active labor policy tool decreased, as only a little more than one-half of those who had such training contracts were inserted into the labor market (Censis 1998:239, Table 30, 1999:188, Table 3; CNEL 1994:86–87).

Also the Italian laws aimed at favoring the reemployment of unemployed workers by making it easier than before to hire and dismiss workers (laws 223/1991 and 236/1993) do not seem to have achieved significant results. Among those who are registered in the mobility lists only a strong minority—mostly in the southern regions—have succeeded in finding a job (CNEL 1994:84–85). Through the financial support of the European Social Fund, training interventions and interventions aimed at a reintroduction into the labor market have achieved more relevant, though hardly conclusive results. These interventions have reached (as an annual average) 6 percent of the long-term unemployed acknowledged by the authorities, and 13 percent of the young in search of their first employment (ISFOL 1999:406–8). One survey showed that, in comparison with a homogeneous national sample, for the young and the long-term unemployed who received these training interventions, "professional training has . . . a positive impact, disregarding the influence that the personal characteristics or the educational qualification of the subjects might have on it" (ibid.:304). This "positive impact" not only involves the possibility of finding a job thanks to these interventions, but also the quality and duration of this job (ibid.:303–8). This encouraging conclusion is, however, balanced by the consideration that only a restricted minority of the young or long-term unemployed is entitled to receive the training interventions financed by the European Social Fund.

The institution of limited-duration and part-time contracts has met with greater success, and these types of contracts have provided jobs to a growing and considerable number of persons during the 1990s.[17] But this success should be evaluated bearing in mind that many of these persons transformed their full-time contracts into part-time ones (CNEL 1994:113, Table 21), and that among the new employed, some percentage would in any case have been employed even without these measures. Despite these restrictions, according to a research institute on training and employment policies, "the analysis of the results apparently indicates that part-time and limited-duration jobs are actually tools making more fluent and flexible the entry of young people into the labor market, and the way out for elderly people" (ISFOL 1999:86). In contrast, the benefits of law 44/1986 (promotion of juvenile entrepreneurship) have been modest at a national level, although not negligible in some southern area, with about 24,000 persons employed in new companies financed by this law (CNEL 1994:90).

Active labor policies for drug addicts have apparently proved particularly ineffective. Within the "prevention and rehabilitation programs for potential or proclaimed drug addict subjects, . . . the projects aimed at reintroducing into the labor market" (Turco 1998:12), and at socially rehabilitating them in general, had a particular importance when carried out by residential communities. This was so even before the issuing of the Consolidated Act (law 309/1990) (ISFOL 1999:149). Their effectiveness cannot be established, as an overall and systematic evaluation of the rehabilitation and prevention projects provided for by the National Intervention Fund (law 309/1990) has not been made so far. Past and present experiences, however, are not encouraging: in the 1980s, prevention and rehabilitation activities were carried out within, respectively, either schools and therapeutic communities or public health centers but, depending on cases, with questionable success or none at all.[18]

Therefore, as for drug addicts, it does not seem in general that before law 309/1990 any effective social rehabilitation action had been carried out.[19] Nor after the enactment of law 309/1990 did the effectiveness of rehabilitation prove satisfactory. The recent institution of the Drogatel telephone service has highlighted that presently most (57 percent) heroin addicts who turn to it are unemployed (presumably this percentage includes also persons who are not unemployed, but outside the labor market) (Turco 1998:9). The effort to introduce or reintroduce drug addicts into the labor market, despite the funds made available by the European Social Fund, has involved a small percentage (a few thousand people) of the potential beneficiaries. These nonabundant financial resources have been preferentially addressed to the disabled (ISFOL 1999:408–9). We shall later examine the reasons for this limited success, indicated by the inconsistency between aims and expected outcomes, and by the production of perverse effects.

Housing policies have proved absolutely inadequate, both in terms of quality and quantity, to cover the needs of those who have an inadequate income (Tosi 1984:250). Since the end of the Second World War, the average number of persons per room has considerably decreased, but barriers to owning or renting a house have strengthened because of an insufficiency of public housing. By the mid-1990s this was estimated as 5 percent of the overall housing on the market) (ISMU 1995:230). These barriers have also strengthened because of the "scarce utilization municipalities subject to controlled rents have made of the Social Fund" (Testa 1987:17).

There has also been a progressive deterioration, both physical and in terms of quality of social life, of the old areas in the historical town centers. The relatively new, but poorly serviced housing projects built by public and private firms in the 1950s and 1960s have also deteriorated (Negri and Saraceno 1996:179–83; Sidoti 1989:136–45; Testa 1987:30–31). The funds made available to local authorities through law 266/1997 and law decree 225/1998, aimed at restoring dilapidated urban areas, have given the opportunity to local authorities to develop and start some intervention programs (Selmini 1999:127–29). In Genoa, in particular, the city made use of these funds, in addition to other regional funds and to the contribution of local trade and handicraft associations, to implement a program aimed at promoting entrepreneurial activities. This was in conjunction with an existing program for the recovery of the historical town center, financed by the Ministry of Public Works (Comune di Genova 1998). An evaluation of these programs, and hence of the effectiveness of law 266/1997, is, however, premature.

The lack of economically affordable housing also for needy persons and families (only about 7 percent of them lived in public flats by the mid-1980s) (Testa 1987:13–14) has contributed to the creation of a relatively widespread homeless population.[20] This condition, however, also stems from the previously mentioned interconnected causes that put and maintain deprived subjects in a condition of poverty and social marginalization, both in economic and social-institutional terms. It lowers, in particular, their "ability to use the resources made available by the institutional authorities" (Commissione d'indagine sulla povertà e l'emarginazione 1992:93). Paradoxically, those who desperately need a house—the homeless—often do not formally have the right to one and, if they do, it is highly improbable that they ever succeed in getting it.

Particularly needy, from this point of view, are many immigrants from developing countries: even if they have a residence permit, they are in practice excluded from property and come up against serious obstacles—though they may have a regular job—in finding apartments. Sometimes strong political and social resistance emerges when public apartments are assigned to immigrants, although they are entitled to receive them, and there is even stronger resistance when reception and aid centers provided for by the Martelli Law are set up. The (scant) sums the regions have made available since 1990 to provide temporary or permanent accommodation to immigrants do not seem to have significantly mitigated their discomfort. Generally speaking, we can say that disadvantaged (in economic and social terms) persons find themselves either homeless or with poor-quality apartments in rundown neighborhoods, and in both cases have great difficulty in improving their housing condition (Forti 1991; ISMU 1995:228–49; Negri and Saraceno 1996:164–84; Italia-Razzismo 1991).

The benefits of public policies on *education* should meet the universalistic aims of providing all citizens with an education not below a conventional minimum, and of granting them equal opportunities of access to high school education. The growing schooling rate of the Italian school-age population conforms to both objectives. There has been, accordingly, a reduction in 1996 of youth in the fifteen to twenty-four segment without educational qualifications, or with only a primary school education, to less than 2 percent of the overall youth population (against almost 9 percent in 1983). Correspondingly, there has been a strong percentage increase of young people who have finished high school (from one-third in 1983 to over 92 percent in 1996) (Censis 1990:172, Table 66; Volino 1997:409, Table 5). The increase in schooling has been going on since the end of the war, with a percentage increase of high school graduates, and even more, of those holding a junior high school diploma (Censis 1994:201, Table 54).

Currently, the number of children three to five years old attending nursery schools has stabilized at around 95 percent, after having previously gradually increased. As for the students of primary and secondary schools, schooling exceeds 100 percent. This is not only due to anticipated or late registrations, repeated years, and reentries into the school system, but also to the entry into the Italian school system of non–European Union citizens, and in general foreign minors, who represent a fast-growing percentage of the total student population (Censis 1990:172, Table 66; 1998:160–61, Tables 34, 36; 1999:151, 152, 154, 160, Tables 20, 22, 26). In particular, the continuous growth of the proportion of young people who enter high school meets the objective of equalizing the opportunities of access to high school education. From a little more than three-fourths in 1982–83 this percentage increased to over 92 percent in 1996–97, and to almost 95 percent in 1997–98 (Bentivegna 1990:373, Table 20; Censis 1998:161, Table 36; 1999:153, Table 24).

The overall growth in the schooling rate has not, however, prevented the persistence of inequalities in educational opportunities, both in terms of quality (cultural prestige of the type of education) and quantity (overall education period).[21] Regarding quantity, the employment status and the educational degree of parents keep heavily influencing the educational level achieved by their children, as in the past. Nonetheless, the by now almost universal junior high school diploma, and a generalized access to high school education, have shifted the advantage of a privileged social origin toward higher educational levels (high school diploma and university degree), for they are less frequently achieved. A privileged social origin leads nowadays, accordingly, to higher educational levels than before, but there has been no relative improvement in the educational opportunities of those having an unprivileged social origin. The probability of not being able to successfully complete one's studies, and consequently the dropout rate, are growing according to the educational level. A little more than one-fourth do not continue their education after the junior high school diploma, but over 60 percent do not continue their studies after completing high school (Censis 1998:123, Picture 1).

As for quality, since the early 1980s a constant relation—probably already existing before—has been noted between the students' social privilege, and the cultural prestige of their education. The children of parents with a modest cultural level and with low job prestige generally turn to professional and technical institutes (Cobalti 1996; Gasperoni 1997:33–38; Shavit and Westerbeeck 1997; Trivellato 1984:211–14). In turn, the level of education has been and continues to be related to the level of job attained, even disregarding the original social background (Schizzerotto 1988, 1994). Therefore, in Italy there is a transmission, which is partly mediated by the school system, of relative deprivation from one generation to another.

This condition of the social structure, which is not generally considered desirable, does not seem to have been substantially moderated by the establishment of professional training courses. These are mostly organized by the regions or through contributions from regional funds, in addition to funds from the European Social Fund. As a matter of fact, training activities provided by local authorities "too often turn into a sort of fragmentation, scarcely aware of the needs of both the labor market, and those who ask for training" (Negri and Saraceno 1996:240–41; cf. also Bàculo

1997:410; Censis 1998:191–92). The need for further training for almost 40 percent of the new employment that was foreseen in 1998–99 underlined the limited usefulness of these professional training courses for companies. The percentage of newly employed persons who need training grows fast in correspondence with their schooling rate. In fact, as many as 68 percent of university graduates need training (Censis 1998:150–51 and Table 30).

The benefits of the policies concerning *health* can scarcely be evaluated, since up to now the National Health Service has not committed itself to caring for the public health needs of non–European Union citizens. For European Union citizens, the coverage is in any case incomplete in terms of services provided and financial support. The gradual improvement of health conditions in Italy is an established fact, as the lowering of the child mortality rate and the growth of life expectancy indicate. The child mortality rate has steadily decreased from almost 30 percent in 1970 to less than 15 percent in 1980, about 8 percent in 1990, 7 percent in 1995, 5.5 percent in 1997, and 5.3 percent in 1998 (Censis 1994:337, Table 26, 1998:302, Table 15, 1999:315, Table 24; World Health Organization 1996:A-6, Table A-1). Life expectancy has also grown. It was estimated to be over seventy-eight years in 1995, with an increase of about four years for both sexes in comparison with 1981 (ISTAT 1996:21; World Health Organization 1996:A-6, Table A-1). However, the difference in health (measured by the life expectancy) of persons with different educational degrees seems to have grown to the benefit of those who are better educated.

Considering the strong relation between education and social class, this difference in health conditions, and even more so its growth, is evidence that there is not coverage of health needs for all citizens, without distinction. The universalistic goal, which in 1978 inspired the establishment of the National Health Service, has then not been fully achieved. The neediest and less-educated strata seem to find it difficult to completely exploit the available free medical resources (or those available at reduced fees). Moreover, they are more frequently exposed to unhealthy life conditions. They also live in areas in which there are fewer and lower quality public (or operating within public health) health services. There are still considerable differences between the center-north and the south of Italy regarding the provision of medical services, particularly preventive medicine, and therefore in the health conditions of the population (Negri and Saraceno 1996:189–206).

The reform of public health was implemented through law decrees 502/1992 and 517/1993, subsequent regulations (ministerial decrees of 15 April 1994 and 14 December 1994; ministerial guidelines 1/1995, law 419/1998), and the regional decentralization of the management and financial control authority. The reform introduced entrepreneurial principles into public health management. The new legislation has not thus far achieved the benefit of reducing the expenditure of the National Health

Service and the local health units. On the contrary, this expenditure has grown considerably, both in absolute terms and in comparison with the gross national income, in the years that immediately followed the reform (1996 and 1997). Nor has it increased users' satisfaction. This is usually rather high, with regard to the services provided by the public and private health service, but in most cases the reform does not seem to have produced any substantial changes in this opinion (Censis 1998:262, 318–19, Tables 27, 29). Furthermore, it has the worrisome ability to generate perverse effects in terms of health service expenditure and quality of provided services (these perverse effects and the ways legislators have tried to control them will be later discussed). On the other hand, this reform has succeeded in eliminating a perverse effect produced by the previous public health law system, for it encouraged the expansion of the quantity of employed resources, and hence health expenditure (Albini 1999; Vanara 1997:25).

The Prevalence of Drugs in Italy

The failure of drug prevention and rehabilitation policies through reintroduction of users and addicts into society, particularly into the educational system and the labor market, is longstanding. Prevention was carried out in schools during the 1980s through public financing in the name of "an emergency ideology" (Ravenna 1993:320). However, according to the IARD (Investment Adviser Registration Depository), a research institute, reports on the condition of youth in Italy based on a very large sample, it did not prevent a growth in percentage from 1983 to 1992, and particularly from 1987 to 1992, of fifteen- to twenty-four-year-olds who considered marijuana use admissible. These youth did not even rule out the possibility that they might actually also use marijuana. Nor did it prevent an increased exposition of youth to environments in which drugs circulate. Open-minded attitudes were less frequent only with regard to heroin (Cavalli and de Lillo 1993:200–4). The following, more recent report has pointed out that—in comparison to the 1992 report—"the transactions concerning hashish and marijuana are on the increase, but those concerning heroin and cocaine are stable" (Buzzi 1997:189, note 7). But, as we shall see, that stability has been merely relative.

Occasional marijuana smokers (or rather, those who do not rule out the possibility for themselves) went from 6.3 percent in 1987 to 11.6 percent in 1992, and to 19.3 percent in 1996. Moreover, while in 1987 those who had contacts with drug users were a minority among the young, they became a majority in 1996. Furthermore, since the 1980s, an increasingly high number of young people have been offered to try or buy drugs (36.8 percent in 1996 in comparison with 21.1 percent in 1983). Also, the percentage of those who wish or have the fancy to experiment with this kind of substances has grown as well (from 4.5 percent in 1987 to 14 percent in 1996). If estimates are reliable, the number of users of the so-called new drugs of synthetic origin is relatively high. This number is estimated at about 400,000 subjects. The estimate, if correct, would indicate a consumer population of about 1 percent out of the whole Italian population in the fourteen to sixty-five age segment, and therefore a much higher proportion within the juvenile population (Bagozzi 1999:21; Censis 1999:314, Table 23; Piccone Stella 1999:41). However, a lack of estimates using the same criteria in other countries does not allow a comparison. Finally, the personal willingness to take heavy drugs is limited to a restricted minority, which is however growing, from 0.9 percent in 1987 to 1.4 percent, to 2.1 percent in 1996 (Buzzi 1997:186–90; Buzzi, Cavalli, and de Lillo 1997:421, 443–45).[22]

The past and present number of Italian drug addicts is still unknown: estimates on this subject are uncertain and divergent since—among other factors—different indicators, which are not always valid measures of this phenomenon, are used.[23] Estimates on opiate drug users—who are not necessarily drug addicts—in the early 1980s range between 100,000–110,000 and 180,000–240,000 subjects (Ravenna 1994:63–66). Current evaluations carried out by the European Monitoring Center on drug addiction and made widely public by the Italian Union for Fighting AIDS seem to indicate that this number is rapidly growing. The number of opiate drug addicts (who are only a part of the overall users) would range in Italy from 180,000 to 313,000 subjects, giving them a prevalence in the general population of 3.3–5.4 percent, the same rate as in the United States. This epidemiological datum is indirectly confirmed by a survey carried out by Adiconsum, a consumers' association, which identified 150,000 families with one or more dependent drug addicts (*La Stampa,* 15 June 1999, p. 16, 19 June 1999, p. 15; cf. also Piccone Stella 1996:587).

An increase in AIDS infections noted by the authorities indicates heroin spreading throughout the country, but also indicates the absence in Italy, at least until the early 1990s, of public policies on health prevention or damage reduction (Piccone Stella 1999:107; Turco 1998:12–13; see also Regione Emilia-Romagna 1996:8; Regione Marche 1996:12; Selmini 1999:129). AIDS cases per 100,000 inhabitants counted in Italy increased from 1.7 percent in 1985 to 4.2 percent in 1990, to 9.6 percent in 1995, and dropped to 5.5 percent in 1997 (Censis 1994:341, Table 30, 1998:307, Table 19). Therefore, it does not seem that the intervention programs provided for by the above-mentioned law 135/1990 were immediately successful. And it is not possible to reasonably say that they proved successful in the long term. On the contrary, they proved completely unsuccessful or even counterproductive, since the decrease in the spreading of AIDS cases that occurred in Italy by the mid-1990s was much lower than the corresponding decrease all over Europe and all over the world.[24]

In light of these data, and particularly bearing in mind the youth's growing inclination to take heavy drugs, the aging of drug addicts provides evidence that contrasts with the opinion of the minister for social solidarity. The evidence is not, in other words, that "the information and sensitization activity addressed to youth through schools and media" has achieved "positive results" (Turco 1998:13). Several years usually pass from the first contacts with heroin or other heavy drugs to the condition of drug addiction. Moreover, the systematic "information and sensitization activity addressed to youth" mentioned by the minister was started after 1990, the year in which law 309/1990 was promulgated. The growth of the average age of drug addicts can therefore be attributed with greater validity to unknown previous factors.

The aging of the drug addict population during the 1990s seems to demonstrate the temporary decrease that occurred for whatever causes in the 1980s (1983–87) in the inclination of youth to take heavy drugs (Cavalli and de Lillo 1988:207–8; Negri and Saraceno 1996:269; Piccone Stella 1999:37–38). The aging of this population occurred also elsewhere, in countries that, compared to Italy and to each other, implemented different prevention policies in terms of contents and historical continuity. Therefore, the causes of this process cannot be easily identified: we shall provide some indications on this subject regarding the benefits of these policies in Sweden, the United States, and Italy in the next chapter.

NOTES

1. For a definition of "uneasiness" as "the manifestation in the new generations of the difficulty of fulfilling the growth tasks that the social context requires of them in order to achieve a personal identity and acquire the necessary skills for a satisfactory management of everyday relations," cf. Neresini and Ranci (1994:131).

2. In this regard, cf. Arzuffi (1991:447–49), Ascoli (1992b:525–26), Devastato (1999:131–34), Pasquinelli (1993:288–89), and Rei (1997:137–39, 141–43). The current government has proposed an intervention plan that still includes prevention and rehabilitation, but limits methadone distribution and confers a greater role on the rehabilitation communities (*La Stampa,* 15 February 2002, p. 6).

3. For a recent introduction to the theme of the "third sector," particularly focused on the norms that regulate it, cf. Devastato (1999).

4. Cf. Censis (1998:267–69), Colozzi (1994:159–61), Commissione d'indagine sulla povertà e l'emarginazione (1995), Negri and Saraceno (1996:52–54), Nevola (1991:175–78), and Saraceno (1999:61–64).

5. Cf. Commissione d'indagine sulla povertà e l'emarginazione (1992:109–15), Negri and Saraceno (1996:37–38), Rei (1997:122), and Saraceno (1995:46–49).

6. We disregard here the liberalization of the labor market that the current government has decided to carry out, if parliament consents to it (*La Stampa,* 12 April 2002, p. 11). For all information concerning labor policies enacted in Italy, cf. Censis (1994:246–49, 1998:218–20, 1999:213–15), CNEL (1994:85–90), ISFOL (1999:75–90), *La Stampa* (13 January 2000, p. 16), Negri and Saraceno (1996:57–85, 99), and Reyneri (1996:Chapters 11 and 12). The book by Negri and Saraceno, which in-

cludes one of the best introductions to this subject in terms of thoroughness and clarity, considers mobility lists only as a measure of passive labor policy. This opinion is justified when these lists are considered as an income protection tool for the unemployed, whereas "the goal . . . of facilitating a reintroduction in the labor market" (1996:69) places these lists among active policy measures. With regard to the new law on immigration (text and comments), cf. *Come* [1 March 1998, 53 (monograph issue), 15 March 1998, 54, p. 7]. Regarding social or placement cooperatives, cf. also Rei (1997:141–43), particularly on the reintroduction of drug addicts in the labor market; cf. also the speech of the Minister for Social Solidarity at the 12th Commission of the Chamber of Deputies, in *Forum* (1998, 11:10).

7. For an introduction to the provisions of the law regulating the housing market in Italy, cf. Negri and Saraceno (1996:157–60).

8. For a distinction between quantitative and distributive housing policies, cf. Tosi (1984:239–42).

9. An introduction to the public policies in force concerning education and professional training can be found in Negri and Saraceno (1996:86, 208–16).

10. Cf. *Corriere della Sera* (21 July 1999, p. 15), ISFOL (1999:330–35), and *La Stampa* (9 July 1999, p. 5, 14 September 1999, p. 13, 23 September 1999, p. 5).

11. The Italian state, like other states, uses the national fiscal system to pay for the deficit of the National Health Service. Regarding public health, in fact, "more or less considerable losses are unavoidable and after all, they affect the whole community" (Coppini, 1994:210–11).

12. The impact evaluation uses consolidated social balance sheets that report the services provided by different entities to the same recipients (Rei 1997:47).

13. Cf. on this subject Censis (1998:328, Table 42), Labos (1993:62–66, 102–7), Negri and Saraceno (1996:270–71, and Table 7.6), and Piccone Stella (1999:79–90).

14. A special committee at the Ministry of Justice is currently studying "therapeutic programs outside the prison structures," whose effects cannot be evaluated so far (Turco 1998:11).

15. Cf. Censis (1999:58), Commissione d'indagine sulla povertà e l'emarginazione (1992:25–45), ISTAT (1998:87–105), *La Stampa* (15 July 1999, p. 3, 26 May 2002, p. 18), Negri and Saraceno (1996:119–55), and Saraceno (1999:56–60, 2002:86).

16. Cf. Cavalli and de Lillo (1988:36, Table II.a), Censis (1990:275, Table 31, 1994:259, Table 24, 1998:234, Table 25), ISFOL (1999:310–11), and ISTAT (1998:189). The figures concerning youth unemployment provided by Censis are not perfectly comparable, since the definition of "young" changes. According to less recent ISTAT sources, this term refers to persons included in the fourteen to twenty-nine age group (cf. Censis, 1990:275, Table 31). However, in ISTAT sources from 1993 on, this term refers to the fifteen to twenty-nine age group (cf. Censis 1994:259, Table 24).

17. In 1998, the number of new part-time workers who entered the labor market totaled 1,478,000, and 1,246,000 limited-duration-job workers. In 1999, these figures, respectively, grew to 1,631,000 and 1,447,000, an increase in the total number of the employed workforce of, respectively, 7.9 and 7 percent. Cf. Censis (1998:239, Table 30, 1999:187, 188, Table 3), ISFOL (1999:75–76, 85).

18. Concerning the failure of prevention activities carried out in schools, cf. Battaglia and Coletti (1987:39–43). As for the doubtful, and in any case unchecked, success of the rehabilitation interventions carried out in the 1980s, cf. Cagossi (1988:262–63) and Ravenna (1993:320–21).

19. An early 1980s inquiry concerning some hundreds of drug addicts from Bologna who had turned to a public therapeutic center demonstrated in fact that 31 percent of them—in the fourteen to twenty-three age group—were neither studying nor working (Simoni 1985:100–1). On the contrary, another contemporary study of a national youth sample in the fifteen to twenty-four age group found only 25 percent neither studying nor working (Cavalli and de Lillo 1988:173, Table 15b).

20. Until 1 January 1998, the minimum monthly pension totaled 626,450 lire. The proportion of pensions that were equal to or lower than this minimum amount was 28.6 percent (cf. Censis, 1998:324, Table 36).

21. In fact, "similar educational coverage levels may conceal considerable qualitative differences" (Trivellato 1984:213).

22. Compared to IARD's inquiry, another empirical inquiry, also concerning the percentage of young people who, in 1987, had direct or indirect contacts with drugs, provided a greater or smaller difference in results, depending on the particular category of young people and drugs that have been considered (Chiari, Francescutti, and Libralato 1992). In fact, the inquiry carried out by Chiari et al. showed less frequent contact with drugs (Buzzi, Cavalli, and de Lillo, 1997:425, Table 34; Chiari, Francescutti, and Libralato, 1992:92, Table 3). This difference might be explained either by the younger age of the sample (14–19 as opposed to 25–24 years in IARD's sample), by different sampling procedures (in particular, the sample of the inquiry by Chiari et al. overrepresents the student population), or finally by a more limited representativeness of the sample in Chiari et al. That inquiry was aimed at representing the young living in the area of Pordenone, instead of Italian youth in general. On the other hand, the sample in Chiari et al. provides precious information on drug consumption among the student population. This information will be used during international comparisons and cannot be found in IARD's inquiry.

23. In particular, the increase in drug addicts under treatment at the public health services should not necessarily be considered an indicator of an increase in heavy drug consumption, since it might also be "an effect of growing information on the problem of drug addiction" (Negri and Saraceno 1996:268).

24. In Italy, the decrease in cases from 1995 to 1996, a rate of about 14 percent, is lower than the 21.5 percent rate recorded all over Europe and the 41 percent rate recorded all over the world during the same period (United Nations, Department of Economic and Social Affairs, Statistics Division, 1997:101, 107).

7   The Benefits of the Social Policies

A Comparison

BENEFITS OF SOCIAL POLICIES: A COMPARISON AMONG
ITALY, THE UNITED STATES, AND SWEDEN

In making a comparison, we shall first of all examine rehabilitation and secondary prevention policies, and then primary prevention policies. A systematic and centralized drug addict rehabilitation policy began in Italy through the progressive implementation of law 309/1990, and was carried out mainly by regional authorities, often in cooperation with the so-called nonprofit sector. Before this law, however, rehabilitation activities—in the sense of social reinsertion—were already being carried out by therapeutic communities through public financing, whereas methadone was administrated by local social-sanitary units and by hospitals. The goal was to create the physical conditions for the social reinsertion of drug addicts. In contrast with what happened in the United States, the Italian authorities, by entrusting this task to organizations of the National Health Service, never discouraged the administration of methadone, trying on the contrary to make it available.

As in the United States, however, the lack of a unitary regulatory framework before law 309/1990 had allowed a number of public and private initiatives—the latter often partially financed by public support—on detoxification and social rehabilitation. It had also produced, however, their fragmentation and spread, jeopardizing in this way their effectiveness, and making it difficult to publicly monitor their management. Law 309/1990, together with the laws of the early 1990s on public acknowledgment, regulation, and financing of nonprofit associations, provided the previously absent normative framework. This would have allowed, in principle, the benefits of Italian drug policies to approximate the corresponding Swedish policies, which also follow normative provisions, and to mark on the contrary their distance from the American policies, which do not have a unitary character. However, far fewer overall benefits are ac-

151

tually provided in Italy, even considering only rehabilitation and secondary prevention.

The very fast growth in the last fifteen years of the number of drug addicts who have undergone treatment provided by public health services has been much higher than the growth either of the number of those who turn to therapeutic communities or of the assumed overall number of drug addicts. This suggests that Italian authorities have been more successful, in comparison with the U.S. ones, in pursuing the objective of the detoxification of all drug addicts. It is an objective the United States has never seriously pursued at any administrative level, though the specialized literature agrees in reporting the effectiveness of treatments, even without detoxification, for the social rehabilitation of drug addicts.

There were about 94,000 drug addicts under treatment in Italy as late as 31 March 1994 (perhaps 30 percent out of the overall number) and their number increased to 138,000 subjects in 1999 (almost all exclusively or mainly heroin addicts), apparently without any significant variations in the overall number of the overall addict population. In the United States, on the contrary, 115,000 drug addicts were undergoing treatment (perhaps 1 percent out of all drug addicts with a frequency of use of at least once a month with regard to opiate derivatives, and about 15–20 percent of the subjects who use heroin at least once a week). Another indicator of the different commitment to rehabilitation is a more limited geographical distribution in the United States of treatment centers: while they have been located for many years throughout Italy, in 1993 they were present in the United States in only forty out of the fifty states (Censis 1994:367, Table 55; Grosso 1999:37; *La Stampa,* 17 January 2000, p. 5).

In comparison with Italy, however, Sweden has pursued the goal of detoxification with greater determination, and for a longer time. This is the only country in which, since the early 1980s, the authorities have tried—apparently with good results—to approach all drug abusers in order to detoxify them, whereas in Italy this task has been entrusted for the time being to local initiatives, leaving at the national level only a simple intention proclaimed by the minister for social solidarity (Piccone Stella 1999:43–44; Turco 1998:9). Again, Sweden anticipated Italy by many years in carrying out systematic prevention activity in secondary schools, which in Italy had been previously left to local initiatives, as it still is in the United States. Sweden is also the only country in which the government has decided to implement a systematic efficiency evaluation of rehabilitation and detoxification programs.

Also regarding primary drug prevention programs, which are general welfare programs, Italian authorities have neither achieved the benefits obtained in Sweden, nor in some cases have they intended to do so. In comparison with Sweden (but not with the United States), Italy is a country with a relatively pronounced inequality in the distribution of income, and hence with a high relative deprivation (ISTAT 1996:44–45; for the United States, cf. Danziger and Gottschalk 1995:42, Table 3.1). Nevertheless, as we shall later see, benefits have been considerable in the area of public health. Though lower than in Sweden, they have been higher than those of the United States, despite its higher per capita income. Public health, together with education, is the only area among social services that is granted as a citizenship right. It is the only one in which Italy has approximated the Swedish welfare system. Since the public provision of a minimum income for the purpose of reinsertion into society has an experimental nature, social assistance in Italy is not yet a right that is fully exercised by all entitled citizens.

Concerning the elderly and some other protected categories, money transfers for the purpose of social assistance (if not integrated by other kinds of income, and particularly by social insurance money transfers) are in any case insufficient.[1] The proportion of the Italian population below the poverty line—10–12 percent—though by some percentage points lower than the U.S. one, is from two to four times higher (depending on the calculation criteria) than the corresponding share of Swedish population.[2] The better results of the Swedish assistance system in comparison with the Italian system not only derive from a greater amount of subsidies and from the existing reintroduction active policies for those who are assisted, but also from the universalistic character of the assistance services, in contrast with differentiated access in Italy, depending on entitlement categories, the budget constraints of municipalities, and the decisions made by individual social workers (Kazepov 1999:110–12).

In the absence of an adequate unemployment subsidy, the effectiveness of passive policies against unemployment in granting an income to the unemployed is limited to the minority of unemployed persons who succeed in getting this benefit. Even for them, this effectiveness is usually limited to very meager income transfers. Often, the other unemployed are left in a condition of poverty. Income transfers to the unemployed are not enough to keep them above the poverty line, and do not include the total number or even the majority of the unemployed. Italy and the United States share this condition, though only in the latter is there a real unemployment subsidy. In contrast, the liberality and breadth of these subsidies are more than adequate in Sweden. The modest restrictions introduced during the first half of the 1990s were later partially canceled.

We cannot find throughout the 1990s a linear connection between commitment to active labor policies (measured by appropriation related to gross national income) and unemployment rate (either overall or long-term unemployment). In comparison with Italy and Sweden, since 1993 there has been a lower overall and long-term unemployment rate in the United States, to which a minimum appropriation has corresponded. Yet— as previously mentioned—in comparison to Sweden, the new jobs created in the United States have been mainly of a lower quality with regard to wages, stability, and degree of social protection, and the difference between unemployment rates in the United States and Sweden considerably diminished in 1998.

On the other hand, Sweden—which more than any other country has been committed to active policies—has continuously had a lower unemployment rate than Italy. The high Italian unemployment rate stands out (with 12 percent in spring 1999, it was nearly twice the Swedish rate, which was 6.8 percent, and three times the American rate, which was 4.2 percent). In particular, long-term unemployment, two-thirds of the total, was about four times higher than in Sweden, and seven times higher than the rate in the United States (which is, however, underestimated). The jobs available in Italy for the majority of the young are not only precarious, but are also characterized by low wages and low skill qualifications. Accordingly, they are not adapted to professional training (*La Stampa*, 27 June 1999, p. 3, 7 July 1999, p. 16; Reyneri 1996:188–91), as they are in the United States. Unemployment of youth, which has remained steady, never went below 27 percent in the period 1991–97, reaching 33 percent in 1997 and 32 percent in May 1999: it is a lower overall rate than in the United States, but higher than in Sweden.[3]

Since there has never been in Italy a labor policy aimed at encouraging women's entry into the labor market (unlike what has been tried on behalf of the young) we cannot, strictly speaking, examine the benefits. Nevertheless, we should consider the consequences of this absence of social policies on the rate of women's labor, that is, women's share of the overall labor force. Regarding the characteristics of women's participation in the labor market and its impact on family income, Italy is in some aspects in a particularly unfavorable position. In some other aspects it is closer to the United States than to Sweden, though since the 1970s some of these characteristics have rendered Italy closer to Sweden. In particular:[4]

1. Throughout the 1970s and 1980s, the rate of women's participation in the labor force in Italy was much lower than in the United States, and even lower than in Sweden. In the 1990s, however, the rate of women's participation in Sweden stagnated at about 50 percent, and decreased after 1994 to about 48 percent (which is in any case one of the highest rates anywhere in the world). The continuously growing American rate was in 1996 only two percentage points lower than in Sweden, and finally, the Italian rate, also continuously rising, reached about 31 percent in 1991 and about 35 percent in 1998 (44 percent according to different sources). This rate was still much lower than the rate of the two other countries and than the European average rate. This figure suggests that double-income families, which are "optimum from the point of view of [reducing] poverty" (Esping-Andersen 1997:43–44), are less frequent in Italy. Part-time jobs meet the requirements of mothers with under age children particularly well. Their

relatively scarce diffusion within the Italian labor force, and particularly the female labor force, has contributed to this condition (Censis 1999:22, Table 12; *La Stampa,* 27 June 1999, p. 3; OECD 1997:178, Table F). On the other hand, in Italy—as in other Mediterranean countries, but not as in Sweden—part-time jobs are often precarious (Reyneri 1996:99). Therefore, they can hardly enable women to give a substantial and lasting contribution to their husbands' income.

2. This conclusion is strengthened if we bear in mind that women's contribution to family income depends in Italy, more than on their active participation in the labor market, on their unemployment rates, which are comparatively much higher. In fact, in 1997, unemployment affected about 17 percent of Italian working women in comparison with about 8 percent of Swedish women and 5 percent of American women. We should also consider that Italian women's unemployment is long-term in two-thirds of the cases, and is more frequent than in the other two countries.[5] Also for this aspect, Italy is in a particularly unfavorable position.

3. Most Italian unemployed women (similarly to men) are not in a position to contribute to family income. Similar to but even more pronounced than in the United States, for most of the unemployed of both sexes there are in Italy not sufficiently widespread, liberal, or lasting unemployment benefits, nor are there any other effective measure for the protection of family income. Family allowances would be a case in point, if they were not so meager and given only to the unemployed who had previously a regular job (Saraceno 1995:48–49). Accordingly, the unemployed female labor force in Italy shares with the United States a condition of relative privation, and sometimes even of absolute deprivation.

4. Nonetheless, Italy shares with Sweden a high concentration of female labor force in the service sector, particularly in public administration. In Italy, too, as in Scandinavia, "We can say that the offer of women's labor has created at least in part a demand for it" (Reyneri 1996:118). As a matter of fact, public and private (but often with public financial support) welfare services, mainly carried out by female personnel, have made it possible for many women who are engaged in work away from home to meet their family demands.

From a comparative point of view, the inadequacies of the public housing policies implemented in Italy closely resemble those noted in the United States. In both countries, the serious lack of public housing has been made worse since 1980s by the sales to the existing tenants of apartments that have not been replaced by new buildings. As a consequence, the majority of the needy population cannot secure an apartment at reasonable rent, nor has it been substantially aided in covering the costs of renting a house on the market. All this has happened although these public policies have been directed at meeting the accommodation requirements of those who cannot turn to the market. Authorities, furthermore, have built new

public housing at reduced rents, have allocated subsidies for paying market rents to tenants with an insufficient income, and in some cases have
provided them with temporary accommodations in boarding houses or
free hostels. These efforts, however, have been inadequate.

What is more, in both countries, building projects have had from the
start many serious design and maintenance deficiencies, later increased
by inadequate control of antisocial behaviors, and particularly by the lack
of attention of the building managers toward vandalism and defaulting
tenants. In this way, these projects have often become areas with a bad
reputation, decay physically, and criminal activities become widespread.
Among these activities, the sale and use of drugs by residents have a strong
impact on other urban residents and on the police. A much better result has
been achieved by the other objective, shared by the U.S. and Italian decision-makers, of expanding the real estate market by facilitating house purchases (Tosi 1984:259–61). In particular, first-time purchases of houses
have been made easier through low-interest loans and the allocation of
subsidies to private building companies that serve needy customers.

However, the analogy between the results achieved by U.S. and Italian
housing policies is not complete. In comparison with the corresponding
U.S. population, a greater proportion of the economically disadvantaged
Italian population receives some form of public aid. In Italy, the building
of housing projects went on until the last decade, and there has been an attempt to restore buildings keeping the existing tenants, thus avoiding a
gentrification effect (whether perverse even considering the extent of the respective urban populations). On the other hand, in the United States regulations similar to the Italian law on rent control (392/1978), substantially
modified by the introduction of agreements granting exceptions to some
regulations (law 359/1992), have been provided for only some municipalities. The lack of such regulations can be indirectly considered as a benefit.
For law 392/1978 has proved ineffective in attaining its goal of securing
housing at reasonable rental rates for the whole or at least to a great part
of the economically disadvantaged population. It has also shown perverse
effects, which we shall mention later. In spite of these differences, regarding the aim of covering needs, Italian and U.S. public housing policies are
linked by a quantitative and qualitative failure, which is highlighted by a
comparison with the corresponding Swedish policies. In terms of quality
and quantity, public housing in Sweden has very few analogies elsewhere,
and surely not in Italy or in the United States. It must be pointed out,
though, that the political-administrative authorities of Sweden have been
less successful in this case than in some other areas of intervention. They
have not fully succeeded in avoiding some of the inconveniences (long
waiting lists, social and ethnic segregation, crime) that are in any case
much more widespread elsewhere.[6]

Concerning the effectiveness of welfare services in the educational area, and considering them from a comparative point of view, the common goal of equality in educational opportunities has not been achieved in any country. The transmission, partly mediated by the school system, of a given socioeconomic origin (and in case, also of a condition of relative deprivation) from one generation to another does not only occur in Italy, but generally also elsewhere (Schizzerotto 1992:52).

There has been no empirical research that specifically compares, for Italy, the United States, and Sweden, the respective possibilities of securing an elementary and high school education for persons coming from different social classes (no matter how defined).[7] It is possible, however, to resort to indirect indicators of how socially accessible, and in this sense how effective, are the educational institutions in these countries. The enrollment rates in primary and secondary schools are one indirect indicator of effectiveness. In Italy—despite a continuous and rapid growth—this rate not only remains lower than the average rate of the European Union countries, but also much lower than the corresponding enrollment rates in the United States and Sweden (Censis 1998:171, Table 54; UNESCO 1997, I-4, I-8).

Another indirect indicator of effectiveness derives from the conclusions of two studies. They examined first of all the change in the influence of social origin on educational opportunities (measured by the number of education years, and by the possibility of transition to higher levels of schooling) over the years in a number of countries, among which Italy, Sweden, and the United States. Second, they examined and compared the present influence of social origin on educational opportunities in some countries, including Sweden and the United States, but not Italy. The first study showed an overall continuous or growing influence (depending on the school level) of social origins on educational opportunities in the United States, a continuous influence in Italy, and a decreasing influence in Sweden. The second study showed that in Sweden the influence of social origins on educational opportunities is relatively low, and in particular, lower than in the United States (Blossfeld and Shavit 1992:165–71; Goldthorpe 1996:495–500).[8]

Examination of the two studies, bearing in mind the strong influence that social origins have on educational opportunities in Italy, yields the following conclusions. The influence of social origin is greater in Italy than in Sweden, but it is roughly as strong in Italy as in the United States, taking into account that in the United States it has been historically growing, and is currently stronger than in Sweden. Considering all the indirect indicators of effectiveness of the respective school systems, in view of the common goal of providing equal educational opportunities to the whole population, Sweden has the most effective educational system, Italy the least effective, while the United States holds an intermediate position.

Health policy is the only area in which Italian policies are not only favorably comparable to the corresponding U.S. policies in terms of their results, that is, their effectiveness, but are also sometimes not very far in this respect from Swedish policies. We now compare the following conventional indicators of efficiency of the respective public health policies. These indicators are supplied by international sources, taking 1995 as reference year:

1. In 1995, the rates of child mortality, both within the first year and the fifth year of life, were minimum in Sweden, and slightly higher in the United States and in Italy (in the first year, 6.9 percent live births in the United States and 7 percent in Italy, against 5.5 percent in Sweden, according to sources of the World Health Organization).[9] The differences among Sweden, Italy, and United States decreased, without however disappearing, throughout the 1980s and the 1990s. Italy, in particular, achieved considerable progress in this regard, shortening the distance with Sweden and other economically developed countries. In 1970, in comparison with a 23.4 percent average rate of child mortality within the first year of life among the current fifteen member countries of the European Union, the Swedish rate was 11 percent (the lowest), while the Italian rate was 29.6 percent, 2.7 times higher than the Swedish rate. In 1998, the average European rate was 5.2 percent, the Swedish rate was 3.5 percent (still the lowest and the only one below 4 percent), and finally the Italian rate was 5.3 percent, almost in line with the European average rate and only one and a half times higher than the Swedish rate.

2. Life expectancy at birth was in 1995, according to the figures provided by the World Health Organization, the highest in Sweden with seventy-nine years, only seven to eight months lower in Italy, but lower by over two years in the United States.[10]

3. AIDS cases in Italy ranged between 6.7 and 9.6 per 100,000 inhabitants from 1991 to 1995, and dropped to 5.6 in 1997 and to 3.2 in 1998. For comparative purposes, the data on Italy, Sweden, and the United States are obtained from a single source, the *United Nations Statistical Yearbook*. Also, we consider both the average annual number of AIDS cases made public by health authorities for the years 1995 and 1996, and the total number of cases through December 1996. We are able to draw some interesting conclusions on relationships between the respective prevalence rates and, indirectly, on the effectiveness of the respective health policies on the prevention of drug addiction. An annual average rate of 9.1 AIDS cases per 100,000 inhabitants were obtained in Italy in the period 1995–96. Accordingly, Italy holds an intermediate position between the United States (18.5 cases per 100,000 inhabitants, more than twice as much as Italy) and Sweden (1.8 cases per 100,000 inhabitants, about one-fifth the rate of Italy and one-tenth that of the United States).

The total number of cases per 100,000 inhabitants through December 1996–220.1 in the United States, 66.1 in Italy, 16.6 in Sweden—confirms the intermediate position of Italy, but also indicates that by the mid-1990s Italy's rate approached that of the United States and drew further away from that of Sweden, thus worsening its position. Among those who contracted the infection, an unknown percentage, perhaps one-third (like in the United States) or one-fourth (like in Sweden), included drug addicts.[11]

Similar results can be drawn from a comparative analysis of the prevalence of drug addiction in these three countries. The previously reported data, though for the last decade, often involve different years, and the reliability of statistics on this subject is usually low. Bearing this in mind, throughout the 1990s the data on the number of regular heroin users were as follows: 0.3–0.7 percent in Sweden, 2.5 percent in the United States, and 3.3–5.4 percent in Italy (but this refers to the wider number of all opiate addicts).

Among the latter addicts, we can, however, reasonably guess that a non-negligible number (perhaps somewhat over one-seventh, as in Sweden, according to official estimates made in the early 1990s)[12] include exclusively or also heroin addicts, considering the marked ability of this substance to create addiction, if regularly used (Trad 1994:163). The prevalence of heroin addicts in Italy is thus roughly intermediate between the estimated rates in the United States and Sweden. Similarly, if we consider the overall number of opiate addicts, the evaluation of the respective rates—about 20 percent in the United States, 3.3–5.4 percent in Italy, 1.5–2 percent in Sweden—also demonstrates Italy's intermediate position in comparison with the other two countries. Referring to the widest estimate among those we previously reported, the total number of opiate addicts in each country would be 313,000 in Italy, 6,000,000 in the United States, and 20,000 in Sweden. The respective rates would be therefore 5.4, 23, and 2 percent. This would involve, as for Italy, a rate almost three times higher and, for the United States, a rate eleven times higher than in Sweden.

THE COSTS OF SOCIAL POLICIES: A COMPARISON OF ITALY, THE UNITED STATES, AND SWEDEN

A consideration of the costs of Italian policies in comparison with the corresponding American and Swedish policies is necessary for evaluating their respective efficiency. The impact on the national income of the respective public expenditure on social welfare is an indicator of public commitment in this direction. According to Eurostat sources referring to the period 1992–96, the share of gross national income absorbed in Italy by social protection, that is by the national welfare system, totals about 25 percent with a slight tendency to decrease in comparison with the previous decade. It indicates an overall expenditure that is much lower than the corresponding Swedish one, equal to 36–38 percent of the GDP (gross do-

mestic product) with a stronger tendency to decrease. Lower, too, is the
share of GDP absorbed in Italy by taxes and social (insurance) contributions, totaling 43.5 percent in 1998 (a large increase compared to 29.5 percent in 1979, though substantially steady since 1996), against a 53 percent
share in Sweden in 1998 (a slight increase compared to 49 percent in 1979).

The Italian share of GDP engaged in social protection expenditure
(about 25 percent, as previously stated) is, on the other hand, higher than
the corresponding proportion of the U.S. GDP, totaling about 20 percent,
without significant changes from 1975 to 1995.

The heavy cuts in social programs decided in the early 1980s under Reagan's presidency were, in fact, partly canceled by subsequent federal laws.
With a 43.5 percent rate compared to 28.5 percent in the United States (a
modest increase compared to about 26 percent during the period 1976–86),
the share of GDP absorbed in Italy by taxes and social (insurance) contributions is much higher, too.[13]

In Italy, however, as elsewhere, the major part of social expenditure is
allocated for social insurance purposes and has therefore neither the aim
nor the effect of socially redistributing income, or life opportunities in general. The share of public expenditure strictly directed to social assistance
engaged in 1997 a little more than 3 percent of the total Italian expenditure
for social protection, and about 0.8 percent of the GDP. These percentages
were, respectively, less than 3 and 0.7 percent in 1998 (Censis 1998:311, 313,
Tables 21, 23, 1999:329–30, Tables 45–46). This share of public expenditure
for assistance is allocated in the form of social pensions and social assistance to counteract an acknowledged condition of economic discomfort,
and therefore is net of money transfers for persons considered in need of
economic support because of physical disabilities.

The latter percentage is lower in comparison with the U.S. one, which
covers a larger share of the population. In both countries, public assistance
is inadequate to raise persons and families over the official poverty line.
The share of GDP spent for mere assistance purposes in Italy is, on the
other hand, slightly higher than in Sweden. In Sweden the much lower
proportion of needy people, however, is assisted with much greater liberality, not only regarding money transfers. Sweden and Italy traditionally
have a "social" orientation in public expenditure, but a different orientation in their respective welfare systems (Esping-Andersen 1990:27–28). In
this regard, a comparison between the two countries is significant for the
share of GDP allocated to finance the provision of social services. In 1995,
these shares were, respectively, 8.2 percent in Sweden and 3.3 percent in
Italy (National Board of Health and Welfare 1996:179, Table 5; Economist
Intelligence Unit 1996:3; Censis 1998:312, Table 22).

The majority of money transfers for the benefit of families is included in
the Italian assistance expenditure. It is necessary to add to family allowances, which are an important component of this expenditure, further

allowances for maternity (borne by social insurance) and for nursery schools (borne by local authorities). The overall benefits to families have absorbed a decreasing share of gross national income, as they dropped from 4 percent in 1960 (compared to 2.8 percent in Sweden and 0.4 percent in the United States) to 1.4 percent in 1980 (compared to 2.2 percent in Sweden and 0.8 percent in the United States). Currently, this share is much lower not only than the corresponding Swedish share, but also than the average share of OECD countries. Nevertheless, Italy is roughly in line with the average OECD rate regarding the value of the aid package provided to

1. children from relatively large and needy families;
2. single-parent families;
3. children in general (like elsewhere, in an inverse relation with family income).

Furthermore, unlike many other European Union countries, and particularly Sweden, in 1996 there was in Italy a substantial increase in the percentage of the average yearly income of a relatively needy couple, with two children of school age, that equals the value of tax allowances and money benefits. The financial law of 1998 (article 3, subparagraph 3) provided for further increases in family allowances. Currently, the rate of this income is higher than the average European rate, whereas it was much lower in 1995 (Bradshaw 1998:105, 113–16; Kamerman and Kahn 1998:81, 95–96; Turco 1998:12).

Italian public expenditure for labor policies, compared to the gross national income, is higher than the U.S. but much lower than the Swedish expenditure. This difference concerns both active policies (in 1997, 1.08 percent of the GDP in Italy, 0.25 percent in the United States, and 2.09 percent in Sweden) and passive policies (0.88 percent for Italy, 0.50 percent for the United States, and 2.16 percent for Sweden). The United States spends therefore relatively little money in labor policies, and concentrates its expenditure for active policies on workfare projects (that is, assistance with compulsory work) and for passive policies on unemployment benefits. In the United States, there is not a systematic commitment to the costs of retraining the marginal labor force to be borne by the public treasury. The U.S. political-administrative authorities have traditionally preferred to entrust to the market the task of absorbing unemployment. Until the end of the 1980s—as previously mentioned—the United States had a higher unemployment rate than the average rate of OECD countries and that of Sweden, whereas during the 1990 this rate decreased. Trusting in the labor market to reduce the unemployment rate has, however, contributed to enlarging the unregulated, as well as its distance from the regulated, labor market, or at least not to contrast the tendency to an ever-greater share of the unregulated labor market. This tendency, though, depends on exogenous economic factors that cannot be controlled by the authorities responsible for economic policy.

The U.S. authorities have rarely had recourse to public expenditure in counteracting unemployment by active policies. Consequently, there is practically no social policy in this sense. It does not then make much sense to comparatively evaluate the efficiency of these policies in terms of public expenditure. The efficiency of passive policies seems modest. Compared to the national income, the commitment of the United States to expenditure is even lower than the commitment of some European Union countries, such as Luxembourg and Holland, which have lower unemployment rates than the United States. This low expenditure commitment corresponds to even less of an ability to confront a condition of economic disadvantage in the unemployed labor force, as unemployment benefits in the United States are often not enough to prevent a condition of poverty. In the United States, though, this disadvantage is more a result of low wages than unemployment. Perhaps the most important factor accounting for the economic disadvantage of the unemployed is, however, that a considerable part of the unemployed labor force does not pay compulsory social insurance contributions, as it works in the informal labor market and is not consequently entitled to receive these subsidies.[14]

A comparison with other countries that spend much more money on labor policies than the United States, such as Italy and Sweden, highlights—as we previously stated—a high and lasting youth and overall unemployment rate in Italy, in comparison with the Swedish rate. This rate has always been lower than the Italian one and has been decreasing for some years. An examination of the specific items of expenditure shows the respective degrees of efficiency in pursuing the common aim of fighting unemployment through public labor policies. With regard to active policies, with reference to the years 1996–97, both countries—but Italy much more than Sweden—seem to financially privilege subsidized labor, which absorbs 56 percent of the overall expenditure in Italy and one-third in Sweden. As regards the rest, however, the respective public expenditure mix is quite different.

Italy has spent almost 40 percent of its budget resources for active policies on measures specifically addressed to youth, against only 1 percent in Sweden. Some of these measures have proven very expensive if compared to their results. In 1993, for example, the funds allocated by law 44/1986 to promote youth entrepreneurship totaled over 1,100 billion lire (approximately $500 million), but resulted in jobs for only 24,000 persons (CNEL 1994:90), at a cost of 46 million lire (approximately $21,000) cost per employed person.[15] On the contrary, Sweden has invested nonnegligible shares of its budget resources for active policies (from one-eighth to one-third, depending on which policy) on measures that in all have absorbed in Italy only one-twentieth of the expenditure for active policies. These measures have involved placement and professional training services, and measures for the disabled (Censis 1998:247, Table 43).

There is a considerable gap—about four percentage points in 1998—between their respective unemployment rates, and a much higher youth unemployment rate (for the fifteen to twenty-four age segment, 22 percent in Sweden in 1997, strongly decreasing in comparison with the preceding years, and 38 percent in Italy, with slight variations in comparison with the preceding years). Furthermore, there is a more reduced incidence of long-term unemployment (in 1997, almost one-fourth of the Italian unemployed had been in this condition for at least four years, against practically nobody in Sweden). All these factors suggest an efficient use of the conspicuous resources allocated in Sweden to reduce unemployment, and an inefficient use of the relatively more modest resources allocated in Italy for this purpose (Censis 1998:245–47, Tables 40–43).

Sweden stands out in comparison with the other two countries with regard to the incidence of public expenditure for education on the GDP. According to UNESCO statistics and with reference to two different years (1994 and 1996), this incidence was respectively 8.4 and 8.3 percent in Sweden, but 5.2 and 4.7 percent in Italy, and 5.5 and 5.4 percent in the United States. In comparison with other European Union countries, Sweden spends a particularly high percentage and Italy a particularly low percentage of the GDP in education in general, especially in subsidies granted to families for this purpose (Censis 1999:92, Table 2).[16] The considerable Swedish expenditure commitment in this field does not correspond to a particularly long average period of school attendance, which is slightly higher than the Italian and much lower than the U.S. attendance period (UNESCO 1997, I-5, I-9; 1998, I-5, I-7, I-8).[17] Considering that the educational opportunities for individuals from the lower classes are relatively good in Sweden, and relatively bad in Italy and in the United States, the United States has successfully striven to keep the majority of the population in school as long as possible, neglecting the others. In Sweden, efforts have been mainly focused on the goal—achieved to some extent, though particularly onerous in financial terms—of also allowing the possibility of access to high school education to socially disadvantaged persons. Finally, there has been a lower expenditure commitment in Italy, and correspondingly poorer results, to the goal of providing high school education to a large number of citizens, and also allowing individuals from the lower classes the opportunity to reach this educational level. On the other hand, the Italian authorities have institutionally aimed only at the latter, and not at the former objective.

Regarding health, the public expenditure commitment in Italy, compared to the gross national income, totaled about 5–6 percent throughout the 1980s and the 1990s, and 5.5 percent in 1997 and 1998. This expenditure commitment, as well as the overall one (including private health and totaling in 1997 7.5 percent of the GDP), was and continues to be (compared to the gross national income, and in terms of expenditure per inhabitant) close to the average rate of the European Union countries. In recent years, it has even approached Sweden (totaling in turn 7.5 percent of the GDP in 1995, a decrease due to a 21 percent reduction in public health expenditure from 1990 to 1994). It is much lower, though, than the corresponding expenditure commitment in the United States (currently estimated at about 13 percent of the gross national income). Public health absorbs 70 percent of the overall health expenditure in Italy, against 84 percent in Sweden (a decrease compared to 91–92 percent during the 1980s) and about 40 percent in the United States. A comparison among the respective amounts of health expenditure based on the purchasing power of the respective countries gives similar results. In 1990, the individual health expenditure rate, as a percentage of the corresponding expenditure rate in the United States was 56 percent in Sweden and 49.8 percent in Italy.[18]

Despite different forms of welfare mix within health services in all three countries, health service is mostly public in Italy and even more so in Sweden, whereas in the United States it is mostly private. As previously remarked, Sweden has the most effective health system according to all indicators. Considering the respective rates of child mortality as an indicator, the Italian health system is in line with the U.S. system, but is more effective according to other indicators (average life expectancy, and the spread of drug addiction and AIDS infection). There is apparently a positive relationship between the effectiveness of a national health system and the degree to which public organizations operate within it.

This consideration is partly mitigated by the following further considerations. First of all, the Swedish health system has further increased its effectiveness, in spite of a (moderate) privatization process. Second, the American health system has considerably improved its effectiveness though remaining mainly private. We can therefore state that a prevalently public instead of private management of a health system favors its effectiveness, on condition that this prevalence is not overwhelming. Furthermore, a fair degree of effectiveness (in comparison with other economically developed countries) may also be achieved by a health system that—in terms of health expenditure—prevalently includes private organizations. With reference to Italy, United States, and Sweden, how are effectiveness and efficiency related?

In this regard, we should bear in mind that in Italy and in Sweden the effectiveness of the respective health systems has continued to improve, compared to the past and to other developed countries. A considerable position has been thus achieved in Italy, and an eminent one in Sweden. In Italy, however, health expenditure has been steady for many years. It is currently equal, in comparison with the GDP, to the expenditure of Sweden, which on the contrary has considerably decreased in recent years. We can therefore infer that:

1. The Swedish health system is more effective than the Italian one;

2. Considering that Italian and Swedish health expenditures compared to national income do not move very far from the average expenditure of the European Union countries, the performances of the Swedish health system qualify it as one of the most efficient in the world, and perhaps the most efficient, worldwide;

3. After the recent cuts in expenditure, Sweden seems to have achieved an optimum ratio between cost and performance.

On the contrary, the considerable development in terms of effectiveness of the U.S. health system has been achieved at very high (compared to the GDP), rapidly and continuously growing costs, without (even currently) achieving significant results in the overall health condition of the population. Thus, it turns out to be the most inefficient health system not only in comparison with Sweden, but also to some extent with Italy and the other European Union countries. A relative inefficiency can be noted, too, within the specific area of drug addict rehabilitation.

An efficiency evaluation of the public expenditure in this area is hampered by problems about the validity and reliability of the available statistics on the number of drug addicts and the expenditure commitment to rehabilitate them. The number of drug addicts can hardly be estimated, since the condition of drug addiction is not steady. Furthermore, this condition has not been unequivocally established, confirmed, and recorded over the years, or in a given period, by authorities of different countries, or even of the same country, as long as they remain insufficiently coordinated. The expenditure commitment to rehabilitation also includes in Italy, but not explicitly in Sweden and in the United States, prevention expenditure. Therefore, an efficiency evaluation might only provide results that are merely indicative. Since drug addiction often involves many kinds of substances (most of all in countries like Sweden, where it is difficult to find opiates), we shall not examine in this section the statistics on addiction to a specific substance, such as heroin. Moreover, it is impossible to distinguish the share of budget items engaged in rehabilitation from the share (if present) engaged in prevention.

Bear in mind that expenditure items for the period 1990–92 (in which the data of all three countries are available) are as follows:

- in Italy, 230 billion lire (in 1992, but almost the same amount in the following years), including promotion and rehabilitation activities entrusted to the national and local administrations, and rehabilitation and social reintroduction activities entrusted to the local social-health units and private associations (Corte dei Conti 1996:17–18, Notes 7, 9; Turco 1998:13);
- in Sweden, 2.3 billion crowns (1992) (National Board of Health and Welfare 1994:43);
- in the United States, $3 billion (1990) (Reuter 1998:317–18).[19]

In connection with the GDP for each country and for the reference year, the shares actually allocated to rehabilitation, reintroduction, and prevention are as follows: 0.15 percent in Italy, 0.56 percent in the United States, 1.5 percent in Sweden. These shares of the public expenditure budget should, however, be compared, with great uncertainty, to the assumed number of drug addicts, so as to create a rough indicator of the commitment of the authorities of each country to these aims (rehabilitation, reintroduction, and prevention) with regard to each drug addict. In fact, even a relatively high share of gross national income allocated for these purposes would prove insufficient if drug addicts were a numerically high part of the population, whereas smaller shares would be enough if drug addicts were a small minority.

Using the prevalence rates drawn from the largest estimates of the number of opiate addicts (0.53 percent in Italy, 0.23 percent in the United States, 0.2 percent in Sweden), the following inferences may be drawn. Italy spends (compared to the gross national income) ten times less money than Sweden to socially rehabilitate these addicts, and has almost three times as many opiate addicts. On the contrary, the United States, with a prevalence almost eleven times higher than that of Sweden, spends (compared to the gross national income) less than four-tenths of that money. However, out of the total number of U.S. drug addicts the proportion is unknown (with certainty, not even in Sweden) of those who, after having undergone treatment, have been later actually rehabilitated. Rehabilitation, in this sense, means that they permanently keep away from drug use and have a regular job or family role. The ratio of this proportion as a proportion of the expenditure for rehabilitation, in relation to the gross national income, is consequently also unknown. If this ratio were known, it might become an efficiency indicator.

We might infer from the respective estimates of the rates of opiate addicts a greater efficiency of the Italian compared to the U.S. policies, for Italy proportionally spends about one-fourth as much as the United States, with about one-fifth as many addicts. This would also be the case in comparison with the Swedish policies, because in Italy public expenditure compared to the national income is ten times lower, but the estimated number of drug addicts is less than three times smaller. These would be, however, misleading deductions. Not only are these estimates quite uncertain, except perhaps for Sweden, but also they do not provide any indication of the success rates that these attempts of rehabilitation and social reintroduction (systematically conducted only in Sweden) have achieved in all three countries.

In Italy public expenditure aimed at rehabilitation and social reintroduction of drug addicts and at prevention of the use and abuse of drugs, in comparison with the national income, is one-tenth the expenditure of Sweden. The efficiency of the respective public policies in this area can, however, hardly be evaluated. In fact, their benefits are only approximately known in Sweden or not at all in Italy. That the public expenditure allocated in Italy to rehabilitation and social reintroduction is only one-fourth the expenditure of the United States is an even less indicative evidence of efficiency. This is so not only because in the United States (as in Italy) systematic evaluations of benefits are not available, but also because the estimate of public expenditure does not include, for the United States, expenditures for prevention.

More specifically, the overall proportion of former drug addicts rehabilitated and socially reintroduced is not well known (for Sweden), or only known in a conjectural way (for the other two countries). Only in Sweden has a systematic investigation of the behavior of former drug addicts after their discharge from therapeutic centers (*follow-up studies*) been carried out. More in-depth information has thus been acquired on the rates of discharged persons who abstain from drug use than on those, among them, who succeed in socially reinserting themselves. In the United States and in Italy, on the contrary, these follow-up studies have never been systematically carried out. Fortunately, the few studies done provide useful indications in this sense. The available information on the three countries, and the consequent efficiency evaluations, can be summarized as follows:

(a) Sweden is the only one of the three countries in which social services have succeeded in establishing relations with most opiate addicts (80 percent of whom live in Stockholm, according to an official estimate), alcoholics, or those addicted to a combination of these substances. Sweden is also the only country in which all treatment centers have decided to follow up their patients after discharge. These activities have enormously facilitated welfare authorities in carrying out follow-up studies aimed at achieving reliable effectiveness and efficiency evaluations. These studies concern dozens of rehabilitation centers and many hundreds of former patients, who were followed for six months or one year, depending on the particular study. The conclusions have been summarized in an official Swedish publication, with apparently excessive pessimism, in the phrase "high costs and scarce results" (National Board of Health and Welfare 1994:43). In fact, about 40–50 percent of the patients who are former opiate addicts have abstained from abusing these substances during the follow-up study. The majority of them (over 70 percent) have also abstained from abusing alcohol. The number of successful cases have been much lower for the minority (10–20 percent) of drug addicts who were subjected to a forced treatment. These persons are usually jobless, and mostly homeless, at the moment of their treatment, with no other income but the aid provided by social assistance. After their discharge, these subjects usually find themselves in much better physical and mental condition, and with improved opportunities to find housing and work. While many of them resume their previous life, more than one-fourth of them give up abusing drugs or reduce their use, and roughly the same percentage of them express a willingness to continue treatment. Psychiatric support services, and—after their discharge—-counseling and training services to help them reenter the labor market are in general available to opiate addicts and alcoholics, whether they undergo a voluntary or forced treatment.

Former drug addicts who remain unemployed share with the other unemployed the opportunity to secure work completely or partly financed by the state within the framework of active labor policies. Thus, they become formally a part of the employed labor force. We do not know how many drug addicts have been rehabilitated in this way, but a substantial use of financial resources and skilled personnel has allowed Sweden to achieve—at high costs—noteworthy results in the short term, but lesser ones in the long term. Success mostly depends on the addict's previous work and on the family relations that have not been destroyed by drug addiction. Considering only benefits in terms of social rehabilitation, we can therefore evaluate as intermediate the efficiency of the relevant Swedish policies.[20]

(b) In the United States, the little available information on the biographical course of current and former drug addicts includes both their abstaining from use and their social reintroduction. It shows the great difficulties in which these persons find themselves, as they are generally left to themselves and to their limited psychological, economic, and social personal resources. As in Sweden, nonparticipation in work and family roles very frequently precedes, at the beginning of adulthood, the use of heavy drugs. To this, dropping out of school should also be added, at least in the United States. Unemployment effects have been shown by a longitudinal survey focused on the behavior of a sample of hundreds of persons living in Harlem (New York), and periodically interviewed for over twenty years. It showed that over one-half of all drug addicts, and a little less than one-half of all former drug addicts, are unemployed. This percentage may be compared to about 20 percent of a test group with similar characteristics, but without a past or current of drug addiction. The attention that authorities paid to them has been limited to social control through imprisonment (which 60 percent of the sample group, compared to 20 percent of the test group, has experienced). Furthermore, 40 percent of the sample group has sought treatment one or more times during that period, on its own initiative and often unsuccessfully (there have been twice as many untimely deaths among those who have undergone treatment compared to those who have not).

Usually, the treatment that is most in demand, and generally the only one that can be actually obtained, is the administration of methadone in specialized centers. If these centers are public and free (but also in centers for payment), this administration is not accompanied with psychiatric support activities and can be stopped suddenly if there are not enough funds.

Access to these centers is possible only via a long waiting list, because the number of available places is not proportionate to the demand. Neither further psychiatric support services for former users, nor support from social services, nor any other form of advice and aid are provided for during the relation with the center or after it. It is not surprising that, as the results of the above-mentioned survey show, the unemployment rate of discharged persons is just a little lower than the rate of current users (Brunswick and Titus 1998; Hunt and Rosenbaum 1998). Extremely modest results, and hence a low efficiency of the relevant U.S. policies, correlate with a relatively small financial effort. A scarce allocation of funds, but also the allocation procedures and the presence of perverse effects that derive from the frequent imprisonment of drug addicts and drug users in general, may account for this state of affairs.

(c) In Italy, only a small minority of residential communities carry out follow-up studies, making use of different and not always compatible indicators of effectiveness. Most Italian drug addicts undergoing treatment prefer, however, to turn to public health organizations, even though these do not seem to do their best to follow their patients after their discharge. The numerous prevention, care, and rehabilitation projects financed by the fund established by law 309/1990 have given results whose effectiveness is so far unknown. The reason is that the responsible department's administration has failed, at least until recent times, to provide effectiveness evaluations.

Some obstacles prevent comparative effectiveness evaluations. The available data on U.S. public expenditures to curb the use and abuse of drugs do not include outlays for prevention. Further, the benefits achieved in Italy in the area of social rehabilitation are not known. These obstacles might be overcome, if

1. the estimates concerning drug addiction prevalence were accepted, though these estimates are only rough indicators for the United States and Italy.

2. the overall public expenditure for social protection, as a proportion of national income, were considered. In this case, the portion assigned to rehabilitation, and possibly also the portion allocated to primary and secondary prevention specifically addressed to youth, would be left out of consideration.

In fact, the specialized literature has highlighted (as previously noted in evaluating the consistency between goals and expected results in Sweden) how important welfare expenditure is in making effective primary prevention policies possible.

Comparing the overall public expenditure for social protection to the national income makes possible a comparative efficiency evaluation that includes Italy as well. In Sweden, this expenditure has been proportionally 85 percent higher than in the United States, whereas in Italy it has been 25 percent higher. Spending, in comparison with the national income, less than twice as much as the United States, Sweden has achieved an eleven times lower rate of drug addiction. Italy, with a public expenditure proportionately higher by one-fourth, has achieved rates lower by one-fourth. According to this efficiency evaluation, Italy would stay in an intermediate position between Sweden, whose public expenditure has been surprisingly efficient from this point of view, and the United States, with a surprisingly inefficient public expenditure. There are, however, some problems with this evaluation.

There is, first of all, the previously mentioned uncertainty as to the estimates of the prevalence rates. Also, the purposes of the expenditure for social protection are mostly for social insurance, health, and assistance, and therefore not mainly the prevention of deviant behaviors. Both Swedish and Italian welfare authorities have in any case considered this goal. As the U.S. welfare system is not and has never been oriented to achieve this particular goal, not even as a secondary objective, it is not correct to evaluate its efficiency in this regard. A common objective, which makes comparative evaluations of efficiency possible, is the repression of drug selling and also use through imprisonment (in the United States and Sweden). In 1993, the overall amount of funds allocated in Italy for the prison administration was 880 billion lire (Negri and Saraceno 1996:303), totaling about 0.5 percent of the gross domestic product. Approximately in the same period (1994), this same proportion is found in Sweden, but only one-tenth of this proportion is found in the United States.

Considering the wider extent of drugs in that country, the use of repression as a major public policy instrument to limit and control the use of these substances has proved particularly inefficient. The United States has achieved far less benefit at proportionally much higher cost in comparison with Italy and Sweden. Comparing these two countries to one another, the extent of these substances is much more limited in Sweden, costs being equal in comparison with the national income. Imprisonment rates were (in 1993–94) relatively low in Sweden not only in comparison with the United States (about one-tenth), but also in comparison with Italy (about one-half),[21] although only in Italy is drug use decriminalized. The lower recourse to imprisonment as a tool of social control has gone along in Sweden with a much more limited distribution of these substances. A greater effort to reintroduce the inmate population into society, particularly in the case of drug addicts, may account for the higher costs per imprisoned person recorded in Sweden, in comparison with Italy. One-quarter of prison inmates in Sweden were drug addicts in the early 1990s. This compares with about 15 percent of Milan's prison population in 1991, and currently with almost 30 percent of the entire Italian prison population (*La Stampa*, 17 January 2000, p. 5; Movimento per la Rifondazione Comunista 1991:7–8; Swedish National Institute of Public Health 1995:22).

THE CONSISTENCY BETWEEN AIMS
AND EXPECTED RESULTS

As mentioned, Italian prevention policies—both the enacted policies and those implemented by public authorities, or private subjects operating under their control and within the existing regulations—have been addressed to the goals of primary and secondary prevention. The school environment has been privileged with regard to secondary prevention, with the goal of discouraging students from experimenting with drugs. Primary prevention—among its other purposes—has been aimed at limiting relative and absolute deprivation through assistance measures, and at limiting relative deprivation through active and passive labor policies, and also through housing, education, and health policies. The influential opinion of some social science researchers may help establish consistency between these goals and the expected outcomes of Italian public policies, but also an inconsistency between the enacting procedures of prevention policies and their expected outcomes.

Considering the regulations in force, and particularly the Consolidated Act, which regulates Italian public policies on drugs (presidential decree 309/1990), the consistency of its contents with the recommendations of specialized researchers in this area may be ascertained. Among Italian researchers, an authoritative opinion expressed immediately after the passage of the Consolidated Act stands out. According to this opinion, as "the policies concerning drug addiction" involve the official acknowledgment of therapeutic communities, they represent "in Italy the most advanced cooperation frontier in the area of public services addressed to the people" (Ascoli 1992b:528). Providing for a unified regulatory discipline, financing, and coordinating of intervention projects, and establishing a systematic monitoring of their enacting procedures—besides a permanent Observatory on drug diffusion—the Consolidated Act also complies with the recommendations of international experts concerning prevention.

One of the best-known researchers, Gilbert J. Botvin of Cornell University, is the author of an exhaustive review concerning dozens of preventive interventions in schools. These interventions have used both traditional methods (such as information dissemination, instilling fear of the consequences, moral exhortations) and advanced methods, such as offering alternatives in the organization of time, and training students to develop resistance to the pressure of fellow students, as well as personal and social skills. They have also involved an evaluation of the outcomes. These interventions are hardly comparable to each other, due to a variety of methods used, and often have serious methodological problems that raise doubts as to their reliability and validity. Nonetheless, the review carried out by Botvin allowed him to conclude that traditional methods are ineffective and that the other methods are only partially effective. According to Botvin, an effective prevention action cannot be limited to the school environment, but should also include interventions involving families, social institutions, and the larger community (Botvin 1990:461, cf. also pp. 507–12). Some other experts concur with his conclusions. They point accordingly to the methodological difficulties in carrying out comparative evaluations of effectiveness and impact, the ineffectiveness of traditional methods, the only partial effectiveness of the remaining methods, and the need to intervene also in the external society, including local communities. They do so in light of the large amount of literature concerning not only prevention, but also the etiological factors of propensity to drug use and abuse (Hawkins et al. 1995: particularly pp. 402–6; Morgan 1998:128–30).

According to the provisions of the Consolidated Act, a variety of public and private subjects, the latter belonging to nonprofit organizations, may formulate intervention projects financed by the National Fund for Interventions Aimed at Fighting Drugs. Their aims are reinserting drug addicts into their families, helping them to enter or reenter the labor market, and in general helping them to perform socially acknowledged roles. These aims go along with activities of education about health, which are financed by the Ministry of Public Education according to an intervention program, as previously mentioned. Complete consistency may then be found between the goal of secondary prevention and the expected outcome (namely, a lower prevalence of drugs).

This consistency, however, is less apparent or, in some cases, disappears completely if the implementation of the law on rehabilitation and prevention is considered instead of its provisions. As for rehabilitation, the Italian and other literature on this subject demonstrates that damage reduction interventions (such as the administration of drug antagonists or substitutive medicines, and sometimes the supply of sterile syringes) often effectively contribute to social reintroduction (particularly in the labor market) of drug addicts. This occurs only provided that these actions are accompanied by the support of specialized personnel who can establish relationships with the service users, and gain their trust.[22] Rehabilitation interventions have taken and still take place in Italy through the administration of methadone or different medicines, with public financial support and at no cost for users. This is evidence of a much higher consistency level between goals and expected outcomes in Italy than in the United States, where—as noticed—this consistency is very partial and unsatisfactory.

On the other hand, a comparison with Sweden is unfavorable for Italy. In both countries, unlike the United States, rehabilitation interventions are carried out according to the same directions all over the country. However, only in Sweden do these directives actually involve (Swedish Institute 1995; Swedish National Institute of Public Health 1995:24–30)

1. systematic effectiveness evaluations, carried out by public (mainly municipal) authorities;

2. professional, and even psychiatric, assistance available to all drug addicts in contact with social services;

3. extension of rehabilitation interventions to the majority of drug addicts, and among them, particularly to all those who are imprisoned;

4. introduction of young drug addicts, if they wish so, into regular families who have been prepared to receive them by specialized consultants;

5. coordination between all public and private organizations addressed to drug addicts, including justice and police institutions;

6. forced health treatments, for a limited maximum period established by the law, for drug addicts considered dangerous to themselves and others.

In Italy, by way of contrast, similar provisions are not provided for or, depending on the case, not systematically implemented or remain to be carried out. In particular,

1. Effectiveness evaluations have been belatedly started, and the overall results are so far still unknown.

2. Services to drug addicts are frequently provided by insufficiently trained personnel, and professional services are not always available.

3. No efforts have been made to reach all drug addicts with suitable rehabilitation interventions through the social services.

4. There has been no coordination among all the organizations that are empowered, each in its own way, to be in contact with these users.

5. Forced health treatments are not prescribed to drug addicts. Failing a regulatory framework to control this matter, it is not even clear which professional figures (such as psychiatrists or social workers) are entitled to determine the degree of danger a drug addict poses for him- or herself and others.

We leave aside the Swedish practice of introducing drug addicts into regular families, whose evaluation does not seem to have appeared in the international literature. Let us instead consider the extension of rehabilitating interventions to the majority of those who abuse drugs. In Sweden, as compared to Italy, such interventions involve an average longer contact with specialized services, such as experts recommend (Anglin and Hser 1990:432–32, 442). Regarding all the other aspects, the Swedish approach to rehabilitation is favorably judged by the specialized literature (ibid.: 438–39; 442–43). The deviations that have occurred in the rehabilitation procedures followed in Italy, with respect to the Swedish approach, involve a lower degree of consistency between the goals and the expected results.

As for prevention, the literature has lately provided some useful guidelines concerning preliminary conditions of effectiveness in prevention activities. In Italy, the implementation of primary and secondary prevention policies does not seem to have sufficiently considered these indications. Within primary prevention policies, Italian and non-Italian literatures emphasize a causal relation (other things being equal) between relative deprivation and the spread of drugs, especially if deprivation is concentrated in families and urban areas marked by poverty and a lack of or difficulties in interpersonal relations.[23] The actions carried out in Italy in a plurality of intervention areas—educational institutions, introduction into the labor market, public health—do not entirely (and sometimes not at all) conform to the knowledge provided by the social sciences.

Regarding schools, and particularly high schools, some influential researchers observed that educational institutions display little ability to support, through special courses, students with learning difficulties. Actually, there is not a clear organizational and regulatory framework in which these review and follow-up courses, recently established after the abolition of autumn session exams, can be placed. From a regulatory point of view, there is no unequivocal definition of this follow-up activity, and hence young people with learning difficulties and those belonging to socially and economically disadvantaged families are penalized. From an organizational viewpoint, further and objective learning difficulties derive from an overload of teaching hours in courses that have to be added to those institutionally provided. The achieved levels of reintroduction into the school system often prove unsatisfactory because of problems that may be easily grasped, and that could be overcome in the light of already existing effectiveness evaluations (Negri and Saraceno 1996:216).

The activities aimed at preventing use and abuse of drugs, which have been carried out in schools for many years, do not seem to take into account the by now available information in this field. In fact, the contents of prevention programs for schools in Italy consist of spreading information—not necessarily accurate—on the pharmacological properties and consequences of drugs, based on the—usually mistaken—belief that these information campaigns may turn youth away from experimenting with those substances. The recent efforts made by the Ministry of Public Education, in cooperation with the Ministry of Health, in starting information campaigns aimed at education on health and by controlling their implementation ("monitoring") (Turco 1998:8–9) show the government's commitment to carry out prevention activities in the school. These activities are not limited to financing, as in the past, prevention programs left to the well-intentioned but unprepared actions of single principals or teachers (Battaglia and Coletti 1987:32–33, 79–91).

The centralization of these campaigns, in terms of contents and implementation procedures, is an important distinctive feature not only with respect to what Italy has done up to now, but also with respect to the plethora of actions started in the primary and secondary schools of the United States. A 1990s review reported thirty-five actions started between 1972 and 1989, different regarding recipients, intervention methods, and—obviously—results (which, in turn, were evaluated by different methods) (Botvin 1990:479–86). Centralization of school prevention programs improves their effectiveness, on condition that these programs are updated in light of the available information. As mentioned, there is no reason to believe, generally speaking, that this may have happened or is going to happen in Italy.

On 25 March 1998, during a hearing at the Twelfth Commission of the Chamber of Deputies, the then minister for social solidarity, Livia Turco, announced a "program of interventions." The program was "aimed at education on health, and hence at prevention, to be carried out at any school level in the year 1998." It also provided for:

1. The promotion among students, also with the aid of a new educational organization, of "relations with the social framework," of their "affectivity" and "personal motivations," "for a better prevention of uneasiness and drug addictions."

2. The "strengthening in high schools, in agreement with the social-health services, of information and consultancy centers, as well as support for communication processes and psychosocial dynamics," the declared scope being to identify protection and risk factors "in the school environment, in groups of friends, and in families."

3. An active involvement of families and teachers, the latter obliged to attend training courses, "in order to implement effective teaching and school reintroduction strategies particularly addressed to borderline subjects."

4. Systematic efficiency and effectiveness evaluations of prevention activities carried out in schools.

5. The distribution to secondary and high school students of monographs dealing with issues in connection with the education on health, among which *HIV/AIDS, Drug, Alcohol and Tobacco Prevention*, together with a *Guidebook for Teachers* to help them plan activities conforming to those issues (Turco 1998:8).

We get the impression of a plurality of intentions, among which are

- identifying subjects at risk of deviance, and particularly of drug addiction;
- determining the psychological and social-psychological causes leading to that condition of risk or protecting from it;
- involving family members and the teaching staff in a prevention and rehabilitation effort;
- informing students on how to prevent some infectious diseases, and on the consequences of using and abusing drugs and other mind-altering substances.

This vague declaration of intentions does not, however, clarify the following points that the specialized literature, on the contrary, considers important for the effectiveness of prevention programs:[24]

1. Avoiding, as ineffective and often counterproductive, prevention pro-

grams that include alarming (*scare tactics*) and/or unreliable information, or are limited to the supply of information concerning the psychophysical effects of drug use.

2. Training the teaching staff, in the specific sense of making them prepared and willing to listen to their students, offer them support and encouragement, and personally take an interest in them, something widely desired by students.

3. Teaching students—particularly those who are considered borderline students—how to resist the influence of their fellow students who are inclined to use drugs, and how to strengthen their personal and social skills (resistance skills training, and personal and social skills training). This kind of teaching should be carried out with the active cooperation of students recognized as *leaders* by the other students.

4. Considering the variety, heterogeneity, and mutual influence of the sources of risk, involving a variety of institutions and organizations in prevention and rehabilitation activities for those youth who are already drug users or are considered at risk, and trying to coordinate their actions. Therefore, it is not enough to involve only teachers and families. Nor are all families in a position to cooperate. Especially ill-suited are families who, due to their lifestyle, internal communication, and educational practices, predispose their children to experiment with drugs. Hence, it is necessary to make all possible efforts to involve the social services and the managers of local organizations, in addition to the police.[25]

During the same hearing, the minister announced the start, "in agreement with the other competent ministers," of an "information campaign for the prevention of drug abuse, which . . . will be focused on the abuse of synthetic or new drugs." This should occur through "numerous actions focused on the territory, aimed at approaching the young in their leisure and meeting places, such as discotheques, gym halls, sport plants, etc." (Turco 1998:9). This purpose is in line with the recommendations of experts to focus on situations at risk deriving from (Tittle, Burke, and Jackson 1986:particularly pp. 423–24; Uhl 1998:112–17)

1. personal attitudes and subcultural rules favoring the use of drugs;
2. influence of fellow students to this effect;
3. local availability of these substances.

This would be evidence of a consistency between goals and expected results. A few years have now elapsed since the minister's hearing before the parliamentary commission. Knowledge has now been obtained on the spread of synthetic drugs in Italy in general (*La Stampa,* 23 November 1999, p. 13; Piccone Stella 1999:40–43), particularly inside or in the neighborhood of discotheques (Rossi 1999). The available knowledge indicates that so far this information campaign does not seem to have had any effect. Perhaps this is because the information did not reach the recipients (this would be a further example of the ineffectiveness of Italian prevention policies), or because it did not conform to the prevailing convictions and rules of the youth groups, and therefore was not considered credible. This further drawback is underlined by the specialized literature, which holds that authorities might overcome this failure by using and coordinating the efforts made by the mass media and the various local authorities. They would play the role of formal or informal guards of groups of youths in the places where drugs are used, and seek the cooperation of other students and *leaders* who are trusted by the public of potential users. The effectiveness of prevention programs requires that all these sources be prepared to declare that drug use is morally unacceptable (soft drugs included).

As in the schools, also in situations at risk—particularly at discotheques—the spread of information is insufficient to make prevention effective.[26] Municipalities, Public Services for Drug Addictions (SERTs), and associations that belong to nonprofit organizations (among them, in particular, the association Gruppo Abele) have very recently made encouraging progress, in the sense of a greater consistency between goals and expected outcomes. These organizations do their utmost to approach, near the discotheques or other meeting places, young users (either real or potential) of the so-called new drugs. They not only inform them of the risks in connection with the use of these drugs, but also offer them assistance, entertainment, and drug-free places to get together. They have also tried—but we do not know the results—to convince discotheque managers to play the role of informal guardians. To these secondary prevention activities, Gruppo Abele adds a training program on synthetic drugs, addressed to high school teachers: this program integrates pharmacological ideas with ideas on the psychology of adolescence (Bagozzi 1999:22; Veglia 1999:23, 25).

Within labor policies, too, there has been a low degree of consistency between goals (introduction in the labor market, preferably in the primary market) and expected outcomes (that is, the actual introduction possibilities in light of the available information). According to some experts on social policy, the previously noted limited effectiveness of training courses is a consequence of their frequent irrelevance to the requirements of labor force demand, and hence the demand of enterprises. The international literature is divided on the effectiveness of active labor policies (Dropping et al. 1999:157–58). Italian experts on economic and social policies suggest that the likely ineffectiveness of these training courses (in spite of a recent increase in their number, as well as in the number of students) should be attributed to the prevalence of passive labor policies in Italy.

Therefore, there would be far too little public commitment to help the unemployed (those in the strict sense of the word, and those who are looking for their first employment) in their efforts to enter the labor market. Some expenditure items concerning active labor policies support this opinion. With reference to 1996 for Italy and to 1997 for Sweden, the ratio of gross domestic product allocated for active policies in Italy compared to that in Sweden totaled a little more than one-half. Particularly with regard to public expenditure for professional training, Italy proportionally spent only one-third what Sweden did. The only cases of university training favorably welcomed by enterprises are the recently established university diplomas, roughly equivalent to American college diplomas. For their holders, the overall employment offer exceeds—as previously noted—the overall demand. The meager appropriations for professional training and the limited number of diplomas made available do not lead to an evaluation of consistency in the previously mentioned sense. It is not then surprising that the evaluation made in 1999 by the European Commission on the interventions of the individual member countries concerning youth and long-term unemployment attributed only to Sweden and the United Kingdom full compliance with the directives of the Commission. On the contrary, Italy—together with Greece and Belgium—received an evaluation of complete nonconformity with these directives.[27]

Italian housing policy has also been strongly criticized, not only because of its lack of effectiveness, but also because of the perverse effects caused by the criteria followed in the planning of buildings and residential areas. "Lines of big buildings one after the other, jam containers filled with bricks, in a total lack of equipment, services, green areas," wrote an expert in social policies, referring in particular to the cities of southern Italy. Furthermore, the author stated in this regard "the havoc played by public housing" bears comparison "with the similar one played by private housing" (Sidoti 1989:137). In this case, however, instead of these perverse effects (which we shall later examine) particularly important are the repeated examples of the municipal authorities' lack of consideration for the conclusions reached by environmental criminology. The criticism made by qualified sources of the officials responsible for housing policies in Italy and abroad are also relevant in this connection.

Environmental criminology has focused its attention on the opportunities to commit crimes deriving from the project design of buildings and areas, particularly if destined for residents who share a condition of marginality with respect to the labor market, the family, and other institutions. In these circumstances, a condition of social disorganization, and hence of widespread crime, may result from a faulty project design of buildings and residential environments, which in turn would hamper the creation of permanent nondeviant relations and the possibility of exerting effective social control. A faulty project design in this sense is characterized by physical elements that make it difficult to exert social control, such as the length of corridors, or the presence of a large number of accesses to buildings and to building areas.

The effects of poor planning are increased, according to the specialized literature, by a mix of resident population favoring the absence of relations with neighbors, and hence anonymity. These effects are

- high rates of lodgers and residents without family ties;
- strong ethnic heterogeneity;
- high residential density by area (average number of persons per unit of area);
- high residential density per block (average number of persons and flats per block).

Italian researchers have identified many of these characteristics in housing projects built after World War II. The public officials responsible for urban planning, the planning of low-income buildings and areas, and the allocation criteria of apartments in public housing have not been apparently familiar with or have not taken into account the body of relevant information already available in the 1970s, if not earlier. We should, however, consider that the practice of municipalities of allocating apartments in public housing without contractual time limitations and of selling them to the tenants who live in them to some extent prevent the disorganization of a particular urban area and promotes lasting relations among neighbors. The relative deprivation of the national population is, on the contrary, enhanced, damaging those who are most in need of low rents. However, there is no reason to believe that the available literature on urban sociology or criminology has inspired this practice.[28]

As far as the health sector is concerned, the reforms provided for by law decrees 502/1992 and 517/1993, and the consequent "corporatization" of large hospitals and local social-sanitary units conform to free-market principles. They recommend the introduction, also in the case of the health sector, of competitiveness mechanisms between private and public health, thus reducing costs (Stein and Doerfer 1992:58–59). Authorities tried, however, to take into account the consequences of introducing services for payment in the Italian National Health System. Payments should be made according to *homogeneous diagnostic groups* (ROD), based on the model of the similar diagnostic related groups (DRG) provided for in 1983 in the United States by federal law.

These consequences were critically examined by the specialized U.S. literature, particularly in a series of articles published by the influential *New England Journal of Medicine,* before or in concomitance with law decree 517/1993, and later in 1999. The contributions of this literature were cited above in the evaluation of consistency and perverse effects. The majority of the corresponding Italian literature (in part already available in 1994, immediately after the reforms) expressed itself at least in one case (Giorgi 1999) against a radical corporatization of public health, with explicit reference to the negative evaluations in some U.S. medical circles. Italian criticism, in short, disputed a number of theses:

- Public services could be evaluated through the same criteria used in evaluating market-provided services;

- The privatization of public health would necessarily involve greater efficiency and better quality; and
- Recipients of health services would be able to evaluate their quality themselves.[29]

Through the ministerial decrees of 15 April 1994 and 14 December 1994, establishing the reimbursement tariff required by health organizations, and ministerial guidelines 1/1995, legislators took into account the "international experience" and the "major theoretical contributions on this subject" (Vanara 1997:15, 26). The new set of rules enacted progressive reductions in these tariffs when they exceed preestablished sales amounts, and in the reimbursements to be borne by the National Health Service, in case the difference between actual and programmed hospitalizations exceeds a preestablished threshold. This set of rules also introduced systematic inspections of hospital discharge cards on which the calculation of the tariff compensation is based. The correctives introduced to avoid undesired effects from the reform of the National Health System seem—according to the specialized literature—in a position to limit future costs, and to safeguard at the same time the quality of health assistance (ibid.:19, 25). In this case, the consistency evaluation between goals pursued and results expected is positive. Nevertheless:

1. The literature on this subject is still scarce.

2. The introduction of the tariff reform, which has only taken place in many regions since 1996–97, is still of an experimental nature.

3. The new position of general manager in local health organizations, who is solely responsible for their management, cannot be carried out in a satisfactory way as long as the management accounting tools introduced by the tariff reform are unknown or are not suitably applied.

4. New goods and services are acquired based on their purchasing price rather than on real needs (Albini 1999:59; Campari and De Negri 1999: 77–79).

By way of conclusion, a comparative consistency evaluation highlights the relatively low consistency of Italian social policies compared to Swedish policies. The specialized literature endorses the goals, pursued by the Italian and the Swedish administrations alike, of rehabilitating drug addicts economically and socially, and freely distributing substitutive or antagonist medicines. This literature discourages merely repressive interventions in order to deal with the social problem of use and abuse of drugs. Nevertheless, unlike Sweden, in Italy the effectiveness evaluation of interventions was started too late. The staff charged with supporting drug addicts is not suitably trained, nor is it in a position to provide a complete program of services. Many drug addicts—probably most of them—are not reached by social services, which are not coordinated anyway. Finally, forced health programs for drug addicts considered dangerous to themselves and others are not provided for, though the literature has emphasized their effectiveness in many cases.

PERVERSE EFFECTS

Italian social policies have produced effects that contrast with their explicit goals and expected outcomes. We shall deal in this section with the acknowledged perverse effects, or even only with those that are likely, bearing in mind similar experiences in other countries. Some of these effects concern, in economic and social terms, the most disadvantaged part of the population. It is these people whom social policies having a character of social assistance, social insurance, or general social services aim at supporting through measures of income redistribution or, in general, of life opportunities. Other perverse effects involve the youth population, and further effects concern the overall population. In this section, we shall mostly—but not exclusively—study the effects to the detriment of already disadvantaged persons.

With respect to assistance policies, perverse effects have been produced by the implementation of housing policies. Law 392/1978, which established rent controls, has achieved the following effects, probably neither welcomed nor wanted:

1. Diminishing the availability of houses for rent at reduced costs, for it is not profitable for private proprietors to sign contracts at controlled rents, and the quantity of buildings built since the 1980s with public funds for subsidized housing has not been sufficient.

2. Allocating a non-negligible part of this housing to families with a relatively high income. Among the reasons accounting for this policy are actually tolerated unlawful occupations; the opportunity for many relatively well-to-do tenants to purchase their apartments, thus becoming proprietors; the practice of keeping families who are no longer in economic conditions of poverty.

The liberalization of the housing market through law 392/1992 has not gone along with a strong public commitment to allow low-income persons or families to secure apartments at reduced rents, and has therefore decreased the availability for those who actually need them. We should also add a further perverse effect: the project design and building criteria of subsidized housing projects have often contributed to create and consolidate ghettos of poverty and crime. The very same effect has been brought about by questionable criteria in the allocation of houses, and the quantitative and qualitative deficiencies in the available local services (Negri and Saraceno 1996:159–62, 178–84; Testa 1987:31; Tosi 1984:246–51).

As for the public pension and social insurance system, there are "situations of relative privilege, [as well as] disconnected and reciprocally contradictory tendencies, which often lack any social justification" (Regonini 1984:113). Excluded from this system are those who do not have a regular position in the labor market. Among other factors, the reaction of enterprises, since the 1980s, to the "constraints provided for by the rigid labor regulations in force" has increased the number of these persons in Italy. These regulations were first replaced within companies by informal regulations of this relation, and later first by a "creeping" and then by an open deregulation of formal work relations (Reyneri 1996:361, and in general pp. 359–77; cf. also Regini 1991:186–93, 209–12, 1997:106–9).

Perverse effects in the social insurance system have particularly affected the young, who have been or are at risk of being harmed in the future, for two reasons:

1. Because they finance, through the current redistributive pension scheme based on a pay-as-you-go system, the pensions of those who have left the labor market, without any assurance of recuperating in the future their paid-up contributions in the form of pensions (Rei 1997:122).

2. Because—considering the current "widespread protection of full-time and open-end labor" in Italy (Negri and Saraceno 1996:109) and the spreading of irregular labor among young people[30]—they are more frequently excluded from the public and private pension schemes (Busana Banterle 1993:273). These were neither the explicit goal of the Italian policymakers, nor the results they expected.

Furthermore, quite a few young persons might be harmed by the recent reform of the school system. Education policies are addressed to the whole school-age population, have a universalistic aim, and hence have a social service character. And yet, ineffective professional training has prevented the facilitation of entry into the labor market for the young. Moreover, it has been mandatory for sixteen- to eighteen-year-olds who have not remained in the school system. As a likely effect, there will be an increase in relative deprivation for those who attend these courses, in comparison with the social advantage of the teenagers who remain in the school system. A condition of "relative frustration" for some students may ensue from the likely lower prestige of these training courses (compared to the regular school course until the age of eighteen), and the "condition of disastrous competition to which the freedom of access to the long high school education period binds them." A frustration depending on the fact that, after having started a regular school course, sooner or later these students are obliged to switch to the less prestigious alternative of training courses, without even profiting from them to enter the labor market (Boudon 1981:124, 130).

During their school attendance period, these students or their school peers are also subject to the further perverse effect of being encouraged to experiment with drugs, as a consequence of the prevention efforts made in the school through the ministerial programs and ministerial financial support. The large international experience in prevention within the school evidences that a spreading of information on this subject might even produce or increase young people's interest in these substances and diminish their fear of using them. On the other hand, the attempts to instill fear are often counterproductive, since an exaggerated stress on the bad effects of drugs clashes with the personal experience—deemed more reliable, as it is direct or transmitted by persons of the same age—of the youth audience. In this way, the reliability of information and the authority of teachers, or other adults who transmit it, are undermined (Botvin 1990:479, 487; Morgan 1998:102, 128; Uhl 1998:102).

Finally, the health policy—which, from the point of view of benefits pursued, is in principle of a universalistic nature, too—seems to have produced perverse effects for the whole population, and mainly for persons with limited economic possibilities. On the other hand, the costs of the health service compared to the GDP have not decreased. On the contrary, the health policy has increased these costs in absolute terms without decreasing the deficit of the National Health Service. The reform of the health system has actually produced some perverse effects in consequence of the introduction of the tariff-payment per service system:

1. A reduction in the possibilities of access to medical services—particularly the most expensive ones—for low-income users. The limitation of the average stay period in hospitals introduced by independent hospitals involves, in fact, a deviation of patients who need lasting and expensive cares but are not solvent, to financially nonindependent hospitals. Consequently, those hospitals are overloaded and, in short, there is likely to be a deterioration in the quality of the health care they are able to provide.

2. The growth of health expenditure. The growing orientation of users to private health services, mainly motivated by inadequacies in public health services, and consequently a competitive system between private and public health organizations, have not involved a reduction in health expenditure as a proportion of GDP. The expenditure rate fluctuated around 5.5 percent in the period 1995–98. On the contrary, these factors have gone along with a much higher increase, in absolute terms and in comparison with the inflation rate, and with a rapid growth of the budget deficit of the National Health Service. In fact, this deficit grew by over twenty times in a period of only three years (1995–97). This increase can be at least partly explained by the introduction of the tariff-payment per service system, which would encourage resorting for health services to private organizations operating within the National Health Service.

3. Insufficient coverage of the expenses borne by large hospitals, and in general wherever specialized and complex sanitary services are provided, due to the nonadjustment of tariffs by homogeneous group of diagnoses.[31]

These perverse effects can be summarized as "opportunistic behaviors of manufacturers in the presence of a 'pure' remuneration mechanism" and of "allocating distortions" (Vanara 1997:17). To contrast these effects, the regions, which are entrusted with the payment of health services, tried to find a remedy in the previously mentioned ways during the consistency evaluation.

From a comparative point of view, with respect to the corresponding U.S. social policies, Italian policies have produced different and peculiar perverse effects. In fact, public policies producing these perverse effects have neither been implemented nor pursued in Italy with a similar determination. The authorities have not systematically resorted to imprisonment as a social control tool for persons who are considered socially dangerous. The social expenditure compared to the national income, which is still much higher than the U.S. expenditure but lower than the Swedish, has not decreased. Furthermore, the social and—to some extent—ethnic segregation produced by city-planning policies, although real, has never been as marked as in the United States. Therefore, perverse effects in Italy depend on different circumstances. In particular:

1. The ghettos of poverty and criminality are not only the result of errors made in the planning of tenement houses and housing projects areas, or of a quantitative insufficiency of inexpensive houses and qualitative material and maintenance deficiencies (as in the United States). They are also the result of the allocation—mostly in southern Italy—of working-class houses to criminal families, which produced the effect of discouraging conventional economic undertakings and forcing noncriminal families away from these areas.

2. The effect of increasing relative deprivation through particular criteria followed in the allocation of apartments in public property tenements can be defined as perverse only in Italy, since the redistribution of life opportunities in the United States has never been a goal pursued with determination. In the United States this effect appears in a more accentuated way, with local gentrification processes produced by the demolition of old tenement houses not followed by their rebuilding.

3. The Italian school system, of a universalistic and in principle nondiscriminating nature, is different from the U.S. system, of a meritocratic and hence selective nature. Moreover, the Italian school system is centralized, whereas the U.S. system is decentralized. The perverse effects produced by the Italian system are peculiar. Due to the raising of the age for compulsory education and to the inability of professional training to be equivalent to regular school courses from the viewpoint of the potential employers, the reform of the Italian school system runs the risk of increasing the number of those who drop out. It will also increase the present and future handicap of the young who attend these training courses. Relative deprivation is increased for all of them. Second, the centralization of the Italian system intensifies the perverse effect of encouraging drug use, due to prevention campaigns carried out in obsolete ways (messages underlining the dan-

gerous consequences of drug use presented in a merely informative context, or deemed capable of producing fear).

4. Finally, relative deprivation might be further increased by an insufficient (in terms of extension, quality, and money) insurance coverage of the needs of the population granted by the public social security system, particularly as regards the economically disadvantaged part of it. Though this effect occurs in both countries, it becomes perverse in Italy as this country has pursued the goal of redistribution. This effect follows—as mentioned—from widespread nonregulated work relations, but also from a regulation of the labor market that enterprises consider excessive. With regard to the health service, in the United States the reform of the provisions for the safeguard of the right to health of the elderly (Medicare) and the needy (Medicaid)—the latter of an assistance nature—has caused perverse effects. These effects have not fully appeared in Italy after the reform of the National Health Service. This would depend on the fact that the regions introduced tariff correctives with the (apparently achieved, at least in part) aim of mitigating the undesired effects of a corporatization of the health system.

NOTES

1. Cf. Chapter 6, note 21.

2. Different calculation criteria provide, as for both the United States and Sweden, different results, which, however, agree in indicating a much higher share in the United States (cf. Ginsburg 1992:200–1; Jaentti and Danziger 1994:62–63).

3. For these data, cf. Censis (1994:256, Table 18, 1998:234, 246–47, Tables 25, 42–43), ISTAT (1999:189), *La Stampa*, 11 May 1999, p. 17, 27 June 1999, p. 3, 7 July 1999, p. 16), OECD (1997:178, Table F, 180, Table H), and OECD Statistics Directorate (1997:12–13, 76–77). In Italy, the official ISTAT statistics report a youth unemployment rate starting at the age of fifteen instead of sixteen, as reported by international statistical sources.

4. Unless otherwise stated, with regard to all of the following points, see Censis (1998:234, Table 23), ISTAT (1996:65, Picture 3.1), OECD (1997:178, Table F, 180, Table H), OECD Statistics Directorate (1997:12–13, 76–77), and Reyneri (1996:Chapter 4, particularly p. 92, Table 4.1).

5. Cf. Censis (1998:232, Table 19), OECD Statistics Directorate (1997:12–13, 76–77, 180–82), and ISTAT (1998:188). Different sources likewise underscore the relatively high women's unemployment rate in Italy (both overall and long-term unemployment), however providing different quantitative estimates. Cf. Censis (1999:180–81, Table 1 and Picture 1).

6. These phenomena occur in a variety of capitalist countries. The thesis according to which these phenomena would constitute part of a combination of consequences necessarily brought about by the post-Fordist model of labor organization (Wacquant 1996) neglects the large variety of forms and the intensity through which these consequences reveal themselves.

7. An important comparative survey of ten industrial countries was carried out by Ishida, Mueller, and Ridge (1995), focusing on the relations between class of origin, education, and class of destination in all of them. Unfortunately, this inquiry includes Sweden but not the United States and Italy.

8. We leave aside the interesting (but nonrelevant, in this case) theoretical discussion included in Goldthorpe's article (1996).

9. The data provided by the World Health Organization do not coincide with those of Eurostat, to which we refer, unless otherwise stated.

10. Cf. Censis (1998:302, Table 15, 1999:315, Table 24), Gortmaker and Wise (1997:149–50), United Nations, Department of Economic and Social Affairs, Statistics Division (1997:95, 98), and World Health Organization (1996, A-5, A-6, A-7, A-12, A-13, 1998, B-738–40).

11. Cf. on this subject Censis (1998:307, Table 19, 1999:328, Table 38), Kinlock et al. (1998:18–19), Kornblum and Julian (1995:44, 46), Swedish National Institute of Public Health (1995:15), and United Nations, Department of Economic and Social Affairs, Statistics Division (1997:104, 107).

12. Cf. Swedish Institute (1995) and Swedish National Institute of Public Health (1995:14).

13. Cf. Censis (1998:311, Table 21, 562, Table 21, 1999:328, Table 44), Ginsburg (1992:197, Table A.1), Danziger and Gottschalk (1995:21–37), Jencks (1992:76, Table 2.2), Kamerman and Kahn (1998:79, Table 1), and *La Stampa* (7 November 1999, p. 16).

14. Cf. Censis (1998:247, Table 43), Danziger and Gottschalk (1995:124–50), Ginsburg (1992:109–11), Jaentti and Danziger (1994:57–61), and Lichter (1997:135–36).

15. It should be noted that the training courses financed by the European Social Fund, but managed by the regions, have allowed about one-fourth of those who attended them to enter the labor market within one year after the end of the training period. The unit cost per employed person totaled about 18 million lire (cf. ISFOL 1999:297–98, 403). Therefore, these courses were twice as efficient in creating employment as the incentives to juvenile entrepreneurship.

16. The recent growth in Italy of regional expenditures for professional training—almost doubled in absolute values from 1994 to 1999—might however indicate a greater public commitment to fight youth unemployment (ISFOL 1999:284–85).

17. The statistics provided by UNESCO are diverge slightly from those provided by OCSE. Regarding the latter, cf. Censis (1998:171, Table 55, 1999:164, Table 45).

18. Cf. Censis (1994:354, Table 38, 1998:302, 318, Tables 15, 27, 1999:335, Table 12), Economist Intelligence Unit (1996–97:23), Ginsburg (1992, Table A.19), ISTAT (1998:149), Lehto et al. (1999:105, Table 5.1, 114), and OECD (1993:16–18).

19. We accept this evaluation, instead of others, although the author defines it as a "coarse" one. The author, however, argues it in a sufficiently convincing way, combining an analysis of official data sources with references to already existing evaluations considered reliable. Cf. Reuter (1998:317–18 and 333–34, note 16).

20. Cf. National Board of Health and Welfare (1994:42–43), Swedish Institute (1995), and Swedish National Institute of Public Health (1995:28–29).

21. For data concerning the Italian prison population, cf. Negri and Saraceno (1996:302–3).

22. Cf. for Italy, Piccone Stella (1996:605–6); for the United States, Anglin and Hser (1990:444–46), Hunt and Rosenbaum (1998:207–11), and Platt et al. (1998:179–81).

23. For some references to the literature published in the 1980s and in the 1990s concerning the relation between relative privation (in terms of income, educational qualification, and work position) and deficiencies in interpersonal relationships on the one hand, and use and abuse of drugs on the other hand, cf. for Italy, Baraldi (1994a:148–57), Labos (1993:132–34), Negri and Saraceno (1996:260), Piccone Stella (1999:44), and Serpelloni et al. (1986:141–42); for the United States, cf. Gorman (1996:514), Johnson et al. (1990), and Morgan (1998:117). All of this literature warns that relative or absolute privation is neither a necessary nor a sufficient condition for using and abusing drugs. The lack of a direct relation between privation and drug addiction was underscored, for example, by Baraldi (1994a:147–48), Labos (1993:133), and Morgan (1998:118). Wright et al. (1999) highlighted the existing curvilinear relation between socioeconomic status and the commission of crimes, including those in connection with the use of drugs.

24. An evaluation of efficiency should involve knowledge, which in this case is not available, of the public funds set aside for this "program of interventions aimed at education on health."

25. Cf. Botvin (1990:487–512), Eggert, Seyl, and Nicholas (1990), Hawkins et al. (1995:383–85, 388–91, 397–402), and Uhl (1998:102–22).

26. Cf. Battaglia and Coletti (1987:56–57), Mazerolle et al. (1998), Meier and Johnson (1977), Silbereisen et al. (1995:529–33), and Uhl (1998:118–21).

27. Cf. Censis (1998:127, 141, 145, 166, Tables 45 and 46, 190, 247, Table 43, 1999:182–83, Table 1), Esping-Andersen (1999:155–60). Cf. also Negri and Saraceno (1996:240–41). We should, however, bear in mind that the negative evaluation of the effectiveness of public policies aimed at fighting unemployment expressed by the European Commission does not seem to take into account the heavy increase in the aggregate regional expenditure for professional training. It also does not consider the possible future benefits of recent law 144/1999, which raised the age of compulsory education and professional training to eighteen years.

28. Cf. for Italy, Negri and Saraceno (1996:177–84) and Tosi (1984:247); for the United States, cf. Roncek (1981). This latter source (pp. 80–81), as well as Felson (1998:152–58), specifies the characteristics—that here are partially reported—of faulty planning of quarters and single buildings. Felson (1998) provides a recent and well-informed introduction to the literature on environmental criminology. The works of Lewis Mumford, a pioneer of urban planning studies, appeared long before the 1970s.

29. For a critical reception of a radical corporatization of the Italian health service, based on the U.S. model, cf. Giorgi (1999) and Riboldi (1994:55).

30. In 1996, one-sixth of young workers had an irregular work relation, as opposed to one-eighth of the overall employed labor force in 1994 (Censis 1994:174, Table 5; Chiesi 1997:63, Table 3.4).

31. On this subject, cf. Albini (1999:59), Ardigò (1999:10), Ascoli 1992a:432, Censis (1990:343, 1994:284, 1998:264–65, 318, Table 27, 1999:335, Table 52), Riboldi (1994:55), Sirchia (1999:81), and Vanara (1997:24).

8   Conclusion

In this study we have presented and compared the drug policies that have been carried out in Sweden, the United States, and Italy in order to control drug trafficking, socially rehabilitate those who use drugs, and prevent the spread and use of drugs. The study has had two objectives:

1. A theoretical objective, to assess which drug or welfare policies have been the most effective and efficient, and for which reasons. We have tried to demonstrate that (a) Swedish drug policies have been a sufficient (albeit not necessary) condition to determine the limited use of these substances in Sweden; (b) in the United States the opposite direction of several of the corresponding public policies has been a sufficient (albeit not necessary) condition of the widespread use of these drugs.

Other factors, concerning in particular the consequences of the peers' and the families' milieu, have been considered here as possible effects of any particular social policy, but apart from that they have deliberately been ignored.

2. A practical objective, to provide the political and administrative authorities with information that would help them in their repressive, rehabilitative, and preventive actions.

The description of the Swedish and U.S. drug policies has shed light on (a) the common "prohibitive" choice, namely, a repressive policy not only on trafficking but also on the use of drugs, and (b) furthermore the presence in both countries of rehabilitative and preventive activities, in conjunction with repression. There are also many considerable differences, however.

The U.S. authorities, with the support of public opinion, have preferred to repress the use and trafficking of drugs to the detriment of other activities, and have generally worked in a noncoordinated way. On the contrary, the Swedish authorities, who have also been supported by public opinion but who have acted in a tightly coordinated way, have endeavored to accompany the repressive policies with rehabilitation, even if forced, of the drug addicts, and with preventive measures. The preventive measures have been both of a primary nature, aimed as a matter of principle at everyone considered to be at risk, and also of a secondary nature, aimed at all those who find themselves in a condition of relative deprivation. The two very different approaches to limiting the deprivation of the most disadvantaged have been brought to light by an overview of the respective policies. These policies have included redistributing income, financially supporting the unemployed, and constructing housing with public funding.

The efficacy of these policies has been evaluated using criteria that took into account the benefits (intended as the capacity to achieve the objectives), the expected results, and those obtained. More specifically, the comparative analysis of the efficacy of the policies has attempted to determine:

1. The respective capability to pursue the common objective to repress the use and abuse of drugs, and also the objectives, which have been followed more so in Sweden than in the United States, to rehabilitate drug addicts and prevent the consumption of these substances.

2. The congruence between the objectives that have been pursued and the results that have been expected, according to the conclusions on the subject that have been reached by experts in the field.

3. The congruence between the results that have been obtained, and the results that have been expected. This congruence indicates the capacity to avoid perverse effects. In order to evaluate the efficiency of the Swedish and U.S. policies on drugs we have proceeded instead to a comparative evaluation of the costs and benefits.

The analysis of the capacity to reach the objectives is important for the evaluation of efficacy and efficiency. This analysis has considered the rehabilitation and prevention activities that have been carried out within each of the welfare systems. We have demonstrated the Swedish authorities' much greater commitment to the aim of rehabilitation (in terms of the services that have been offered, and the proportion of drug addicts who have been helped by the social services). The primary and secondary prevention activities that have been carried out in Sweden have had considerable success in limiting the disadvantages of unprivileged social strata and ethnic groups. Compared with the United States, the Swedish welfare state has taken advantage of income-redistributing policies. Accordingly, it has been in a better position to achieve its institutional aims. Among these aims was limiting the risk of poverty (defined according to conventional criteria) and of other sources of hardship (inadequate health conditions and housing, long-term youth unemployment), and also reducing their concentration within the minority ethnic groups. Among the benefits, the lower prevalence of both hard and soft drugs in Sweden, as compared to the United States, has been emphasized. The proportion of regular users of hard drugs is three times greater in the United States than in Sweden. The amount of regular users of soft drugs in relation to the entire youth population is more than three times higher in the United States.

The comparative cost analysis, with reference to the respective GNPs, has brought to light the different orientation of the drug policies and relative public spending. Sweden spends relatively little on its prison inmates, not so much because the daily maintenance of the prisoners is less expensive than in the United States, but rather because (a) there are far fewer prison inmates; (b) each prisoner spends on average less time in prison, and the probability of returning to prison is far less.

More generally, Sweden spends far less (a sixth of what the United States spends, in relation to its GNP) to repress the violation of laws that prohibit drug use and trafficking. On the other hand, Sweden spends proportionately more on rehabilitation and prevention. Public spending on the rehabilitation of people with addictions to drugs (including alcohol) amounts to 0.15 percent of the GNP: it is therefore possible for all known drug addicts to undergo rehabilitation (voluntary or coerced). As far as it has been possible to verify, the corresponding evaluations for the United States are lacking. Still, the literature available in this field has highlighted the problem of insufficient funding, worsened by the funding reductions of the eighties, to rehabilitate all drug addicts and even to complete the rehabilitation that was already under way.

Furthermore, unlike the United States, Sweden also spends considerably on activities of secondary prevention, which aim at dissuading people who are considered to be potential drug users from taking these substances. Secondary prevention is carried out, for the most part, by the social services, whose costs amount to 8 percent of the GNP, about one-quarter of the total social spending. This figure, as a percentage of GNP, is more than one and one-half times the corresponding percentage in the United States, whereas the percentage of GNP absorbed by all public spending (including social spending) in Sweden is twice as high. This difference is not due so much to the increased spending commitment in Sweden on social pensions, and does not depend at all on higher spending on welfare and health (which is, in relation to GNP, much higher in the United States).

Rather, most of the social spending comes from expenditure items (all of which, except for health, are of greater import in Sweden) that are part of the vast category called social security, which does not have a social insurance nature but is financed by the treasury. It therefore provides benefits to all citizens (Ferrera 1993:59). These services, which are very expensive, are provided by the Swedish welfare state for citizens and foreign residents who find themselves for some reason or other in difficulty. These are not only people who belong to families with problems, prison inmates, and drug addicts, but also people who, because of an inadequate income, cannot find affordable housing, or the jobless who are in need of financial aid or professional training. Thus, compared to the United States, Sweden spends a higher percentage of GNP on public housing, and even more on active and passive labor policies.

According to criminologists and experts on social policies, the congruence between the objectives that have been pursued and the results that have been expected is characteristic of Swedish drug policies, whereas U.S. policies stand out for their incongruence. As the "new penology" school of criminology contends, the inclination toward crime connotes well-defined categories of people who are easily identifiable, and whose imprisonment would not influence their future behavior. These arguments have been known as being unfounded and counterproductive since the eighties. Nevertheless, this idea continues to be popular with politicians and a significant portion of U.S. public opinion. During the eighties Charles Murray's arguments enjoyed similar popularity in conservative circles. As Murray (1984) maintained, welfare leads to a "culture of dependence" and therefore to less inclination toward marriage and work, and ultimately to a higher level of poverty. These claims have led to research that has demonstrated, on the contrary:

1. The inclination toward work and marriage is a result of income and work opportunities.

2. Social assistance transfers have not created dependence and have significantly eased poverty, whereas the funding cuts at the beginning of the eighties have made poverty more widespread and severe.

A new social assistance policy, which asserted itself in the second half of the eighties with the support of the Democrats and Republicans and the endorsement of scholars in the field, has provided low-income workers with tax refunds. This has turned out to be, however, not very effective and capable of generating perverse effects. Other measures, which may be more effective, would not obtain enough public support.

An incongruence between the objectives and the expected results of these policies has not been found in Sweden. Rehabilitation, which has been going on for years, conforms to the current recommendations of U.S. scholars. The Swedish social services strive to reach all drug addicts, offering them psychiatric care and counseling to help them overcome work and family problems. The social services also supply certain categories of drug addicts with methadone, but under the strict supervision of medical staff and social services. The (relatively few) Swedish drug addicts therefore are not left to themselves. There is a systematic attempt to detoxify them and rehabilitate them socially in a context that psychologically supports the person, as is recommended in the literature but is rarely available in the United States. The effectiveness of rehabilitation is then systematically evaluated.

In terms of spending, rehabilitation remains nevertheless subordinate to activities of primary and secondary prevention. Primary prevention has helped limit ethnic and social inequalities, as well as unemployment and exit from the labor market, by means of heavy investments in education and professional retraining. Secondary prevention has enabled families,

schools, and youth organizations to carry out the task, in collaboration
with the authorities, of properly socializing and exerting social control
over youth. Primary and secondary prevention and rehabilitation have
been mutually supportive, in conformity with the lessons that U.S. experts
have learned from the disastrous experience of poverty, race discrimination, crime, and the spread of drugs in the urban ghettos, and more generally on the national level. The Swedish welfare system, which includes
prevention and rehabilitation policies, has recently been modified toward
a welfare mix. To this end, services have been contracted out to nonprofit
private organizations that work autonomously, but under public control.
Even if the peculiar Swedish welfare mix has not succeeded in reducing
the costs of services considerably, it may eventually reduce the distance between the citizens and those who provide the services. The literature has
emphasized this distance as a danger to the "state-based" welfare systems,
such as the Swedish one.

The discrepancy between the explicit objectives and expected results of
the policies on the one hand, and their effects on the other, shows that perverse effects have ensued. In the United States the repressive policies on
drugs, and criminal deviance as a whole, have generalized the prison experience to a broad fraction of the underclass, principally those belonging
to racial or other ethnic minorities, with many undesirable consequences.
Among them are the difficulties male ex-convicts experience in trying to
reenter the labor market and form new families. Furthermore, widespread
imprisonment has produced a scarcity of men who do not have a criminal
background, and who are therefore considered eligible marriage partners—hence the proliferation of single-parent families headed by women
who have been forced to live off social assistance. The scarcity of employment and intact families has in turn produced difficult interpersonal relationships in some city neighborhoods. It has also reduced social control,
and thereby increased crime, particularly that connected to drug trafficking. As a consequence, opportunities to find employment in illegal activities have also increased, while it has become even more difficult to enlist
the support of the inhabitants in neighborhood rehabilitation or to persuade them to collaborate with the authorities.

The spread of crime and the local population's involvement in it, either
voluntarily or involuntarily, result in the area and its inhabitants being
negatively labeled by public opinion and the police. This leads to longer
and more frequent detention periods for those who are considered—
wrongly or rightly—to be criminals. Resorting systematically to imprisonment, without giving young males the opportunity to work and fit in
socially, is a self-feeding process, and is therefore inefficient and counterproductive as an instrument to keep crime, and in particular drug trafficking and use, under control. Due to the high costs of imprisonment, the
fact that imprisonment is preferred as the way of controlling crime leads

to other undesirable consequences. In addition to causing a vicious circle of imprisonment and crime, fewer funds become available for welfare. The use and distribution of drugs spread and consolidate also for these reasons.

The lack of funds allocated to the rehabilitation of drug addicts has increased local crime, for the costs of rehabilitation that are available for a fee are too high for most drug addicts, who prefer either to forgo rehabilitation or pay for it by committing crimes. Moreover, welfare measures in the United States have proved to be not only costly and ineffective in preventing crime (not that this was their primary objective), but also counterproductive in other ways. With the aim of reducing social spending, heavy cuts were made at the beginning of the eighties to social assistance transfers, especially for mothers with dependent children, and to social insurance benefits for the unemployed. However, a longer average period of poverty and an increase in the number of poverty-stricken people have resulted from the reduction in the amount of welfare benefits and in the number of those who are legally entitled to receive them. Furthermore, the number of the poor was increased by those formerly employed, who either lost the right to unemployment benefits or received insufficient benefits. The attempt to reduce social spending had no great results, as expenditures were only reduced by a few percentage points, and were still proportionally higher than in Sweden. And yet, against the explicit objectives of the Reagan administration, both the number of poor people—many of whom either received no or insufficient benefits—and the average duration of poverty greatly increased.

This perverse effect has continued, despite the fact that the 1988 Family Support Act moved away from the federal and therefore also local administrations' objective of cutting welfare spending as much as possible. The spread of poverty, on the other hand, has also been a perverse effect of the ethnic-economic segregation produced by public housing policies. The public programs of urban renewal have involved demolishing deteriorated buildings, and have produced a gentrification effect by moving the ethnic and economically underprivileged population elsewhere. This effect contrasts with the declared intention of the Fair Housing Act (1968), to prevent ethnic segregation in the process of residential settlement. In addition, as a further perverse effect, the segregation policy that was de facto pursued by the previous housing policies made it difficult to carry out the new and opposite objective of desegregation, against the probable intentions of the federal authorities.

In Sweden on the other hand, the repression—albeit very strong—of drug trafficking and use does not involve the negative social consequences of imprisonment that have been reported in the literature, since imprisonment is in general neither long nor recurrent. Instead, the authorities endeavor to rehabilitate and reinsert the imprisoned drug addicts, and the inmate population in general, into society. They also try not to create the social conditions to which they themselves rightly attribute the spread of drug addiction. In short, instead of aiming almost exclusively at the repression of drug trafficking and use, the Swedish authorities have preferred to commit themselves to the threefold objective of repression, rehabilitation, and prevention. They have done so with continuity, and by exerting centralized political and administrative authority.

Primary prevention refers to the objective, shared by the Swedish political elite and by most of the population, to limit absolute and relative deprivation. The alleged perverse effects claimed by authors hostile to Swedish social democracy concern the redistribution of income and the availability of free public services. The policies of income redistribution have been put into practice by means of a heavy and steeply progressive taxation system, a rigid labor market, and limited wage differentials. These policies have been blamed for reducing the inclination to work, and therefore for producing economic ruin in the long run. All these contentions are objectionable. First of all, no correlation has been found between the amount of social expenditures, compared with the GNP, and the inclination to work. Furthermore, a pronounced inequality may produce a reduced inclination to work, while, as proved for Sweden, income support measures favor a (female) presence in the job market.

Moreover, the rigidity of the Swedish job market is softened by the widespread existence of part-time work, whereas the deregulation that characterizes the U.S. job market generates poverty. In any case, the causal relationship between the rigidity of the job market and unemployment is dubious. Finally, the difficulties of the Swedish economy in the eighties and above all at the beginning of the nineties—a slowing down of the growth of production and GNP, an increase in inflation and unemployment, an increase in the national debt and budget deficit—cannot apparently be attributed to the social-democratic governments. Rather, they may be imputed to the conservative coalitions that, while in office, put into practice the economic policies that were later criticized. The present significant economic improvement, shown by a number of indicators, has been achieved without having to substantially reduce welfare services by the social-democratic government that returned to power in 1994, after three years of conservative government.

Another contention of the critics of Swedish social democracy is that the public and free availability of social services, in particular regarding education and health, would be inefficient, as too expensive in terms of their quality, which is considered to be inadequate, and also discriminatory toward nonprivileged classes. However, the quality of the Swedish public services, which are dominant by comparison to private services, is generally very high. This is indicated by the high level of education of the population, and particularly by the technical skills of the working class, as well as by the average life span (among the highest in the world) and the infant mortality rate (among the lowest in the world). The Swedish, and in general Scandinavian, welfare mix was reformed in the early nineties by decentralizing to local authorities the responsibility for many public services, such as the detoxification and rehabilitation of drug addicts.

In an attempt to control the high and increasing costs of public services, ample operative space has been left to nonprofit organizations, more so than to the firms that were operating on a profit basis. Still, strict public control has been maintained over the management and budget of these service organizations. This peculiar welfare mix has apparently succeeded in preserving the high level of quality of Swedish social services, maintaining the redistribution effect, and—despite the high cost of this—giving benefits that are compatible with the budget restrictions. The perverse effect of reducing the opportunities of educational mobility has not materialized, for they continue to be very high compared to the United States. Moreover, the distribution of services by private organizations should lead to a reduction in the distance between the administration and the service users. This distance is another one of the alleged perverse effects that literature attributes to "state-based" welfare systems.

A comparison between the social policies enacted in Italy and those in the United States and Sweden shows an overall common repressive line and attribution of power to the local administrative authorities in charge of the preventive and rehabilitative activities. Furthermore, the comparison shows the importance everywhere of the collaboration provided by nonprofit, state-financed, private organizations. Still, in some other respects, the policies enacted in Italy are similar only to the Swedish policies. In both countries repression, rehabilitation, and prevention are coordinated, centralized, and aimed at all consumers, whether actual or potential, even if they are not drug addicts; and there is a commitment to a systematic and centralized evaluation of the outcome of these policies. Finally, there are policies that have been enacted in order to contain relative deprivation. Social welfare, labor policies (active and passive, planned and financed by the central administrations), and housing, education, and health are instrumental to this goal. The objective to redistribute income, and life opportunities in general, shared by all these state policies, has been followed with less determination and consistency in the United States (cf. Tables 1A and 1B).

Having compared the benefits, and considered in particular the policies concerning rehabilitation and the secondary prevention of drug consumption, we have observed that in Italy law 309/1990 put an end to the fragmentation of both public and private initiatives. Their fragmentation had previously marked Italy in the same way as the United States. Later, the centralized management of drug policies together with public recognition for the private nonprofit organizations brought Italy nearer to Sweden.

And yet, only Sweden has seriously pursued the objective of rehabilitating all drug addicts. A systematic activity of prevention has been carried out in schools over many years, and just as systematically the effectiveness of detoxification and rehabilitative programs has been evaluated.

If the benefits of the primary prevention programs in Italy do not stand up to a comparison with the corresponding Swedish programs, they are nevertheless superior to those in the United States. In terms of assistance, Italy has a welfare system that is not particularly effective in limiting the spread of poverty (defined according to conventional criteria). It is less effective than Sweden, but more effective compared to the United States, even though only in the United States is social assistance to the needy the right of every citizen and are unemployment benefits guaranteed in principle (but not in fact) to all the unemployed. Only in Sweden are the unemployed adequately guaranteed against the risk of poverty.

Active labor policies are a tool for combating unemployment that only Sweden has made use of on a large scale. In Italy there has been much legislation on the matter but generally with limited results, above all regarding the youth workforce (which is in most cases unemployed or employed in the secondary labor market). With respect to the United States, and even more so to Sweden, the Italian female labor force is relatively disadvantaged: Italian women are economically active less often than U.S. or Swedish women, and are more often unemployed. They are often (as in the United States) in a condition of relative, or at times even absolute, deprivation. However, the Italian welfare system, which is considerably developed in terms of the number of personnel employed, employs a great proportion of the total female labor force, even if proportionally less than in northern Europe.

The benefits of Italian public housing policies are poor. As with similar policies in the United States, there are quantitative and qualitative failures if the objective of covering the housing needs of the less well-off are considered. However, better—if not totally satisfying—results have been obtained in Sweden. As for the common objective of giving the same educational possibilities to all residents, an evaluation of the efficacy of this has placed Italy after Sweden and the United States. The influence of social origins on educational opportunities in Italy is strong (about the same as in the United States) and the level of schooling of youth is comparatively low (although rapidly increasing). Italian health policies that have been evaluated according to some indicators—infant mortality, life expectancy at birth, spread of AIDS—are relatively effective. Results obtained place Italy in an intermediate position that is better than that of the United States, but the gap with Sweden remains. This conclusion holds true, in particular, for the prevalence of drug addiction (cf Tables 2A and 2B).

Table 1A. Enacted Policies

Normative Framework	
United States	Intransigent prohibition
Sweden	Intransigent prohibition
Italy	Intransigent prohibition

Rehabilitation	
United States	Aimed at only those who want it; not centralized; not coordinated
Sweden	Voluntary or forced; directed at all drug addicts; centralized and coordinated
Italy	Aimed at only those who want it; weak centralization; weak coordination

Primary and Secondary Prevention	
United States	Welfare policies that pursue income redistribution only to a limited extent; in particular, labor policies (active and above all passive) lacking in extension and services; social insurance policies lacking in extension; welfare policies lacking in extension and services; housing policies lacking in quality and quantity; lack of centralization of drug use and abuse prevention policies
Sweden	Centralized and coordinated primary, secondary and tertiary prevention; an institutional commitment to limit the relative deprivation produced by poverty, unequal income distribution, health services, availability and quality of housing
Italy	Primary prevention being reformed; currently social assistance is provided in a variety of ways (in addition to an experimental guaranteed minimum income; disability and old age pensions; ordinary and extraordinary wage guarantee fund; social pensions); many social-welfare policies are the responsibility of private nonprofit organizations
	Labor policies: a heterogeneous and non-coordinated variety of active and passive policies

continued

Table 1A. Continued

> Housing policies: subsidized public housing, financial support for private housing; other housing subsidies for people on low incomes; public financing to recover rundown areas
>
> Education: predominance of public education, compulsory education until the age of 15; public financing for schools at every level, for both public and private non-profit institutions; compulsory training courses until the age of 18 for those who did not attend school after the age of 15
>
> Health: National Health Service available to all citizens, but incomplete in terms of services and financing, together with a fee-paying private health service; regional control of the management, quality, and efficiency of the Health Service

Table 1B. Comparison of Enacted Policies

Normative Framework

United States, Sweden, Italy	Intransigent prohibition

Rehabilitation

United States, Sweden, Italy	Rehabilitation carried out by the local administration, often in collaboration with private organizations (many of them nonprofit organizations), partly state-financed
Sweden, Italy	Centralized and coordinated rehabilitation of drug addicts

Primary and secondary prevention

United States, Sweden, Italy	Preventive interventions by local administrations, often in collaboration with private organizations (many of them nonprofit), partly state-financed
Sweden, Italy	Primary and secondary prevention (more in Sweden than in Italy), directed toward all actual and potential consumers; reduction of relative deprivation through adequate measures of social assistance (recently set up in Italy)

Table 2A. Benefits

Rehabilitation

United States   Lack of money for rehabilitation, relatively few drug
                  addicts undergo therapy; no institutional commitment
                  for their social-professional insertion into society
Sweden   Almost all drug addicts undergo complete therapy
                  (not only pharmacological) with good results;
                  maximum commitment for their social-professional
                  reintegration
Italy   High percentage of drug addicts, but probably only a mi-
                  nority, undergo basic therapy (only pharmacological),
                  complete treatment, or at least not only pharmacologi-
                  cal, often—but not always—available on request; in-
                  sufficient institutional commitment for their social-
                  professional insertion

Prevention

United States   Poor benefits on the whole; strong and increasing inequal-
                  ity of income, relatively widespread poverty; social as-
                  sistance and medical services for poor citizens insuffi-
                  cient in terms of quality and coverage; insufficient
                  passive labor policies in terms of extent and total
                  amount of subsidies; poor active labor policies; work-
                  fare inefficient for the professional retraining and social-
                  professional insertion; housing policies completely
                  insufficient in terms of quantity and quality; soft and
                  heavy drugs very widespread
Sweden   Good benefits; relatively equal distribution of income; lim-
                  ited risk of poverty; public or private, state-supported,
                  services generally excellent in quality; relatively low
                  rate of unemployment; very generous and widely
                  available unemployment benefits; effective active em-
                  ployment policies; fairly good socioeconomic integra-
                  tion of immigrants; relatively low spread of soft drugs,
                  very low spread of heavy drugs; nevertheless relative
                  deprivation has not been completely eliminated, espe-
                  cially in the case of immigrants
Italy   For the moment insufficient welfare social assistance in
                  terms of amount and coverage; social assistance only
                  given to those who request it, with high access barriers
                  and with legislative holes; failed economic and social
                  insertion of socially marginalized

---

continued

Table 2A. Continued

Labor policies: not in favor of most of the unemployed
and of those excluded from the labor market, in particular drug addicts; active labor policies generally
ineffective in opposing unemployment, especially of
youth, and completely ineffective if the unemployed
are drug addicts, even after the promulgation of law
309 / 1990; inadequate housing policies both in quantity
and quality

Education policies: increasing percentage of school enrol-
ment, but inequalities in educational possibilities have
been maintained (in terms of quality and years of education); ineffective professional training

Health policies: progressive improvement in the health situation, but strong social differences in health conditions and access to services; no benefits of the health
reform as yet; strong spread of soft drugs, much more
limited spread of heavy drugs; high prevalence of
drug addictions, and therefore poor efficacy of law
309 / 1990

An evaluation of the efficiency of the drug policies involves a consideration of their cost in terms of the GNP. Proportionally Italy spends overall
about 25 percent more than the United States on social protection, but
around two-thirds of what Sweden spends (despite the recent cuts in public spending). Social assistance, strictly defined, with reference to the GNP
and considered as a whole, is inversely correlated with its effectiveness: it
is highest in the United States, lower in Italy, and lowest in Sweden, where
the poor are paradoxically much better covered, and therefore that cost is
considerably more per capita. Financial transfers to the families, generally
provided as welfare benefits, have grown in Italy over the last years in
absolute and relative terms, after a period of relative decline. Still, this financial aid affects the GNP proportionally less in Italy than in other industrialized countries, in Sweden in particular, despite the cuts in the
social assistance transfers implemented there in the early part of the
nineties. In the United States, proportionally less was spent on social assistance than in Italy or in other OECD countries, even though the percentage of GNP allocated to this expenditure has increased (except during
the Reagan period) since the fifties. Active labor policies are social policies
addressed to all citizens, so that their costs are covered by public funds,
while passive labor policies have a social assistance character when they
are not financed with mandatory national insurance contributions.

Generally speaking, the GNP percentages spent in Italy on active or passive labor policies have been higher than in the United States, and lower than in Sweden, but closer to the former. The available data do not bring to light the low effectiveness (shown by the cost/benefit ratio) of Italian policies in this area. The U.S. authorities have basically handed over the problem of unemployment to the market, and obtained variable results (quite good in the nineties), widespread poverty among the unemployed of the secondary labor market, and a strong dualism in this market, but still by spending relatively little. The Swedish authorities have faced this problem by spending heavily, but limiting the dualism between primary and secondary labor markets, avoiding poverty from unemployment, and containing the numbers of jobless (except in the first half of the nineties). The Italian authorities have spent quite considerable sums as a percentage of the GNP, obtaining, however, one of the highest rates of unemployment among the industrialized countries (especially among youth, women, and the long-term unemployed, which are categories that often overlap), strong dualism, and a frequent condition of poverty among the jobless, especially adults. It seems difficult to compare the efficiency of U.S. and Swedish labor policies, considering that they have been given relatively little importance in the United States, and that the containment of unemployment has been but one of the objectives of the Swedish policies. In any case, both have been much more effective than the corresponding Italian policies.

Likewise, the effectiveness of Italian policies in the area of education has been modest. Public spending in this area has been proportionally slightly less in Italy than in the United States, and very low compared to Sweden. Compared to the United States, there is a shorter average schooling period in Italy, and access to higher education by socially disadvantaged people is much more limited than in Sweden. Until recently, in Italy there was no policy that guaranteed higher education to the broadest number of people: therefore it is not possible to speak of inefficiency in this case. On the other hand in Italy as in Sweden, the objective has been to make education equally available for everyone. The failure to achieve this objective in Italy, as opposed to the partial success in Sweden, suggests that spending on education—despite being proportionally lower—has been more inefficiently allocated in Italy.

Despite the presence of various forms of welfare mix in all three countries, for the most part health spending is private in the United States, but state funded in Italy and Sweden. The percentage of GNP that is thus allocated in these two countries is close to the European Union average. The Italian health situation, measured according to various indicators, can be placed on a European level, and therefore is rather good. On the whole, it is superior to the corresponding U.S. situation, in spite of the latter's continuous and considerable progress. Nevertheless, given that health spending is proportionally the same in Sweden and Italy, whereas the health conditions in Italy are worse than those in Sweden, Italy's policies in this area have proven to be less efficient in comparison to this country. Their efficiency is in line with those of other European countries and, as in them, much higher than the efficiency of U.S. health spending.

A comparative analysis of efficiency should be conducted in terms of the costs and benefits of public spending on the rehabilitation and social insertion of drug addicts, and on the prevention of the use and abuse of drugs. This analysis has not been carried out for the three countries we have studied. A comparative evaluation of efficiency would require more complete, valid, and reliable knowledge of

(a) the total public spending in this area, especially as far as the United States is concerned;

(b) the benefits, in particular, the respective rates of prevalence of drug addiction, and the proportion of drug addicts who have been rehabilitated and reinserted into society in each country.

We have, nevertheless, given indications concerning the respective sums (with reference to the GNP) of the areas of public spending and with reference to the respective prevalence of drug addiction. Furthermore, we have provided information on the relation between the costs and benefits (in terms of social recovery) of public policies in Sweden and the United States, while the information regarding the benefits—so defined—in Italy is completely insufficient. The considerably higher spending commitment in Sweden, compared to the United States, in the area of public policies with recovery objectives seems to be causally related to the effectiveness of these policies.

In short, an increased financial commitment seems to have formed a necessary condition for the achievement of far more satisfactory results. A different indicator of efficiency has also been used. The total amount of public spending on social protection, in relation to the GNP, may be related to the rates of prevalence of drug addiction. As far as primary prevention is concerned, the considerable inefficiency of the U.S. social policies, the considerable efficiency of the Swedish policies, and the intermediate position of the Italian policies, have been brought into light. We have, however, observed that the primary prevention of drug addiction has never been an objective of the U.S. social policies, and therefore an evaluation of efficiency in this case would be inappropriate.

Such an evaluation would, however, be appropriate for public policies that set a common goal. All three countries have made use of policies of social control, specifically of imprisonment. These policies have been an instrument both to control drug dealing, and in the case of Sweden and the United States, to control the use of drugs as well. The mainly repressive goal of the U.S. drug policies has been shown to be very inefficient, in relation to the benefits shown by the prevalence of drug addiction. The corresponding Swedish policies, on the other hand, have been very efficient, while the Italian policies occupy an intermediate position. The degree to which repressive drug policies have taken place has been measured by the total cost of the prison administration (in terms of the GNP percentage), and by the imprisonment rates (number of inmates per thousand inhabitants).

In conclusion, the study has shown the considerable success Sweden has had, compared with the United States and Italy, in reaching the stated objectives of the respective drug policies. The common objective of repressing the use and traffic of drugs has not been reached in the United States and Italy, where the use of drugs is widespread, whereas there has been good, albeit incomplete achievement of these objectives in Sweden. The capacity of the Swedish political-administrative authorities to carry out the objectives of rehabilitating drug addicts without creating the social conditions that further the use of drugs was also high. On the other hand, these objectives have been pursued with much less commitment in the United States and with much less effectiveness in Italy. Swedish social policies have also been more efficient when compared with Italian policies, and even more so compared with U.S. policies, for the objective of containing drug use through repression has been pursued with better results than in the other two countries, and by spending much less (with relation to the GNP) than in the United States.

The comparative evaluation of efficiency becomes less certain if we consider the objectives of rehabilitation and prevention, since they have not been so important—considering the relative spending commitment—in the United States. U.S. authorities have in fact spent proportionally less on the rehabilitation of drug addicts as well as on activities of secondary prevention, and in most cases even primary prevention. Nevertheless, on the whole not negligible sums of money have been committed, compared to which the results that have been obtained have been—to say the least—inadequate. Benefits achieved through rehabilitation and prevention have been limited not only by the insufficient budgets, but also by a lack of coordination in the activities that have been carried out. Recent efforts to coordinate rehabilitation activities that have been carried out in various centers and states may point to a future improvement in the efficiency of these services. Currently, this efficiency is low and greatly inferior in comparison to Sweden. The relative inefficiency of preventive activities in the United States, compared to Sweden, is better highlighted if these activities are compared in the welfare and health areas, in which the spending commitment has been more or less the same. In fact, for both these areas it has been shown that the United States spends more (in proportion to the GNP) despite continuing to have more poor people, a higher average duration of poverty, more frequent periods of poverty, and a population with a worse health situation, above all for the poor.

Their quite distinct capacities of reaching the objectives, and their quite distinct efficiency in putting their policies into practice, are precisely what might have been foreseen by referring to the scholarly literature available already before implementation of the drug policies began. The references to the specialized literature, which often makes use of multivariate analysis techniques, have made it easier to argue the existence of a causal relationship between different welfare policies and the spread of drugs in specific populations of comparable income. The efficacy and efficiency of the primary prevention policies have turned out to be very different in the United States and Sweden, whereas Italy has been an intermediate case. Over the past decades, U.S. political elites, perhaps owing to strong pressure from public opinion, have followed a policy of mass incarceration and substantial reductions in welfare spending, as the best answers to the social problems of crime (including that connected to drugs) and poverty.

That these policies have been useless and dangerous was, and still is, a conviction of most specialized scholars, who already in the eighties were advising rehabilitation, a fight against poverty, and public support for the insertion of rehabilitated drug users into the workplace. Maybe without complete awareness of this advice, the Swedish authorities directed their welfare policies precisely at these objectives, whose efficacy (evaluated before the policies had been actuated and external to them) has been high. Subsequently, the comparative consideration of the perverse effects of the drug policies has confirmed the differing evaluation of external efficacy. The essentially repressive U.S. solution to the drug problem has contributed to spreading the very crimes that it was intended to discourage. In Italy, rehabilitation and prevention have been the objectives of public policies, rather than their results. They have also had perverse effects, though Italian policies have been more effective and efficient compared to U.S. policies. Finally, the Swedish commitment to policies that have been at the same time repressive, rehabilitative, and (above all) preventive has not only considerably limited the spread of drugs, but also has had no perverse effects, as we have argued.

The theoretical objective of the study has been to ascertain which drug policies have been more effective and efficient, and for which reasons: a comparison between Swedish, U.S., and Italian policies has served this purpose. Whether our study will fulfill its practical objective of guiding the authorities in their task of containing the use of drugs we cannot say. The commitment and the capability of the Swedish political-administrative authorities have not had and will not probably in the future have similar results outside Scandinavia. On a negative note, however, the failure of the U.S. experience, which we have dealt with at length, may serve to dissuade politicians and public opinion from undertaking repressive policies that, when not accompanied by activities of rehabilitation and prevention on a large scale, are ineffective, costly, and counterproductive.

References

Abrahamson, P. 1988. *Social Movements and the Welfare State: Comparing The Struggle against Urban Poverty in Scandinavia and the U.S.* Working paper no. 5, Sociologisk Institut, Copenhagen.

Abrahamson, P. 1991. "Welfare and Poverty in the Europe of the 1990s: Social Progress or Social Dumping?" *International Journal of Health Services* 21(2):237–64.

Abrahamson, P. 1993. "Labour Market Insertion: Some International Experiences." Pp. 123–38 in M. Ferrera (Ed.), *The Evaluation of Social Policies: Experiences and Perspectives.* Milan: Giuffrè.

Akerlof, G. A. 1982. "Labor Contracts as Partial Gift Exchange." *Quarterly Journal of Economics* 97(4):541–69.

Akers, R. L. 1991. "Addiction: The Troublesome Concept." *Journal of Drug Issues* 21(4):777–93.

Albanesi, V. 1999. "Un commento finale. Il CNCA e il Welfare State." Pp. 277–97 in U. Ascoli (Ed.), *Il Welfare futuro. Manuale critico del Terzo settore.* Rome: Carocci.

Albini, S. 1999. "Il finanziamento degli ospedali." *Tendenze Nuove* 8(luglio/agosto):58–59.

Allan, E., and Steffensmeier, D. J. 1989. "Youth, Underemployment, and Property Crime: Differential Effects of Job Availability and Job Quality on Juvenile and Young Adult Arrest Rates." *American Sociological Review* 54(February):107–23.

Andersen, J. G., et al. 1999. "The legitimacy of the Nordic welfare states: trends, variations and cleavages." Pp. 235–61 in M. Kautto, M. Heikkila, B. Hvinden, S. Marklund, and N. Plough (Eds.), *Nordic Welfare States in the European Context.* London: Routledge.

Anderson, E. 1993. "Sex Codes and Family Life among Poor Inner-City Youth." Pp. 6–95 in W. J. Wilson (Ed.), *The Ghetto Underclass.* London: Sage.

Angell, M. 1999. "The American Health Care System Revisited." *New England Journal of Medicine* 340(1):48.

Anglin, M. D., and Hser, Y.-I. 1990. "Treatment of Drug Abuse." Pp. 393–460 in M. Tonry and J. Q. Wilson (Eds.), *Drugs and Crime.* Chicago: University of Chicago Press.

Anheier, H. K., and Salomon, L. M. 1997. "Il settore non-profit: una nuova forza globale." Pp. 296–308 in G. Rossi (Ed.), *Terzo settore, stato e mercato nella trasformazione delle politiche sociali in Europa.* Milan: FrancoAngeli.

Ardigò, A. 1999. "L'ospedale tra sistema sociale e ambiente. Impianti concettuali e alcune problematiche empiriche." *Tendenze nuove* 8(luglio/agosto):8–13.

Arnell-Gustafsson, U. 1982. "On Strategies against Socio-economic Residential Segregation." *Acta Sociologica* 25(Supplement):33–40.

Arsanogullari, S. 2000. *Social Assistance in Sweden 1990–1985.* Dept. of Economics, Uppsala University.

Arzuffi, O. 1991. *Emarginazione a-z.* Casale Monferrato: Piemme.

Ascoli, U. 1984. "Il sistema italiano di Welfare." Pp. 5–51 in U. Ascoli (Ed.), *Welfare State all'italiana.* Roma: Laterza.

Ascoli, U. 1987. "Il sistema italiano di Welfare tra ridimensionamento e riforma." Pp. 283–312 in U. Ascoli and R. Catanzaro (Eds.), *La società italiana degli anni ottanta.* Rome: Laterza.

Ascoli, U. 1992a. "L'azione volontaria nei sistemi di welfare." *Polis* 6(3):429–36.

Ascoli, U. 1992b. "Nuovi scenari per le politiche sociali degli anni 90: uno spazio stabile per l'azione volontaria?" *Polis* 6(3):507–33.

Bàculo, L. 1997. "Segni di industrializzazione leggera nel Mezzogiorno." *Stato e Mercato* 51:377–417.

Bagozzi, F. 1999. "Ecstasy: alcune note a margine." *Narcomafie* 7(12):21–22.

Bakanic, V. 1995. "I'm Not Prejudiced But . . . : A Deeper Look at Racial Attitudes." *Sociological Inquiry* 65:67–86.

Baraldi, C. 1994a. *Suoni nel silenzio.* Milan: FrancoAngeli.

Baraldi, C. 1994b. "Comunicazione, socializzazione e droga." Pp. 83–211 in C. Baraldi and M. Ravenna (Eds.), *Fra dipendenza e rifiuto.* Milan: FrancoAngeli.

Barbagli, M. 1998. *Immigrazione e criminalità in Italia.* Bologna: Il Mulino.

Barbetta, G. P. 1993. "Il settore nonprofit: approcci economici." Pp. 61–75 in U. Ascoli and S. Pasquinelli (Eds.), *Il Welfare Mix. Stato sociale e terzo settore.* Milan: FrancoAngeli.

Barbetta, G. P., and Ranci, C. 1997. "Terzo settore e nuove politiche sociali: il caso italiano." Pp. 177–214 in G. Rossi (Ed.), *Terzo settore, stato e mercato nella trasformazione delle politiche sociali in Europa.* Milan: FrancoAngeli.

Battaglia, M., and Coletti, M. 1987. *Come parlare di droga nella scuola. Riflessioni e suggerimenti.* Rome: La Nuova Italia Scientifica.

Bentivegna, S. 1990. "Il tempo della scuola." Pp. 355–90 in Consiglio Nazionale dei Minori, *Secondo rapporto sulla condizione dei minori in Italia.* Milan: FrancoAngeli.

Berk, R. A. 1988. "Causal Inferences from Sociological Data." Pp. 155–72 in N. J. Smelser (Ed.), *Handbook of Sociology.* London, Sage.

Berry, B. J. L. 1985. "Islands of Renewal in Seas of Decay." Pp. 69–96 in P. E. Peterson (Ed.), *The New Urban Reality.* Washington, DC: Brookings Institution.

Berzano, L. 1991. "Il vagabondaggio nella metropoli." Pp. 153–76 in P. Guidicini (Ed.), *Gli studi sulla povertà in Italia.* Milan: FrancoAngeli.

Bianchi, S. 1999. "Feminization and Juvenilization of Poverty. Trends, Relative Risks, Causes, and Consequences." *Annual Review of Sociology* 25:307–33.

Bjorgo, T. 1995. Pp. 182–220 in T. Bjorgo (Ed.), *Terror from the Extreme Right.* London: Frank Cass.

Blau, P. M., and Golden, R. M. 1986. "Metropolitan Structure and Criminal Violence." *Sociological Quarterly* 27(1):15–26.

Blossfeld, H. P., and Shavit, Y. 1992. "Ostacoli permanenti: le disuguaglianze di istruzione in tredici paesi." *Polis* 6(1):147–79.

Bobo, L., and Zubrinsky, C. L. 1996. "Attitudes on Residential Integration: Perceived Status Differences, Mere In-Group Preference, or Racial Prejudice?" *Social Forces* 74(3):883–909.

Bodenheimer, T. 1999a. "The American Health Care System. The Movement for Improved Quality in Health Care." *New England Journal of Medicine* 340(6):488–492.

Bodenheimer, T. 1999b. "The American Health Care System. Physicians and the Changing Medical Marketplace." *New England Journal of Medicine* 340(7):584–88.

Botvin, G. J. 1990. "Substance Abuse Prevention: Theory Practice, and Effectiveness." Pp. 461–519 in M. Tonry and J. Q. Wilson (Eds.), *Drugs and Crime.* Chicago: University of Chicago Press.

Boudon, R. 1981. *Effetti "perversi" dell'azione sociale.* Milan: Feltrinelli.

Bradshaw, J. 1998. "La condivisione dei costi dei figli: i pacchetti di aiuti per i figli nei paesi dell'Unione Europea nel 1996." *Polis* 12(1):101–19.

Bridges, G. S., and Steen, S. 1998. "Racial Disparities in Official Assessments of Juvenile Offenders: Attributional Stereotypes as Mediating Mechanisms." *American Sociological Review* 63:554–70.

Brunswick, A. F., and Titus, S. P. 1998. "Heroin Patterns and Trajectories in an African American Cohort." Pp. 77–108 in J. A. Inciardi and L. D. Harrison (Eds.), *Heroin in the Age of Crack-Cocaine.* London: Sage.

Busana Banterle, C. 1993. "La previdenza integrata in Italia tra flessibilità di impresa e sicurezza dei lavoratori." *Stato e mercato* 38:243–77.

Buzzi, C. 1997. "Percezione delle norme sociali e trasgressione." Pp. 171–90 in C. Buzzi, A. Cavalli, and A. de Lillo (Eds.), *Giovani verso il Duemila.* Bologna: Il Mulino.

Buzzi, C., Cavalli, A., and de Lillo, A. (Eds.). 1997. *Giovani verso il Duemila.* Bologna: Il Mulino.

Cagossi, M. 1988. *Comunità terapeutiche e non.* Rome: Borla.

Campari, M., and De Negri, A. 1999. "Perché è così difficile in sanità raggiungere i risultati sperati?" *Tendenze nuove* 8(luglio/agosto):76–80.

Carrieri, M., and Donolo, C. 1983. "Oltre l'orizzonte neo-corporativo. Alcuni scenari sul futuro politico del sindacato." *Stato e mercato* 9:475–503.

Caspi, A., Wright, B. R. E., Moffitt, T. E., and Silva, P. A. 1998. "Early Failure in the Labor Market: Childhood and Adolescent Predictors of Unemployment in the Transition to Adulthood." *American Sociological Review* 63(June):424–51.

Cavalli, A., and de Lillo, A. (Eds.). 1988. *Giovani anni 80.* Bologna: Il Mulino.

Cavalli, A., and de Lillo, A. (Eds.). 1993. *Giovani anni 90.* Bologna: Il Mulino.

Censis. 1990. *24° Rapporto/1990 sulla situazione sociale del paese.* Milan: FrancoAngeli.

Censis. 1994. *28° Rapporto/1994 sulla situazione sociale del paese.* Milan: FrancoAngeli.

Censis. 1998. *32° Rapporto/1998 sulla situazione sociale del paese.* Milan: FrancoAngeli.

Censis. 1999. *33° Rapporto/1999 sulla situazione sociale del paese.* Milan: FrancoAngeli.

Chamlin, M. B., and Cochran, J. K. 1995. "Assessing Messner and Rosenfeld's Institutional Anomie Theory: A Partial Test." *Criminology* 33(3):411–29.

Chavis, D. M., Speer, P., Resnick, I., and Zippay, A. 1993. "Building Community Capacity to Address Alcohol and Drug Abuse: Getting to the Heart of the Problem." Pp. 251–84 in R. C. Davis, A. J. Lurigio, D. P. Rosenbaum (Eds.), *Drugs and the Community.* Springfield, IL: Charles C. Thomas.

Chiari, G., Francescutti, C., and Libralato, V. 1992. "Droga e alcool negli adolescenti italiani: un modello esplicativo." *Polis* 6(1):83–115.

Chiesi, A. 1997. "Il lavoro. Strategie di risposta alla crisi." Pp. 55–86 in C. Buzzi, A. Cavalli, and A. de Lillo (Eds.), *Giovani verso il Duemila*. Bologna: Il Mulino.

Chitwood, D. D., Comerford, M., and Weatherby, N. L. 1998. "The Initiation of the Use of Heroin in the Age of Crack." Pp. 77–108 in J. A. Inciardi and L. D. Harrison (Eds.), *Heroin in the Age of Crack-Cocaine*. London: Sage.

Christoffersen, H. 1997. "Social Policy in Denmark." Pp. 170–87 in M. Mullard and S. Lee (Eds.), *The Politics of Social Policy in Europe*. Cheltenham: Edward Elgar.

Clarke, J. 2001. "U.S. Welfare: Variations on the Liberal Regime." Pp. 113–52 in A. Cochrane, J. Clarke, and S. Gewirtz (Eds.), *Comparing Welfare States*. London: Sage.

Clasen, J., Kvist, J., and Van Oorschot, W. 2001. "On Condition of Work: Increasing Work Requirements in Unemployment Compensation Schemes." Pp. 198–231 in M. Kautto, J. Fritzell, B. Hvinden, J. Kvist, and H. Uusitalo (Eds.), *Nordic Welfare States in the European Context*. London: Routledge.

Cloward, R. A. 1960. *Delinquency and Opportunity*. New York: Free Press.

Consiglio Nazionale dell'Economia e del Lavoro. 1994. *Occupazione, disoccupazione e aree di crisi*. Rome: Author.

Cobalti, A. 1996 . "Istruzione e mobilità in Italia: recenti analisi dei dati del 1985." *Polis* 10(3):405–29.

Cohen, A. 1997. "Feeding the Flock." *Time* (European Edition), August 25, pp. 30–32.

Cole, P. S., and Weissberg, R. P. 1994. "Substance Use and Abuse among Urban Adolescents." Pp. 92–122 in T. P. Gullotta, G. R. Adams, and R. Montemayor (Eds.), *Substance Misuse in Adolescence*. London: Sage.

Coleman, A. 1987. "The Social Consequences of Urban Design." Pp. 142–53 in B. Robson (Ed.), *Managing the City*. London: Croom Helm.

Colombo, S., and Merlo, G. 1986. "Tossicodipendenza e criminalità: uno studio della situazione a Torino." *Bollettino per le farmacodipendenze e l'alcolismo* 9(1-2-3):92–119.

Colozzi, I. 1994. "Il sistema pensionistico: quale riforma." in R. De Vita, P. Donati, and G. B. Sgritta (Eds.), *La politica sociale oltre la crisi del Welfare State*. Milan: FrancoAngeli.

Colozzi, I. 1997. "Il principio di sussidiarietà come principio regolatore delle politiche sociali." Pp. 24–33 in G. Rossi (Ed.), *Terzo settore, stato e mercato nella trasformazione delle politiche sociali in Europa*. Milan: FrancoAngeli.

Colozzi, I., and Bassi, A. 1995. *Una solidarietà efficiente*. Rome: La Nuova Italia Scientifica.

Colozzi, I., and Bassi, A. 1996. "I modelli istituzionali di terzo settore: una comparazione internazionale." Pp. 43–59 in P. P. Donati (Ed.), *Sociologia del terzo settore*. Rome: La Nuova Italia Scientifica.

Coluzzi, M., and Palmieri, S. 2001. *Welfare a confronto*. Rome: Ediesse.

Commissione d'indagine sulla povertà e l'emarginazione. 1992. *Secondo rapporto sulla povertà in Italia*. Milan: FrancoAngeli.

Commissione d'indagine sulla povertà e l'emarginazione. 1995. "Una proposta sul minimo vitale." *Forum* 11:13–15.

Comune di Genova. 1998. *Programma d'intervento ai sensi dell'art. 14 del Decreto Legislativo 225/1998*. Genova.

Cook, R. F., and Roehl, J. A. 1993. "National Evaluation of the Community Partnership Program: Preliminary Findings." Pp. 225–48 in R. C. Davis, A. J. Lurigio, and D. P. Rosenbaum (Eds.), *Drugs and the Community*. Springfield, IL: Charles C. Thomas.

Coppini, M. A. 1994. *Le ragioni dello stato sociale*. Rome: Ediesse.

Corte dei Conti. 1996. "Gestione del Fondo nazionale di intervento per la lotta alla droga." *Forum* 12:16–32.

Dahrendorf, R. 1995. *Quadrare il cerchio*. Rome: Laterza.

Danziger, S., and Gottschalk, P. 1995. *America Unequal*. Cambridge, MA: Harvard University Press.

David, P. 1984. "Il sistema assistenziale in Italia." Pp. 185–205 in U. Ascoli (Ed.), *Welfare State all'italiana*. Rome: Laterza.

David, P. 1992. "Pubblico e privato nel settore assistenziale." *Stato e mercato* 38:477–86.

Davies, K., and Esseveld, J. 1982. "Unemployment and Identity: A Study of Women Outside the Labour Market." *Acta Sociologica* 25(3):283–93.

Davis, R. C., and Lurigio, M. N. 1996. *Fighting Back. Neighborhood Antidrug Change*. London: Sage.

Davis, R. C., Lurigio, A. J., and Rosenbaum, D. P. (Eds.). 1993a. *Drugs and the Community*. Springfield, IL: Charles C. Thomas.

Davis, R. C., Lurigio, A. J., and Rosenbaum, D. P. 1993b. "Introduction." Pp. xi—xviii in R. C. Davis, A. J. Lurigio, D. P. Rosenbaum (Eds.), *Drugs and the Community*. Springfield, IL: Charles C. Thomas.

De Bernart, M. 1991. "Storie di povertà e di non cittadinanza." Pp. 193–218 in P. Guidicini (Ed.), *Gli studi sulla povertà in Italia*. Milan: FrancoAngeli.

De Leonardis, O. 1996. "I welfare mix. Privatismo e sfera pubblica." *Stato e mercato* 46:51–75.

De Masi, E., and Grossi, B. 1997. "Alla ricerca della qualità nel servizio sanitario nazionale." *Tendenze nuove* (ottobre/dicembre):35–40.

DeHoog, R. 1993. "Benefici e limiti del contracting-out." Pp. 115–28 in U. Ascoli and S. Pasquinelli (Eds.), *Il Welfare Mix. Stato sociale e terzo settore*. Milan: FrancoAngeli.

Deschenes, E. P., and Greenwood, P. W. 1994. "Treating the Juvenile Drug Offender." Pp. 253–80 in D. L. MacKenzie and C. D. Uchida (Eds.), *Drugs and Crime. Evaluating Public Policy Initiatives*. London: Sage.

DeSena, J. N. 1994. "Local Gatekeeping Practices and Residential Segregation." *Sociological Inquiry* 64(3):307–21.

Devastato, G. 1999. "Terzo settore e regolazione pubblica: Dalle leggi del 1991 al nuovo regime fiscale per le ONLUS." Pp. 115–39 in U. Ascoli (Ed.), *Il Welfare futuro. Manuale critico del Terzo settore*. Rome: Carocci.

Dillion, Y. A. 1999. "Does Racism Really Matter? An Analysis of White Americans' Attitudes toward Welfare Spending." Report presented at the Annual Meeting of the American Sociological Association, Chicago, August 9.

DiMaggio, P., and Anheier, H. 1993. "Per una sociologia delle organizzazioni nonprofit." Pp. 35–59 in U. Ascoli and S. Pasquinelli (Eds.), *Il Welfare Mix. Stato sociale e terzo settore*. Milan: FrancoAngeli.

Dole, V., and Nyswander, M. 1998. "Methadone Maintenance: A Theoretical Perspective." Pp. 280–84 in J. A. Inciardi and K. McElrath (Eds.), *The American Drug Scene*. Los Angeles: Roxbury.

Donati, P. P. 1996. "Introduzione. Nuovi orientamenti nell'analisi e nella promozione del terzo settore." Pp. 13–22 in P. P. Donati (Ed.), *Sociologia del terzo settore*. Rome: La Nuova Italia Scientifica.

Donati, P. P. 1997. "L'analisi sociologica del terzo settore: introdurre la distinzione relazionale terzo settore/privato sociale." Pp. 255–95 in G. Rossi (Ed.), *Terzo settore, stato e mercato nella trasformazione delle politiche sociali in Europa*. Milan: FrancoAngeli.

Donziger, S. R. (Ed.). 1996. *The Real War on Crime. The Report of the National Criminal Justice Commission*. New York: HarperCollins.

Dropping, J. A., Hvinden, B., and Vik, K. 1999. "Activation Policies in the Nordic Countries." Pp. 13–158 in M. Kautto, M. Heikkila, B. Hvinden, S. Marklund, and N. Plough (Eds.), *Nordic Social Policy*. London: Routledge.

Duncan, G. J., Yeung, W. J., Brooks-Gunn, J., and Smith, J. R. 1998. "How Much Does Childhood Poverty Affect the Life Chances of Children?" *American Sociological Review* 63(June):406–23.

Dunn, W. N. 1994. *Public Policy Analysis: An Introduction*. Englewood Cliffs, NJ: Prentice Hall.

Economist Intelligence Unit. 1994a. *Country Report. United States of America*. 4th Quarter.

Economist Intelligence Unit. 1994b. *Country Report. Sweden*. 1st Quarter.

Economist Intelligence Unit. 1995. *Country Report. United States of America*. 1st Quarter.

Economist Intelligence Unit. 1996. *Country Report. Sweden*. 1st Quarter.

Economist Intelligence Unit. 1996–97. *Country Profile. Sweden*.

Economist Intelligence Unit. 1997a. *Country Report. Sweden*. 3rd Quarter.

Economist Intelligence Unit. 1997b. *Country Report. United States of America*. 3rd Quarter.

Economist Intelligence Unit. 1997c. *Country Report. Sweden*. 1st Quarter.

Economist Intelligence Unit. 1998a. *Country Report. Sweden*. 2nd Quarter.

Economist Intelligence Unit. 1998b. *Country Report. Sweden*. 3rd Quarter.

Economist Intelligence Unit. 1998c. *Country Report. Sweden*. 4th Quarter.

Economist Intelligence Unit. 1998–99. *Country Profile. Sweden*.

Eggert, L. L., Seyl, C. D., and Nicholas, L. J. 1990. "Effects of a School-Based Prevention Program for Potential High School Dropouts and Drug Abusers." *International Journal of the Addictions* 25(7):773–801.

Elliott, D. S., Huizinga, D., and Ageton, S. S. 1985. *Explaining Delinquency and Drug Use*. London: Sage.

Erikson, R., and Golthorpe, J. H. 1993. *The Constant Flux: A Study of Class Mobility in Industrial Society*. Oxford: Clarendon.

Esping-Andersen, G. 1990. *The Three Worlds of Welfare Capitalism*. Cambridge: Polity.

Esping-Andersen, G. (Ed.). 1993a. *Changing Classes*. London: Sage.

Esping-Andersen, G. 1993b. "Post-Industrial Class Structures: An Analytical Framework." Pp. 7–31 in G. Esping-Andersen (Ed.), *Changing Classes*. London: Sage.

Esping-Andersen, G. 1997. "Uguaglianza o occupazione? L'interazione fra salario, welfare state e trasformazioni sociali." Pp. 34–51 in G. Rossi (Ed.), *Terzo settore, stato e mercato nella trasformazione delle politiche sociali in Europa*. Milan: FrancoAngeli.

Esping-Andersen, G. 1999. *Social Foundations of Postindustrial Economies.* Oxford: Oxford University Press.

Esping-Andersen, G., Assimakopoulou, Z., and van Kersbergen, K. 1993. "Trends in Contemporary Class Structuration. A Six-nation Comparison." Pp. 32–57 in G. Esping-Andersen (Ed.), *Changing Classes.* London: Sage.

Evers, A. 1993. "Quattro ipotesi per l'analisi del welfare mix." Pp. 97–114 in U. Ascoli and S. Pasquinelli (Eds.), *Il Welfare Mix. Stato sociale e terzo settore.* Milan: FrancoAngeli.

Evers, A. 1997. "Tipi diversi di 'welfare pluralism.' Il nuovo scenario delle politiche sociali in Europa." Pp. 13–23 in G. Rossi (Ed.), *Terzo settore, stato e mercato nella trasformazione delle politiche sociali in Europa.* Milan: FrancoAngeli.

Fagan, J. 1996. "Gangs, Drugs, and Neighborhood Change." Pp. 39–74 in C. R. Huff (Ed.), *Gangs in America.* London: Sage.

Farley, R., and Frey, W. H. 1994. "Changes in the Segregation of Whites from Blacks during the 1980s: Small Steps Toward an Integrated Society." *American Sociological Review* 59(February):23–45.

Feeley, M. M., and Simon, J. 1992. "The New Penology: Notes on the Emerging Strategy of Corrections and Its Implications." *Criminology* 30(4):449–74.

Feldstein, M. 1998. "Asking for Trouble." *Time* (European Edition), January 19, p. 21.

Felson, M. 1998. *Crime and Everyday Life.* London: Pine Forge.

Ferrera, M. 1993. *Modelli di solidarietà.* Bologna: Il Mulino.

Folkhaelsoinstitutet, Centralfoerbundet foer alkohol- och narkokaupplysning. 1996. *Alkohol- och narkotikautvecklingen i Sverige,* Stockholm.

Fong, E. 1996. "A Comparative Perspective on Racial Residential Segregation: American and Canadian Experiences." *Sociological Quarterly* 199–226.

Forti, M. 1991. "Monolocale cercasi disperatamente." Pp. 6–18 in Italia-Razzismo (Eds.), *La casa impossibile. La questione delle abitazioni e gli immigrati.* Rome: marzo.

Friis, E. J. 1988. "Sweden." Pp. 506–7 in *The Americana Annual 1988.* Danbury, CT: Grolier.

Fritzell, J. 1993. "Income Inequality Trends in the 1980s: A Five-Country Comparison." *Acta Sociologica* 36:47–62.

Fritzell, J. 1999. "Changes in the Social Patterning of Living Conditions." Pp. 159–84 in M. Kautto, M. Heikkila, B. Hvinden, S. Marklund, and N. Plough (Eds.), *Nordic Social Policy.* London: Routledge.

Fritzell, J. 2001. "Still Different? Income Distribution in the Nordic Countries in a European Comparison." Pp. 18–41 in M. Kautto, J. Fritzell, B. Hvinden, J. Kvist, and H. Uusitalo (Eds.), *Nordic Welfare States in the European Context.* London: Routledge.

Furaker, B., Johansson, L., and Lind, J. 1990. "Unemployment and Labour Market Policies in the Scandinavian Countries." *Acta Sociologica* 33(2):141–64.

Gallino, L. 1999. "La medicina si chiama computer. Paghiamo ancora il ritardo tecnologico." *La Stampa,* 2 November, p. 3.

Gasperoni, G. 1997. "L'esperienza scolastica: scelte, percorsi, giudizi." Pp. 31–53 in C. Buzzi, A. Cavalli, and A. de Lillo (Eds.), *Giovani verso il Duemila.* Bologna: Il Mulino.

Gentilini, R. 1999. "Affitti, via al fondo sociale." *Corriere della Sera,* 21 July, p. 23.

Giddens, A. 1990. *The Consequences of Modernity*. Stanford, CA: Stanford University Press.

Gidron, B., Kramer, R. M., and Salamon, L. 1993. "Stato e terzo settore in prospettiva comparata." Pp. 155–76 in U. Ascoli and S. Pasquinelli (Eds.), *Il Welfare Mix. Stato sociale e terzo settore*. Milan: FrancoAngeli.

Ginsberg, L. 1994. *Understanding Social Problems, Policies, and Programs*. Columbia: University of South Carolina Press.

Ginsburg, N. 1992. *Divisions of Welfare*. London: Sage.

Ginsburg, N. 2001. "Sweden: The Social Democratic Case." Pp. 195–222 in A. Cochrane, J. Clarke, and S. Gewirtz (Eds.). *Comparing Welfare States*. London: Sage.

Giorgi, G. 1999. "Gli strumenti di management ed il controllo di gestione." *Tendenze nuove* 8(luglio/agosto):70–75.

Goldthorpe, J. H. 1996. "Class Analysis and the Reorientation of Class Theory: The Case of Persisting Differentials in Educational Attainment." *British Journal of Sociology* 47(3):481–505.

Golini, A. 1991. *Anziani*. Pp. 245–64 in *Enciclopedia delle Scienze Sociali*. Roma: Istituto dell'Enciclopedia Italiana.

Gori, C. 2002. "Il futuro dei servizi sociali in Italia." *Il Mulino* 51(January/February), 399:92–100.

Gorman, D. M. 1996. "Etiological Theories and the Primary Prevention of Drug Use." *Journal of Drug Issues* 26(2):505–20.

Gornick, J. C., and Jacobs, J. A. 1998. "Gender, The Welfare State, and Public Employment: A Comparative Study of Seven Industrialized Countries." *American Sociological Review* 63:688–710.

Gortmaker, S. L., and Wise, P. H. 1997. "The First Injustice. Socioeconomic Disparities, Health Services Technology, and Infant Mortality." *Annual Review of Sociology* 23:147–70.

Gotham, K. F. 1998. "Blind Faith in the Free Market: Urban Poverty, Residential Segregation, and Federal Housing Retrenchment, 1970–1995." *Sociological Inquiry* 68(1):1–31.

Gould, A. 2001. "Resisting Postmodernity: Swedish Sociale Policy in the 1990s." Paper presented at the Institute for Social Research, Stockholm University, September 18.

Graham, A. 1997. "The UK 1979–95: Myths and Realities of Conservative Capitalism." Pp. 117–32 in C. Crouch and W. Streeck (Eds.), *Political Economy of Modern Capitalism*. London: Sage.

Green, J. H. 1995. "Public Finances, Adjustment Programs, and Debt Dynamics." In D. Lachman, A. Bennett, J. H. Green, R. Hagemann, and R. Ramaswamy. 1995. *Challenges to the Swedish Welfare State*. Washington, DC: International Monetary Fund.

Greenberg, D. F., and Larkin, N. J. 1998. "The Incapacitation of Criminal Opiate Users." *Crime and Delinquency* 44(2):205–28.

Grosso, L. 1999. "Riabilitare con il metadone." *Narcomafie* 7(11):35–38.

Gruberg, M. 1979. *Department of Housing and Urban Development*. P. 496 in *The Encyclopedia*, 14th International Edition. Danbury, CT: Americana Corporation.

Grund, J.-P. C. 1998. "From the Straw to the Needle? Determinants of Heroin Administration Routes." Pp. 215–58 in J. A. Inciardi and L. D. Harrison (Eds.), *Heroin in the Age of Crack-Cocaine*. London: Sage.

Gustafsson, B., et al. 1999. "The Distribution of Income in the Nordic Countries. Changes and Causes." Pp. 215–34 in M. Kautto, M. Heikkila, B. Hvinden, S. Marklund, and N. Plough (Eds.), *Nordic Social Policy*. London: Routledge.

Gynnerstedt, K. 1997. "Social Policy in Sweden: Current Crises and Future Prospects:" Pp. 188–206 in M. Mullard and S. Lee (Eds.), *The Politics of Social Policy in Europe*. Cheltenham: Edward Elgar.

Haen Marshall, I. 1997. "Minorities, Crime, and Criminal Justice in the United States, I." Pp. 1–35 in I. Haen Marshall (Ed.), *Minorities, Migrants, and Crime,* London: Sage.

Hagan, J. 1992. "The Poverty of Classless Criminology: The American Society of Criminology 1991 Presidential Address." *Criminology* 30(1):1–19.

Hagan, J. 1994. *Crime and Disrepute*. London: Pine Forge.

Hagan, J., Hefler, G., Classen, G., Boehnke, K., and Merkens, H. 1998. "Subterranean Sources of Subcultural Delinquency Beyond the American Dream." *Criminology* 36(2):309–41.

Hagan, J., and Peterson, R. D. 1995. "Crime and Inequality in America: Patterns and Consequences." Pp. 14–36 in J. Hagan and R. D. Peterson (Eds.), *Crime and Inequality*. Stanford, CA: Stanford University Press.

Hagemann, R. 1995. "Social Security in Sweden." Pp. 31–46 in D. Lachman, A. Bennett, J. H. Green, R. Hagemann, and R. Ramaswamy. 1995. *Challenges to the Swedish Welfare State*. Washington DC: International Monetary Fund.

Halleroed, B. 1996. "Deprivation and Poverty: A Comparative Analysis of Sweden and Great Britain." *Acta Sociologica* 39:141–68.

Halleroed, B., and Heikkila, M. 1999. "Poverty and Social Exclusion in the Nordic Countries." Pp. 185–214 in M. Kautto, M. Heikkila, B. Hvinden, S. Marklund, and N. Plough (Eds.), *Nordic Social Policy*. London: Routledge.

Handler, A. B. 1979. "Housing." Pp. 481–95 in *The Encyclopedia Americana*. 14th International Edition. Danbury, CT: Americana Corporation.

Harris, K. M. 1993. "Work and Welfare among Single Mothers in Poverty." *American Journal of Sociology* 99(2):317–52.

Harris, K. M. 1996. "Life after Welfare: Women, Work, and Repeat Dependency." *American Sociological Review* 61:407–26

Hasenfeld, Y., and Rafferty, J. A. 1989. "The Determinants of Public Attitudes Toward the Welfare State." *Social Forces* 67(4):1027–48.

Hatland, A. 2001. "Changing Family Patterns: A Challenge to Social Security." Pp. 116–36 in M. Kautto, J. Fritzell, B. Hvinden, J. Kvist, and H. Uusitalo (Eds.), *Nordic Welfare States in the European Context*. London: Routledge.

Hawkins, J. D., Arthur, M. W., and Catalano, R. F. 1995. "Preventing Substance Abuse." Pp. 343–427 in M. Tonry and D. P. Farrington (Eds.), *Building a Safer Society*. Chicago: University of Chicago Press.

Heikkila, M., et al. 1999. "Conclusion: The Nordic Model Stands Stable But on Shaky Ground." Pp. 262–73 in M. Kautto, M. Heikkila, B. Hvinden, S. Marklund, and N. Plough (Eds.), *Nordic Social Policy*. London: Routledge.

Hernandez, R. 1998. "Pataki Eases Parole for Many, But Tightens It for the Violent." *New York Times,* August 3, p. B1.

Hernes, G. 1991. "The Dilemmas of Social Democracies: The Case of Norway and Sweden." *Acta Sociologica* 34:239–60.

Hester, S., and Eglin, P. 1992. *A Sociology of Crime*. London: Routledge.

Hillenbrand, S. W., and Davis, R. C. 1993. "Residents' Perceptions of Drug Activity, Crime, and Neighborhood Satisfaction." Pp. 5–18 in R. C. Davis, A. J. Lurigio, and D. P. Rosenbaum (Eds.), *Drugs and the Community.* Springfield, IL: Charles C. Thomas.

Hodos, J. 1997. "Timing and Tempo: How Public Development Affects Neighborhood Change." Paper presented at the American Sociological Association Meeting, Toronto, August 9–13.

Hollingsworth, J. R. 1997. "The Institutional Embeddedness of American Capitalism." Pp. 133–47 in C. Crouch and W. Streeck (Eds.), *Political Economy of Modern Capitalism.* London: Sage.

Horton, P. B., et al. 1994. *The Sociology of Social Problems.* Englewood, NJ: Prentice Hall.

Howlett, D. 1998. "To Save Housing, City Destroying It." *USA TODAY,* August 17, p. 5A.

Hser, Y.-I., Longshore, D., and Anglin, M. D. 1994. "Prevalence of Drug Use Among Criminal Offender Populations. Implications for Control, Treatment, and Policy." Pp. 18–41 in D. L. MacKenzie and C. D. Uchida (Eds.), *Drugs and Crime. Evaluating Public Policy Initiatives.* London: Sage.

Hunt, G., and Rosenbaum, M. 1998. "'Hustling' within the Clinic: Consumer Perspectives on Methadone Maintenance Treatment." Pp. 188–214 in J. A. Inciardi and L. D. Harrison (Eds.), *Heroin in the Age of Crack-Cocaine.* London: Sage.

Hvinden, B., Heikkila, M., and Kankare, I. 2001. "Towards Activation? The Changing Relationship between Social Protection and Unemployment in Western Europe." Pp. 168–97 in M. Kautto, J. Fritzell, B. Hvinden, J. Kvist, and H. Uusitalo (Eds.), *Nordic Welfare States in the European Context.* London: Routledge.

Iglehart, J. K. 1999a. "Expenditures." *New England Journal of Medicine* 340(1):70–76.

Iglehart, J. K. 1999b. "The American Health Care System. Medicare." *New England Journal of Medicine* 340(4):327–32.

Iglehart, J. K. 1999c. "The American Health Care System. Medicaid." *New England Journal of Medicine* 340(5):403–8.

Inciardi, J. A., and Harrison, L. D. 1998. "The Re-Emergence of Heroin in the Age of Crack-Cocaine." Pp. vii—xxii in J. A. Inciardi and L. D. Harrison (Eds.), *Heroin in the Age of Crack-Cocaine.* London: Sage.

Inciardi, J. A., McBride, D. C., and Surratt, H. L. 1998. "The Heroin Street Addict: Profiling A National Population." Pp. 31–50 in J. A. Inciardi and L. D. Harrison (Eds.), *Heroin in the Age of Crack-Cocaine.* London: Sage.

Inciardi, J. A., and McElrath, K. 1998a. "Introduction." Pp. xi—xiv in J. A. Inciardi and K. McElrath (Eds.), *The American Drug Scene.* Los Angeles: Roxbury.

Inciardi, J. A., and McElrath, K. 1998b. "Policy Considerations." Pp. 285–87 in J. A. Inciardi and K. McElrath (Eds.), *The American Drug Scene.* Los Angeles: Roxbury.

Innis, L. B., and Sittig, J. 1996. "Race, Class, and Support for the Welfare State." *Sociological Inquiry* 66(2):175–96.

ISFOL, 1999. *Formazione e occupazione in Italia e in Europa. Rapporto 1999.* Milan: FrancoAngeli.

Ishida, H., Mueller, W., and Ridge, J. M. 1995. "Class Origin, Class Destination, and Education: A Cross-National Study of Ten Industrial Nations." *American Journal of Sociology* 101:147–93.

ISMU. 1995. *Primo rapporto sulle emigrazioni.* Milan: FrancoAngeli.

ISTAT. 1996. *Rapporto sull'Italia.* Bologna: Il Mulino.

ISTAT. 1998. *Rapporto sull'Italia.* Bologna: Il Mulino.

ISTAT. 1999. *Rapporto sull'Italia.* Bologna: Il Mulino.

Italia-Razzismo. 1991. *La casa impossibile. La questione delle abitazioni e gli immigrati.* Rome: Marzo.

Jacoby, J. E., and Gramckow, H. P. (Eds.). 1994. "Prosecuting Drug Offenders." Pp. 151–71 in D. L. MacKenzie and C. D. Uchida (Eds.), *Drugs and Crime. Evaluating Public Policy Initiatives.* London: Sage.

Jaentti, M., and Danziger, S. 1994. "Child Poverty in Sweden and the United States: The Effect of Social Transfers and Parental Labor Force Participation." *Industrial and Labor Relations Review* 48(1):48–64.

Jaffee, D. 1998. *Levels of Socio-Economic Development.* London: Praeger.

Jankowski, M. S. 1995. "Ethnography, Inequality, and Crime in the Low-Income Community." Pp. 80–94 in J. Hagan and R. D. Peterson (Eds.), *Crime and Inequality.* Stanford, CA: Stanford University Press.

Jargowsky, P. A. 1996. "Take the Money and Run: Economic Segregation in the U.S. Metropolitan Areas." *American Sociological Review* 61(December):984–98.

Jencks, C. 1992. *Rethinking Social Policy.* Cambridge, MA: Harvard University Press.

Jencks, C. 1994. *The Homeless.* Cambridge, MA: Harvard University Press.

Johnson, B. D., Golub, A., and Dunlap, E. 1999. "The Ebbing of Hard Drug Use, Drug Markets, and Violence among Inner-City Young Adults in the 1990s." Paper presented at the Annual Meeting of the American Sociological Association, Chicago, August 10.

Johnson, B. D., Thomas, G., and Golub, A. 1998. "Trends in Heroin Use Among Manhattan Arrestees from the Heroin and Crack Eras." Pp. 109–30 in J. A. Inciardi and L. D. Harrison (Eds.), *Heroin in the Age of Crack-Cocaine.* London: Sage.

Johnson, B. D., Williams, T., Dei, K. A., and Sanabria, H. 1990. "Drug Abuse in the Inner City: Impact on Hard-Drug Users and the Community." Pp. 9–67 in M. Tonry and J. Q. Wilson (Eds.), *Drugs and Crime.* Chicago: University of Chicago Press.

Kamerman, S. B., and Kahn, A. J. 1998. "Le politiche per la famiglia nel secondo dopoguerra: la trasformazione degli impegni nazionali." *Polis* 12(1):77–99.

Kangas, O., and Palme, J. 1998. "Does Social Policy Matter? Poverty Cycles in OECD Countries." Paper presented at the Research Committee 19, 14th World Congress of Sociology, Montreal, Canada, July 26–August 1.

Kasarda, J. D. 1985. "Urban Change and Minority Opportunities." Pp. 33–67 in P. E. Peterson (Ed.), *The New Urban Reality.* Washington, DC: Brookings Institution.

Kasarda, J. D. 1993. "Urban Industrial Transition and the Underclass." Pp. 43–64 in W. J. Wilson (Ed.), *The Ghetto Underclass.* London: Sage.

Kautto, M. 1999. "Changes in Age Structure, Family Stability and Dependency." Pp. 54–78 in M. Kautto, M. Heikkila, B. Hvinden, S. Marklund, and N. Plough (Eds.), *Nordic Social Policy.* London: Routledge.

Kautto, M. 2001. "Moving Closer? Diversity and Convergence in Financing of Welfare States." Pp. 232–61 in M. Kautto, J. Fritzell, B. Hvinden, J. Kvist, and H. Uusitalo (Eds.), *Nordic Welfare States in the European Context.* London: Routledge.

Kautto, M., Fritzell, J., Hvinden, B., Kvist, J., and Uusitalo, H. 2001a. "Conclusion: Nordic Welfare States in the European Context." Pp. 262–72 in M. Kautto, J. Fritzell, B. Hvinden, J. Kvist, and H. Uusitalo (Eds.), *Nordic Welfare States in the European Context*. London: Routledge.

Kautto, M., Fritzell, J., Hvinden, B., Kvist, J., and Uusitalo, H. (Eds.). 2001b. *Nordic Welfare States in the European Context*. London: Routledge.

Kautto, M., Heikkila, M., Hvinden, B., Marklund, S., and Plough, N. 1999a. "Introduction: The Nordic Welfare States in the 1990s." Pp. 1–18 in M. Kautto, M. Heikkila, B. Hvinden, S. Marklund, and N. Plough (Eds.), *Nordic Social Policy*. London: Routledge.

Kautto, M., Heikkila, M., Hvinden, B., Marklund, S., and Plough, N. (Eds.). 1999b. *Nordic Social Policy*. London: Routledge.

Kazepov, Y. 1995. "Ai confini della cittadinanza: il ruolo delle istituzioni nei percorsi di esclusione a Stuttgart e Milano." *Polis* 9(1):45–66.

Kazepov, Y. 1999. "Il ruolo delle istituzioni nel processo sociale di costruzione della povertà." Pp. 105–17 in M. della Campa, M. L. Ghezzi, and U. Melotti (Eds.), *Vecchie e nuove povertà nell'area del Mediterraneo*. Milan: Edizioni della Società Umanitaria.

Keister, L. A., and Moller, S. 2000. "Wealth Inequality in the United States." *Annual Review of Sociology* 26:63–81.

Kenworthy, L. 1999. "Do Social-Welfare Policies Reduce Poverty? A Cross-National Assessment." *Social Forces* 77(3):1119–39.

King, D. S., and Rothstein, B. 1993. "Institutional Choices and Labor Market Policy." *Comparative Political Studies* 26(2):147–77.

Kinlock, T. W., Hanlon, T. E., and Nurco, D. N. 1998. "The Initiation of the Use of Heroin in the Age of Crack." Pp. 51–76 in J. A. Inciardi and L. D. Harrison (Eds.), *Heroin in the Age of Crack-Cocaine*. London: Sage.

Kjeldstad, R. 2001. "Gender Policies and Gender Equality." Pp. 66–97 in M. Kautto, J. Fritzell, B. Hvinden, J. Kvist, and H. Uusitalo (Eds.), *Nordic Welfare States in the European Context*. London: Routledge.

Klausen, K., and Selle, P. 1997. "Il terzo settore in Scandinavia." Pp. 156–73 in G. Rossi (Ed.), *Terzo settore, stato e mercato nella trasformazione delle politiche sociali in Europa*. Milan: FrancoAngeli.

Klizner, M. 1993. "A Public Health/Dynamic Systems Approach to Community-Wide Alcohol and Other Drug Initiatives." Pp. 201–24 in R. C. Davis, A. J. Lurigio, D. P. Rosenbaum (Eds.), *Drugs and the Community*. Springfield, IL: Charles C. Thomas.

Knight, K. R., Rosenbaum, M., Kelley, M. S., Irwin, J., Washburn, A., and Wenger, L. 1996. "Defunding the Poor: The Impact of Lost Access to Methadone Maintenance Treatment on Women Injection Drug Users." *Journal of Drug Issues* 26(4):923–42.

Kohn, M. 1987. "Cross-National Research as an Analytical Strategy." *American Sociological Review* 52:713–31.

Kornblum, W., and Julian, J. 1995. *Social Problems*. Englewood Cliffs, NJ: Prentice Hall.

Korpi, W., and Palme, J. 1998. "The Paradox of Redistribution and Strategies of Equality: Welfare State Institutions, Inequality, and Poverty in the Western Countries." *American Sociological Review* 63(October):661–87.

Kramer, R. M. 1992. "Il ruolo delle organizzazioni volontarie in quattro welfare state: uno studio comparato." *Polis* 6(3):437–65.

Krivo, L. J., and Peterson, R. D. 1996. "Extremely Disadvantaged Neighborhoods and Urban Crime." *Social Forces* 75(2):619–50.

Krohn, M. D., Lizotte, A. J., Thornberry, T. P., Smith, C., and McDowall, D. 1996. "Reciprocal Causal Relationships among Drug Use, Peers, and Beliefs: A Five-Wave Panel Model." *Journal of Drug Issues* 26(2):405–28.

Kuhnle, S., and Selle, P. 1993. "Enti pubblici e organizzazioni volontarie: un approccio relazionale." Pp. 177–99 in U. Ascoli and S. Pasquinelli (Eds.), *Il Welfare Mix. Stato sociale e terzo settore*. Milan: FrancoAngeli.

Kuttner, R. 1999a. "Health Insurance Coverage." *New England Journal of Medicine* 340(2)163–68.

Kuttner, R. 1999b. "The American Health Care System. Employer-Sponsored Health Coverage." *New England Journal of Medicine* 340(3):248–52.

Kuttner, R. 1999c. "The American Health Care System. Wall Street and Health Care." *New England Journal of Medicine* 340(8):664–68.

Kvist, J. 1998. "Patterns of Welfare Reform in the Nordic Countries in the 1990s: Using Fuzzy-set Theory to Access Countries' Conformity to the Nordic Model of Welfare." Paper presented at the Research Committee 19, 14th World Congress of Sociology, Montreal, Canada, July 26–August 1.

Labos. 1993. *Famiglie e percorsi di tossicodipendenza*. Rome: T.E.R.

Lachman, D. 1995. "Overview." Pp. 1–2 in D. Lachman, A. Bennett, J. H. Green, R. Hagemann, and R. Ramaswamy (Eds.), *Challenges to the Swedish Welfare State*. Washington, DC: International Monetary Fund.

Lazarsfeld, P. F., and Rosenberg, M. 1955. *Concepts and Indices. Introduction*. Pp. 15–18 in P. F. Lazarsfeld and M. Rosenberg (Eds.), *The Language of Social Research*. New York: Free Press.

Lehto, J., Moss, N., and Rostgaard, T. 1999. "Universal Public Social Care and Health Services?" Pp. 104–32 in M. Kautto, M. Heikkila, B. Hvinden, S. Marklund, and N. Plough (Eds.), *Nordic Social Policy*. London: Routledge.

Lewis, M. 1993. *The Culture of Inequality*. Amherst, MA: University of Massachusetts Press.

Lichter, D. T. 1988. "Racial Differences in Underemployment in American Cities." *American Journal of Sociology* 93(4):771–92.

Lichter, D. T. 1997. "Poverty and Inequality among Children." *Annual Review of Sociology* 23:121–45.

Lichter, D. T., McLaughlin, D. K., and Ribar, D. C. 1997. "Welfare and the Rise in Female-Headed Families." *American Journal of Sociology* 103(1):112–43.

Lieberson, S. 1991. "Small N's and Big Conclusions: An Examination of the Reasoning in Comparative Studies Based on a Small Number of Cases." *Social Forces* 70(2):307–20.

Lindahl, M. 1979. "Sweden." Pp. 99–106 in *Encyclopedia Americana,* Vol. 26. Danbury, CT: Americana Corporation.

Lindahl, M. 1981. "Sweden." Pp. 511–12 in *The Americana Annual 1981*. Danbury, CT: Grolier.

Lindahl, M. 1983. "Sweden." Pp. 493–94 in *The Americana Annual 1983*. Danbury, CT: Grolier.

Liska, A. E., and Bellair, P. E. 1995. "Violent Crime Rates and Racial Composition: Convergence over Time." *American Journal of Sociology* 101(3):578–610.

Liska, A. E., and Reed, M. D. 1985. "Ties to Conventional Institutions and Delinquency: Estimating Reciprocal Effects." *American Sociological Review* 50 (August):547–60.

Loow, H. 1995. "Racist Violence and Criminal Behavior in Sweden: Myths and Reality." Pp. 119–61 in T: Bjorgo (Ed.), *Terror from the Extreme Right*. London: Frank Cass.

Lundberg, O., and Lahelma, E. 2001. "Nordic Health Inequalities in the European Context." Pp. 42–65 in M. Kautto, J. Fritzell, B. Hvinden, J. Kvist, and H. Uusitalo (Eds.), *Nordic Welfare States in the European Context*. London: Routledge.

Mafstrofski, S. D., Worden, R. E., and Snipes, J. B. 1995. "Law Enforcement in a Time of Community Policing." *Criminology* 33(4):539–63.

Maggi, G. 2002. "L'onda lunga di Enron minaccia il new look della previdenza USA." *La Stampa*, 21 January, p. 18.

Marklund, S. 1990. "Structures of Modern Poverty." *Acta Sociologica* 33(2):125–40.

Marklund, S., and Nordlund, A. 1999. "Economic Problems, Welfare Convergence and Political Instability." Pp. 19–53 in M. Kautto, M. Heikkila, B. Hvinden, S. Marklund, and N. Plough (Eds.), *Nordic Social Policy*. London: Routledge.

Marsden, J., Gossop, M., Farrel, M., and Strang, J. 1998. "Opioid Substitution: Critical Issues and Future Directions." *Journal of Drug Issues* 28(1):243–64.

Marta, C. 1991. "Dall'assimilazionismo al multiculturalismo. Vent'anni di politica e di ricerca sociale sull'immigrazione in Svezia (1966–1985)." *Studi Emigrazione* 28(101):59–81.

Martens, P. L. 1997 "Immigrants, Crime, and the Criminal Justice in Sweden." Pp. 183–255 in M. Tonry (Ed.), *Ethnicity , Crime and Immigration. Comparative and Cross-National Perspectives*. Chicago: University of Chicago Press.

Martini, A. 1981. "La contrattazione in Svezia: politica dei redditi e coesione organizzativa." *Stato e mercato* 2:301–31.

Massey, D. S. 1990. "American Apartheid: Segregation and the Making of the Underclass." *American Journal of Sociology* 96(2)329–57.

Massey, D. S., Condran, G. A., and Denton, N. A. 1987. "The Effect of Residential Segregation on Black Social and Economic Well-Being." *Social Forces* 66(1):29–56.

Massey, D. S., and Denton, N. A. 1988. "Suburbanization and Segregation in U.S. Metropolitan Areas." *American Journal of Sociology* 94(3):592–626.

Massey, D. S., and Eggers, M. L. 1990. "The Ecology of Inequality: Minorities and the Concentration of Poverty, 1970–1980." *American Journal of Sociology* 95(5):1153–88.

Mazerolle, L. G., Kadleck, C., and Roehl, J. 1998. "Controlling Drug and Disorder Problems: The Role of Place Managers." *Criminology* 36(2):371–403.

McKinley, D. G. 1964. *Social Class and Family Life*. New York: Free Press of Glencoe.

McLanahan, S. 1985. "Family Structure and the Reproduction of Poverty." *American Journal of Sociology* 90(4):873–901.

McLanahan, S., and Garfinkel, I. 1993. "Single Mothers, the Underclass, and Social Policy." Pp. 109–21 in W. J. Wilson (Ed.), *The Ghetto Underclass*. London: Sage.

McNamara, J. D. 1997. "A Veteran Chief: Too Many Cops Think It's a War." *Time* (European Edition), September 1, pp. 14–15.

Mead, L. M. 1993. "The Logic of Workfare: The Underclass and Work Policy." Pp. 173–98 in W. J. Wilson (Ed.), *The Ghetto Underclass.* London: Sage.

Meier, R. F., and Johnson, W. T. 1977. "Deterrence as Social Control: The Legal and Extralegal Production of Conformity." *American Sociological Review* 42 (April):292–304.

Messner, S. F. 1989. "Economic Discrimination and Societal Homicide Rates: Further Evidence on the Cost of Inequality." *American Sociological Review* 54 (August):597–611.

Mieczkowski, T. M. 1996. "The Prevalence of Drug Use in the United States." Pp. 349–414 in M. Tonry (Eds.), *Crime and Justice. A Review of Research.* Chicago: University of Chicago Press.

Miethe, T. D., and Meier, R. F. 1994. *Crime and Its Social Context.* Albany: State University of New York Press.

Ministry of Health and Social Affairs. 1997. *Swedish Legislation on Health and Medical Services, and Health and Medical Personnel,* Stockholm.

Morgan, M. 1998. *Evaluation of Substance Use Prevention Programmes: Implications for Illicit Drugs.* Pp. 91–134 in A. Springer and A. Uhl (Eds.), *Cost A6. Evaluation Research in Regard to Primary Prevention of Drug Abuse.* Brussels: European Commission, Social Sciences, Directorate-General Science, Research and Development.

Movimento per la Rifondazione Comunista (Eds.). 1991. *Dossier sulla situazione carceraria milanese.* Milan: July.

Mullard, M. 1997. "A Crisis of Public Expenditure in Europe: Myths and Reality." Pp. 29–51 in M. Mullard and S. Lee (Eds.), *The Politics of Social Policy in Europe.* Cheltenham: Edward Elgar.

Murray, C. 1984. *Losing Ground.* New York: Basic Books.

Nadelmann, E. A. 1998. "Drug Prohibition in the United States: Costs, Consequences, and Alternatives." Pp. 288–303 in J. A. Inciardi and K. McElrath (Eds.), *The American Drug Scene.* Los Angeles: Roxbury.

Nahon, L. 1997. "La psichiatria americana tra conflitti e progresso." *Tendenze nuove* 48(ottobre/dicembre):41–43.

National Board of Health and Welfare (Socialstyrelsen). 1994. *The Social Service and Care in Sweden 1993,* Stockholm.

National Board of Health and Welfare (Socialstyrelsen). 1996. *Social Service, vard och omsorg i Sverige 1996,* Stockholm.

Neckerman, K. M., Aponte, R., and Wilson, W. J. 1988. "Family Structure, Black Unemployment, and American Social Policy." Pp. 397–419 in M. Weir, A. S. Orloff, and T. Skocpol (Eds.), *The Politics of Social Policy in the United States.* Princeton, NJ: Princeton University Press.

Negri, N., and Saraceno, C. 1996. *Le politiche contro la povertà in Italia.* Bologna: Il Mulino.

Nelson, A. C., and Milgroom, J. H. 1995. "Regional Growth Management and Central City Vitality. Comparing Development Patterns in Atlanta, Georgia, and Portland, Oregon." Pp. 1–37 in F. W. Wagner, T. E. Joder, and A. J. Mumphrey (Eds.), *Urban Revitalization. Policies and Programs.* London: Sage.

Neresini, F., and Ranci, C. 1994. *Disagio giovanile e politiche sociali.* Rome: La Nuova Italia Scientifica.

Nersnaes, L. 1988. "Mia's Diary: An Alcohol and Drug Primary Prevention Programme for the Nordic Countries." Pp. 77–90 in A. Springer and A. Uhl (Eds.), *Cost A6. Evaluation Research in Regard to Primary Prevention of Drug Abuse.* Brussels: European Commission, Social Sciences, Directorate-General Science, Research and Development.

Nevola, G. 1991. "Il reddito minimo garantito: due filosofie sociali del welfare state." *Stato e mercato* 31:159–84.

Nicholson, T. 1994. "Social Policy and Adolescent Drug Consumption: The Legalization Option." Pp. 233–47 in T. P. Gullotta., G. R. Adams, and R. Montemayor (Eds.), *Substance Misuse in Adolescence.* London: Sage.

Nielsen, F., and Alderson, A. S. 1997. "The Kuznets Curve and The Great U-Turn: Income Inequality in U. S. Counties, 1970–1990." *American Sociological Review* 62:12–33.

Nonis, M. 1989. "Le condizioni socio-sanitarie degli immigrati del Terzo Mondo a Roma." *Studi Emigrazione* 26(95):338–67.

Nordic Committee on Narcotic Drugs. 1994. *Current Drug Tendencies in the Nordic Area,* Stockholm.

Nurco, D. N., and Lerner, M. 1996. "Vulnerability to Narcotic Addiction: Family Structure and Functioning." *Journal of Drug Issues* 26(4):1007–25.

O'Connor, A. 2000. "Poverty Research and Policy for the Post-Welfare Area." *Annual Review of Sociology* 26:547–62.

Okun, B. 1979. "United States: Population Growth and Characteristics." Pp. 531–38 in *Encyclopedia Americana,* Vol. 27. Danbury, CT: Americana Corporation.

Olsson Hort, S. E. 1993. "Welfare Policy in Sweden." Pp. 71–86 in T. P. Boje and S. E. Olsson Hort (Eds.), *Scandinavia in a New Europe.* Oslo: Scandinavian University Press.

Olsson Hort, S. E. 1995. "Sickness and Unemployment Insurance in Sweden: Recent Changes and Policy Proposals." Pp. 1–10 in E. Brunsdon and M. May (Eds.), *Swedish Welfare: Policy & Provision.* Social Policy Association.

Organisation for Economic Co-operation and Development. 1993. OECD Health Systems. Facts and Trends 1960–1991, Vol. I, Paris.

Organisation for Economic Co-operation and Development. 1997. *Employment Outlook,* July, Paris.

Organisation for Economic Co-operation and Development. 1999. *OECD Economic Outlook,* Vol. 65, June, Paris.

Organisation for Economic Co-operation and Development, Statistics Directorate. 1997. *Quarterly Labour Force Statistics,* no. 3, Paris.

Osgood, D. W., Wilson, J. K., O'Malley, P. M., Bachman, J. C., and Johnston, L. D. 1996. "Routine Activities and Individual Deviant Behavior." *American Sociological Review* 61:635–55.

Palme, J. 1998. "Swedish Pension Reform." Paper presented at the 14th World Congress of Sociology, Research Committee 19, Montreal, Canada, July 26–August 1.

Palme, J. 1999. *The Nordic Model and the Modernisation of Social Protection in Northern Europe.* Copenhagen: Nordic Council of Ministers.

Palme, J. 2001. *Interim Balance Sheet for Welfare in the 1990s.* Stockholm: Government Commission.

Palumbo, M. 1995. "Indicatori e valutazione di efficacia delle policies." *Sociologia e ricerca sociale* 47–48:317–41.

Pampel, F. C., and Williamson, J. B. 1989. *Age, Class, Politics, and the Welfare State.* Cambridge: Cambridge University Press.

Park, R. E. [1925] 1967. "Community Organization and Juvenile Delinquency." Pp. 99–112 in R. E. Park and E. W. Burgess (Eds.), *The City.* Chicago: University of Chicago Press.

Parker, R. N. 1989. "Poverty, Subculture of Violence, and Type of Homicide." *Social Forces* 67(4):983–1007.

Pasquinelli, S. 1993. "Stato sociale e 'terzo settore' in Italia." *Stato e mercato* 38:279–312.

Pasquinelli, S. 1999. "Il Terzo settore nei diversi Welfare States europei." Pp. 95–114 in U. Ascoli (Ed.), *Il Welfare futuro. Manuale critico del terzo settore.* Rome: Carocci.

Patterson, E. B. 1991. "Poverty, Income Inequality, and Community Crime Rates." *Criminology* 29(4):755–76.

Persson, M. 1981. "Time-Perspectives amongst Criminals." *Acta Sociologica* 24(3):149–65.

Peterson, R. D., and Krivo, L. J. 1993. "Racial Segregation and Black Urban Homicide." *Social Forces* 71(4):1021–26.

Physicians for a National Health Program. No date. *It's Time to Make Your Choice,* Chicago.

Piccone Stella, S. 1996. "Giovani e droga: il percorso accidentato della cura." *Rassegna italiana di sociologia* 37(4):585–607.

Piccone Stella, S. 1999. *Droghe e tossicodipendenza.* Bologna: Il Mulino.

Pieretti, G. 1991. "Povertà estreme e povertà silenziose: il ruolo dei processi urbani." Pp. 177–91 in P. Guidicini (Ed.), *Gli studi sulla povertà in Italia.* Milan: FrancoAngeli.

Pierson, P. 1996. "La nuova politica del welfare state: un'analisi comparata degli interventi restrittivi." *Stato e mercato* 46:3–50.

Platt, J. J., Widmann, M., Lidz, V., and Marlowe, D. 1998. "Methadone Maintenance Treatment: Its Development and Effectiveness after 30 Years." Pp. 160–87 in J. A. Inciardi and L. D. Harrison (Eds.), *Heroin in the Age of Crack-Cocaine.* London: Sage.

Plough, N. 1999. "Cuts in and Reform of the Nordic Cash Benefits Systems." Pp. 79–103 in M. Kautto, M. Heikkila, B. Hvinden, S. Marklund, and N. Plough (Eds.), *Nordic Social Policy.* London: Routledge.

Pontusson, J. 1997. "Between Neo-Liberalism and the German Model: Swedish Capitalism in Transition." Pp. 55–70 in C. Crouch and W. Streeck (Eds.), *Political Economy of Modern Capitalism.* London: Sage.

Prina, F. 1999. "Volontariato e impresa sociale di fronte a disagio sociale, marginalità, devianza." Pp. 141–83 in U. Ascoli (Ed.), *Il Welfare futuro. Manuale critico del terzo settore.* Rome: Carocci.

Quadagno, J. 1999. "Creating a Capital Investment Welfare State: The New American Exceptionalism." *American Sociological Review* 64:1–11.

Ragin, C. C. 1987. *The Comparative Method.* Berkeley: University of California Press.

Ragin, C. C. 1994. *Constructing Social Research.* London: Pine Forge.

Ramaswamy, R. 1995. "The Swedish Labor Market." Pp. 12–20 in D. Lachman, A. Bennett, J. H. Green, R. Hagemann, and R. Ramaswamy. 1995. *Challenges to the Swedish Welfare State.* Washington, DC: International Monetary Fund.

Ramaswamy, R., and Green, J. H. 1995. "Recession and Recovery in the 1990s." Pp. 3–11 in D. Lachman, A. Bennett, J. H. Green, R. Hagemann, and R. Ramaswamy. 1995. *Challenges to the Swedish Welfare State.* Washington, DC: International Monetary Fund.

Ranci, C. 1992. "La mobilitazione dell'altruismo: condizioni e processi di diffusione dell'azione volontaria in Italia." *Polis* 6(3):467–505.

Ravenna, M. 1993. *Adolescenti e droga.* Bologna: Il Mulino.

Ravenna, M. 1994. "Fattori interpersonali e personali nell'astensione e nel consumo di droga." Pp. 11–81 in C. Baraldi and M. Ravenna (Eds.), *Fra dipendenza e rifiuto.* Milan: FrancoAngeli.

Regini, M. 1991. *Confini mobili.* Bologna: Il Mulino.

Regini, M. 1996. "Lavoro. Sociologia." Pp. 182–90 in *Enciclopedia delle Scienze Sociali,* Vol. 5. Rome: Istituto della Enciclopedia Italiana.

Regini, M. 1997. "Social Institutions and Production Structure: The Italian Variety of Capitalism in the 1980s." Pp. 102–16 in C. Crouch and W. Streeck (Eds.), *Political Economy of Modern Capitalism.* London: Sage.

Regione Emilia-Romagna. 1996. "Criteri e modalità per il riparto della quota del Fondo nazionale di intervento per la lotta alla droga trasferita alla Regioni ai sensi dell'art. 4 del decreto-legge 19 marzo 1996, n. 130." *Forum* 12:6–10.

Regione Marche. 1996. "Criteri e modalità per il riparto della quota del Fondo nazionale di intervento per la lotta alla droga trasferita alla Regioni ai sensi dell'art. 4 del decreto-legge 19 marzo 1996, n. 130." *Forum* 12:11–15.

Regonini, G. 1984. "Il sistema pensionistico: risorse e vincoli." Pp. 87–117 in U. Ascoli (Ed.), *Welfare State all'italiana.* Rome: Laterza.

Rei, D. 1997. *Servizi sociali e politiche pubbliche.* Rome: La Nuova Italia Scientifica.

Reilly, F. E., Leukefeld, C. G., Gao, J., and Allen, S. 1994. "Substance Misuse Among Rural Adolescents." Pp. 123–46 in T. P. Gullotta., G. R. Adams, and R. Montemayor (Eds.), *Substance Misuse in Adolescence.* London: Sage.

Reiss, A. J., Jr. 1994. "Drug Evaluations in Policy Research: Implications for Drug Control Initiatives." Pp. 9–17 in D. L. MacKenzie and C. D. Uchida (Eds.), *Drugs and Crime. Evaluating Public Policy Initiatives.* London: Sage.

Reuter, P. 1998. "Hawks Ascendant: The Punitive Trend of American Drug Policy." Pp. 314–36 in J. A. Inciardi and K. McElrath (Eds.), *The American Drug Scene.* Los Angeles: Roxbury.

Reyneri, E. 1996. *Sociologia del mercato del lavoro.* Bologna: Il Mulino.

Riboldi, F. 1994. "Quali prospettive per il distretto socio-sanitario di base in Lombardia?" *Percorsi di Integrazione* 3(2):55–57.

Ricolfi, L. 1993. "Esiste il metodo comparato?" *Rassegna Italiana di Sociologia* 34(2):295–305.

Roncek, W. D. 1981. "Dangerous Places: Crime and Residential Environment." *Social Forces* 60(1):74–96.

Rosa, A., Spizzichino, L., and Tempesta, E. 1986. "Prevenzione: scienza o parole? Rassegna delle esperienze internazionali." *Bollettino per le farmacodipendenze e l'alcolismo* 9(1-2-3):23–63.

Rose, D. R., and Clear, T. R. 1998. "Incarceration, Social Capital, and Crime: Implications for Social Disorganization Theory." *Criminology* 38(3):441–79.

Rose, R. 1993. "Welfare: il mix pubblico/privato." Pp. 77–95 in U. Ascoli and S. Pasquinelli (Eds.), *Il Welfare Mix. Stato sociale e terzo settore.* Milan: FrancoAngeli.

Rosenfeld, R. 1986. "Urban Crime Rates: Effects of Inequality, Welfare Dependency, Region, and Race." Pp. 116–30 in J. M. Byrne and R. J. Sampson (Eds.), *The Social Ecology of Crime*. New York: Springer-Verlag.

Rossi, L. 1999. "Il vuoto oltre l'ecstasy." *Specchio*, November 20, pp. 84–98.

Rossi, P. H. 1988. "On Sociological Data." Pp. 131–54 in N. J. Smelser (Ed.), *Handbook of Sociology*. London: Sage.

Rossi, P. H., and Wright, J. D. 1993. "The Urban Homeless: A Portrait of Urban Dislocation." Pp. 149–59 in W. J. Wilson (Ed.), *The Ghetto Underclass*. London: Sage.

Rostgaard, T., and Lehto, J. 2001. "Health and Sociale Care Systems: How Different in the Nordic Model?" Pp. 137–67 in M. Kautto, J. Fritzell, B. Hvinden, J. Kvist, and H. Uusitalo (Eds.), *Nordic Welfare States in the European Context*. London: Routledge.

Ruggie, M. 1992. "The Paradox of Liberal Intervention: Health Policy and the American Welfare State." *American Journal of Sociology* 97(4):919–44.

Runblom, H. 1992. "Scandinavia Faces Multiculturalism. Immigration and Immigrant Policy During the Post-War Period." Paper presented at the Meeting "Mass Migrations in Europe: Implications in East and West," Vienna, March 5–7.

Sampson, R. J. 1987. "Urban Black Violence: The Effect of Male Joblessness and Family Disruption." *American Journal of Sociology* 93(2):348–82.

Sampson, R. J., and Groves, W. B. 1989. "Community Structure and Crime. Testing Social-Disorganization Theory." *American Journal of Sociology* 94(4):774–802.

Sampson, R. J., and Wilson, W. J. 1995. "Toward a Theory of Race, Crime, and Urban Inequality." Pp. 37–54 in J. Hagan and R. D. Peterson (Eds.), *Crime and Inequality*. Stanford, CA: Stanford University Press.

Sanders, J. M. 1990. "Public Transfers: Safety Net or Inducement into Poverty?" *Social Forces* 68(3):813–34.

Saraceno, C. 1995. "Le politiche delle famiglie in Italia." Pp. 37–57 in *Politiche per le famiglie*. Torino: Edizioni Gruppo Abele.

Saraceno, C. 1999. "Bisogni emergenti e nuove povertà." Pp. 55–68 in M. Della Campa, M. L. Ghezzi, and U. Melotti (Eds.), *Vecchie e nuove povertà nell'area del Mediterraneo*. Milan: Edizioni della Società Umanitaria,

Saraceno, C. 2002. "Povertà e famiglie con minori: l'Italia che non vorremmo (vedere)." *Il Mulino* 51(January/February, 399):86–91.

Scheuch, E. K. 1990. "The Development of Comparative Research: Towards Causal Explanations." Pp. 19–37 in E. Oyen (Ed.), *Comparative Methodology. Theory and Practice in International Social Research*. London: Sage.

Schierup, C.-U. 1990. "La situazione svedese. Politica sull'immigrazione e sui rifugiati, politica d'integrazione e di organizzazione etnica." Pp. 125–60 in *Italia, Europa e nuove immigrazioni*. Torino, Edizioni della Fondazione Agnelli.

Schizzerotto, A. 1988. "Il ruolo dell'istruzione nei processi di mobilità sociale." *Polis* 2(1):83–124.

Schizzerotto, A. 1992. "Il concetto di classe sociale: rilevanza e limiti." Pp. 15–68 in A. Schizzerotto (Ed.), *Classi sociali e società contemporanea*. Milan: FrancoAngeli.

Schizzerotto, A. 1994. "Eppure non cambiano." *Polis* 8(3):469–82.

Schmitter, P. C. 1983. "Intermediazione degli interessi e governabilità nei regimi contemporanei dell'Europa Occidentale e dell'America del Nord." Pp. 415–76 in S. Berger (Ed.), *L'organizzazione degli interessi nell'Europa Occidentale*. Bologna: Il Mulino.

Scienza Nuova. "Erba? Chiedamogliela alla polizia. Quella olandese non si scompone." *Scienza Nuova* 1(1):46–47.

Segre, S. 1998. *La devianza giovanile. Cause sociali e politiche di prevenzione.* Milan: FrancoAngeli.

Selmini, R. 1999. "Sicurezza urbana e prevenzione della criminalità: il caso italiano." *Polis* 13(1)121–42.

Serpelloni, G., et al. 1986. "Analisi dei dati sociali, familiari e delle abitudini tossicomaniche di 119 tossicodipendenti da eroina sottoposti a trattamento antiastinenziale." *Bollettino per le farmacodipendenze e l'alcolismo* 9(1-2-3):138–62.

Shavit, Y., and Westerbeeck, K. 1997. "Istruzione e stratificazione in Italia: riforme, espansione e uguaglianza delle opportunità." *Polis* 11(1):91–109.

Shihadeh, E., and Flynn, N. 1996. "Segregation and Crime: The Effect of Black Social Isolation on the Rates of Black Urban Violence." *Social Forces* 74(4)1325–52.

Shihadeh, E. S., and Ousey, G. C. 1996. "Metropolitan Expansion and Black Social Dislocation: The Link between Suburbanization and Center-City Crime." *Social Forces* 75(2):649–66.

Shihadeh, E., and Steffensmeier, D. J. 1994. "Economic Inequality, Family Disruption, and Urban Black Violence: Cities as Units of Stratification and Social Control." *Social Forces* 73(2):729–51.

Shils, E. 1969. "The Intellectuals and the Powers." Pp. 25–48 in P. Rieff (Ed.), *On Intellectuals.* Garden City, NY: Doubleday Anchor.

Sidoti, F. 1989. *Povertà, devianza, criminalità nel'Italia meridionale.* Milan: FrancoAngeli.

Silbereisen, R. K., Robins, L., and Rutter, M. 1995. "Secular Trends in Substance Use: Concepts and Data on the Impact of Social Change on Alcohol and Drug Abuse." Pp. 490–543 in M. Rutter and D. J. Smith (Eds.), *Psychosocial Disorders in Young People.* Chichester: John Wiley & Sons.

Simoni, S. 1985. "I risultati della ricerca: il paradosso della normalità." Pp. 72–110 in CTST-USL 27 (Ed.), *Droga: il paradosso della normalità.* Milan: FrancoAngeli.

Simpson, P. 1999. "Skills Shifts and Changes in Racial Labor Market Allocation over the 1980s." Paper presented at the Annual Meeting of the American Sociological Association, Chicago, August 6–10.

Singer, M., and Needle, R. 1996. "Preventing AIDS among Drug Users: Evaluating Efficacy." *Journal of Drug Issues* 26(3):521–23.

Singh, V. P. 1991. "The Underclass in The United States: Some Correlates of Economic Changes." *Sociological Inquiry* 61(4):505–21.

Sirchia, G. 1999. "Salviamo i grandi ospedali pubblici." *Tendenze nuove* 8(luglio/agosto):81–83.

Sjoegren, A. 1992. "The Mediterranean Next to Stockholm. Integration of Mediterranean People in Botkyrka, a Local Swedish Community." Paper presented at the Meeting "Mass Migrations in Europe. Implications in East and West," Vienna, March 5–7.

Skocpol, T., and Somers, M. 1980. "The Uses of Comparative History in Macrosocial Inquiry." *Comparative Studies in Society and History* 22:174–97.

Skogan, W. G., and Annan, S. O. 1994. "Drugs and Public Housing: Toward an Effective Police Response." Pp. 129–48 in D. L. MacKenzie and C. D. Uchida (Eds.), *Drugs and Crime. Evaluating Public Policy Initiatives.* London: Sage.

Small, M. L., and Newman, K. 2001. "Urban Poverty after The Truly Disadvantaged." *Annual Review of Sociology* 27:23–45.

Smelser, N. J. 1982. *La comparazione nelle scienze sociali.* Bologna: Il Mulino.

Smith, B. E., and R. C. Davis. 1993. "Successful Community Anticrime Programs: What Makes them Work?" Pp. 123–37 in R. C. Davis, A. J. Lurigio, D. P. Rosenbaum (Eds.), *Drugs and the Community.* Springfield, IL: Charles C. Thomas.

Smith, D. J. 1995. "Youth Crime and Conduct Disorders: Trends, Patterns, and Causal Explanations." Pp. 389–489 in M. Rutter, D. J. Smith (Eds.), *Psychosocial Disorders in Young People.* Chichester: John Wiley & Sons.

Social Security Administration. 1996. *Medicare.* SSA Publication No. 05–10043, June. Washington, DC: Author.

Social Security Administration. 1997. *Social Security. Understanding The Benefits.* SSA Publication No. 05–10024, January. Washington, DC: Author.

Sociodata, 1998. "Razzismo e xenofobia in Europa: i risultati di un sondaggio." *Sociodatanews* 3(July):3–10.

Solow, R. 1994. *Il mercato del lavoro come istituzione sociale.* Bologna: Il Mulino.

Somma, P. 1991. *Spazio e razzismo.* Milan: FrancoAngeli.

Sorensen, A. 2001. "Gender Equality in Earnings at Work and at Home." Pp. 98–115 in M. Kautto, J. Fritzell, B. Hvinden, J. Kvist, and H. Uusitalo (Eds.), *Nordic Welfare States in the European Context.* London: Routledge.

South, S. J., and Crowder, A. D. 1998. "Leaving the 'Hood: Residential Mobility Between Black, White, and Integrated Neighborhoods." *American Sociological Review* 63:17–26.

Springer, A. 1998. "Country Reports: An Overview, Including Some Remarks about Socio-Cultural Determinants of Primary Prevention and its Evaluation." Pp. 19–64 in A. Springer and A. Uhl (Eds.), *Cost A6. Evaluation Research in Regard to Primary Prevention of Drug Abuse.* Brussels: European Commission, Social Sciences, Directorate-General Science, Research and Development.

Stahlberg, Ann-Charlotte 1995. "The Swedish Pension System: Past, Present & Future." Pp. 1–10 in E. Brunsdon and M. May (Eds.), *Swedish Welfare: Policy & Provision.* Stockholm: Social Policy Association.

Stahura, J. M. 1986. "Suburban Development, Black Suburbanization and the Civil Rights Movement Since World War II." *American Sociological Review* 51(February):131–44.

Stame, N. 1998. *L'esperienza della valutazione.* Rome: SEAM.

Stark, R. (Ed.). 1975. *Social Problems.* New York: Random House.

Steeh, C., and Schuman, H. 1992. "Young White Adults: Did Racial Attitudes Change in the 1980s?" *American Journal of Sociology* 98(2):340–67.

Steffensmeier, D. J., Allan, E. A., Harer, M. D., and Streifel, C. 1989. "Age and the Distribution of Crime." *American Journal of Sociology* 94(4):803–31.

Steffensmeier, D., Ulmer, J., and Kramer, J. 1998. "The Interaction of Race, Gender, and Age in Criminal Sentencing: The Punishment Cost of Being Young, Black, and Male." *Criminology* 4:763–97.

Stehr, N. 1991. *Praktische Erkenntnis.* Frankfurt: Suhrkamp Verlag.

Stein, P., and Doerfer, I. 1992. "Svezia, il duro risveglio." *Biblioteca della libertà* 27(119):47–79.

Sussman, S., Stacy, A. W., Dent, C. W., Simon, T. R., and Johnson, C. A. 1996. "Marijuana Use: Current Issues and New Research Directions." *Journal of Drug Issues* 26(4):695–733.

Svallfors, S. 1991. "The Politics of Welfare Policy in Sweden: Structural Determinants and Attitudinal Cleavages." *British Journal of Sociology* 42(4):609–34.

228   References

Swedish Institute. 1995. *Alcohol and Narcotics in Sweden,* Stockholm.
Swedish National Institute of Public Health. 1995. Drug Policy. *The Swedish Experience.* Stockholm: Author.
Swedish National Institute of Public Health. 1996. *Alkohol- och narkotikautvecklingen i Sverige. Rapport 96,* Stockholm.
Tahlin, M. 1993. "Class Inequality and Post-industrial Employment in Sweden." Pp. 80–108 in G. Esping-Andersen (Ed.), *Changing Classes.* London: Sage.
Testa, L. 1987. *Emarginazione e disagio nel settore abitativo.* Rome: Labos.
Testa, M., Astone, N. M., Krogh, M., and Neckermann, K. M. 1993. "Employment and Marriage among Inner-City Fathers." Pp. 96–108 in W. J. Wilson (Ed.), *The Ghetto Underclass.* London: Sage.
Teune, H. 1990. "Comparing Countries: Lessons Learned." Pp. 38–62 in E. Oyen (Ed.), *Comparative Methodology. Theory and Practice in International Social Research.* London: Sage.
Thornberry, T. P., and Christenson, R. L. 1984. "Unemployment and Criminal Involvement: An Investigation of Reciprocal Causal Structures." *American Sociological Review* 49(June):398–411.
Tigges, L. M., Browne, I., and Green, G. P. 1998. "Social Isolation of the Urban Poor: Race, Class, and Neighborhood Effects on Social Resources." *Sociological Quarterly* 39(1):53–77.
Tittle, C. R., Burke, M. J., and Jackson, E. F. 1986. "Modeling Sutherland's Theory of Differential Association: Toward an Empirical Clarification." *Social Forces* 65(2):405–32.
Tosi, A. 1984. "La politica della casa." Pp. 239–63 in U. Ascoli (Ed.), *Welfare State all'italiana.* Rome: Laterza.
Trad, P. V. 1994. "The Pharmacological Aspects of Psychoactive Substances: Implications for Medical Management." Pp. 147–74 in T. P. Gullotta, G. R. Adams, and R. Montemayor (Eds.), *Substance Misuse in Adolescence.* London: Sage.
Trivellato, P. 1984. "La politica della scuola." Pp. 207–37 in U. Ascoli (Ed.), *Welfare State all'italiana.* Rome: Laterza.
Turco, L. 1998. "Audizione del Ministro per la Solidarietà Sociale On. Livia Turco presso la Commissione XII della Camera dei Deputati sulle iniziative assunte dal Governo per l'attuazione delle mozioni approvate dalla Camera dei Deputati nel marzo 1997 sulle tossicodipendenze (ex art. 143, comma 3)." *Forum* 11:8–15.
Turco, L. 1999. "Il rischio povertà." *La Stampa,* 23 June, p. 24.
Uchida, C. D., and Forst, B. 1994. "Controlling Street-Level Drug Trafficking: Professional and Community Policing Approaches." Pp. 77–94 in D. L. MacKenzie and C. D. Uchida (Eds.), *Drugs and Crime. Evaluating Public Policy Initiatives.* London: Sage.
Uhl, A. 1998. "Evaluation of Primary Prevention in the Field of Illicit Drugs. Definition-Concepts-Problems." Pp. 135–221 in A. Springer and A. Uhl (Eds.), *Cost A6. Evaluation Research in Regard to Primary Prevention of Drug Abuse.* Brussels: European Commission, Social Sciences, Directorate-General Science, Research and Development.
UNESCO. 1997. *Statistical Yearbook 1996.* Paris: UNESCO Publishing & Bernan.
UNESCO. 1998. *Statistical Yearbook 1998.* Paris: UNESCO Publishing & Bernan.
United Nations, Department for Economic and Social Information and Policy

Analysis. 1997. *Report on the World Social Situation 1997.* New York: United Nations Publications.

United Nations, Department of Economic and Social Affairs, Statistics Division. 1997. *Statistical Yearbook.* New York: United Nations Publications.

Van Voorhis, P., Cullen, F. T., Mathers, R. A., and Chenoweth Garner, C. 1988. "The Impact of Family Structure and Quality on Delinquency: A Comparative Assessment of Structural and Functional Factors." *Criminology* 26(2):235–61.

Vanara, F. 1997. "Esperienze regionali di pagamento a prestazione. Modulazione delle tariffe, qualità delle codifiche e reazione delle unità di offerta." *Tendenze nuove* 48(ottobre/dicembre):15–28.

Veglia, M. 1999. "L'informazione viaggia." *Narcomafie* 7(12):23–25.

Vicarelli, G. 1992. "Politica sanitaria e medicina privata in Italia." *Stato e mercato* 36:457–71.

Volino, A. 1997. "Appendice statistico-metodologica." Pp. 361–446 in C. Buzzi, A. Cavalli, and A. de Lillo (Eds.), *Giovani verso il Duemila.* Bologna: Il Mulino.

Von Hofer, H., Sarnecki, J., and Tham, H. 1997. "Minorities, Crime, and Criminal Justice in Sweden." Pp. 62–85 in I. Haen Marshall (Ed.), *Minorities, Migrants, and Crime,* London: Sage.

Wacquant, L. J. D. 1996. "The Rise of Advanced Marginality: Notes on its Nature and Implications." *Acta Sociologica* 39:121–39.

Wacquant, L. J. D., and Wilson, W. J. 1993. "The Cost of Racial and Class Exclusion in the Inner City." Pp. 25–42 in W. J. Wilson (Ed.), *The Ghetto Underclass.* London: Sage.

Wagner, F. W., Joder, T. E., and Mumphrey, A. J. 1995. "Conclusion." Pp. 203–11 in F. W. Wagner, T. E. Joder, and A. J. Mumphrey (Eds.), *Urban Revitalization: Policies and Programs.* London: Sage.

Wallace, J. M., and Bachmann, J. G. 1991. "Explaining Racial/Ethnic Differences in Adolescent Drug Use: The Impact of Background and Lifestyle." *Social Problems* 38:333–57.

Walters, G. D. 1996. "The Natural History of Substance Misuse in an Incarcerated Criminal Population." *Journal of Drug Issues* 26(4):943–59.

Weber, M. 1974. *Economia e società.* Milan: Comunità.

Weeks, M. R., Himmelgreen, D. A., Singer, M., Woolley, S., Romero-Daza, N., and Grier, M. 1996. "Community-Based Aids Prevention: Preliminary Outcomes of A Program for African American and Latino Injection Drug Users." *Journal of Drug Issues* 26(3):561–90.

Weingart, S. N. 1993. "A Typology of Community Responses to Drugs." Pp. 85–105 in R. C. Davis, A. J. Lurigio, and D. P. Rosenbaum (Eds.), *Drugs and the Community.* Springfield, IL: Charles C. Thomas.

Weir, M., and Skocpol, T. 1985. "State Structures and the Possibilities for 'Keynesian' Responses to the Great Depression in Sweden, Britain, and the United States." Pp. 107–63 in P. B. Evans, D. Rueschemeier, and T. Skocpol (Eds.), *Bringing the State Back In.* Cambridge, Cambridge University Press.

Western, M., and Wright, E. O. 1994. "The Permeability of Class Boundaries to Intergenerational Mobility Among Men in The United States, Canada, Norway and Sweden." *American Sociological Review* 59(August):609–29.

White, H. R. 1996. "Empirical Validity of Theories of Drug Abuse. Introductory Comments." *Journal of Drug Issues* 26(2):279–88.

Wiatrowski, M. D., Griswold, D. B., and Roberts, M. K. 1981. "Social Control Theory and Delinquency." *American Sociological Review* 46:525–41.

Wikstroem, P.-O. H. 1995. "Preventing City-Center Street Crimes." Pp. 429–68 in M. Tonry and D. P. Farrington (Eds.), *Building a Safer Society*. Chicago: University of Chicago Press.

Wilensky, H. L., Luebbert, G. M., Reed, H., and Jamieson, A. M. 1989. *Le politiche sociali. Un'analisi comparata*. Bologna: Il Mulino.

Wilson, B. R. 1997. "Organizzazione religiosa." Pp. 381–95 in *Enciclopedia delle Scienze Sociali*, Vol. 7. Rome: Istituto della Enciclopedia Italiana.

Wilson, J. Q. 1998. "Against the Legalization of Drugs." Pp. 304–13 in J. A. Inciardi and K. McElrath (Eds.), *The American Drug Scene*. Los Angeles: Roxbury.

Wilson, W. J. 1985. "The Urban Underclass in Advanced Industrial Society." Pp. 129–60 in P. E. Peterson (Ed.), *The New Urban Reality*. Washington, DC: Brookings Institution.

World Health Organization. 1996. *World Health Statistics Annual 1995*, Geneva.

World Health Organization. 1998. *World Health Statistics Annual 1996*, Geneva.

Wright, B. R. E., Caspi, A., Moffitt, T. E., Miech, R. A., and Silva, P. A. 1999. "Reconsidering the Relationship between SES and Delinquency: Causation but not Correlation." *Criminology* (1):175–94.

Zimmerman, E., et al. 1991. "La drogue dans l'opinion publique suisse: perception du problème et des mesures à prendre." *Déviance et société* 15(2):153–73.

Zucchini, F. 1994. "Immigrazione e politiche migratorie in Svezia." *Quaderni I.S.M.U.*

Index